Ziggy's
Character Matters

Other *Ziggy* Books

Ziggy & Friends
Ziggy Faces Life
Ziggy's Big Little Book
Life Is Just a Bunch of Ziggys . . .
Alphabet Soup Isn't Supposed to Make Sense
Ziggy's Place
Ziggy's Ups and Downs
Ziggy in the Fast Lane
Ziggy's Follies
Ziggy's School of Hard Knocks
Ziggy on the Outside Looking In . . .
Look Out World . . . Here I Come!
Ziggy . . . A Rumor in His Own Time
A Day in the Life of Ziggy . . .
1-800-ZIGGY
My Life as a Cartoon
The Z Files
Ziggy's Divine Comedy
Get Ziggy with It
The Zen of Ziggy
Ziggy Goes Hollywood
Ziggy's Friends for Life

Treasuries

The Ziggy Treasury
Encore! Encore!!
Ziggy's Star Performances
The First 25 Years Are the Hardest

Ziggy's Character Matters

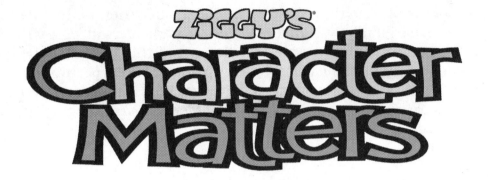

A Ziggy Collection

by Tom Wilson

Andrews McMeel
Publishing

Kansas City

For information, write Andrews McMeel Publishing, an Andrews McMeel Universal company, 4520 Main Street, Kansas City, Missouri 64111.

04 05 06 07 08 BBG 10 9 8 7 6 5 4 3 2 1

ISBN: 0-7407-4732-0

Library of Congress Control Number: 2004106219

www.uComics.com and www.andrewsmcmeel.com

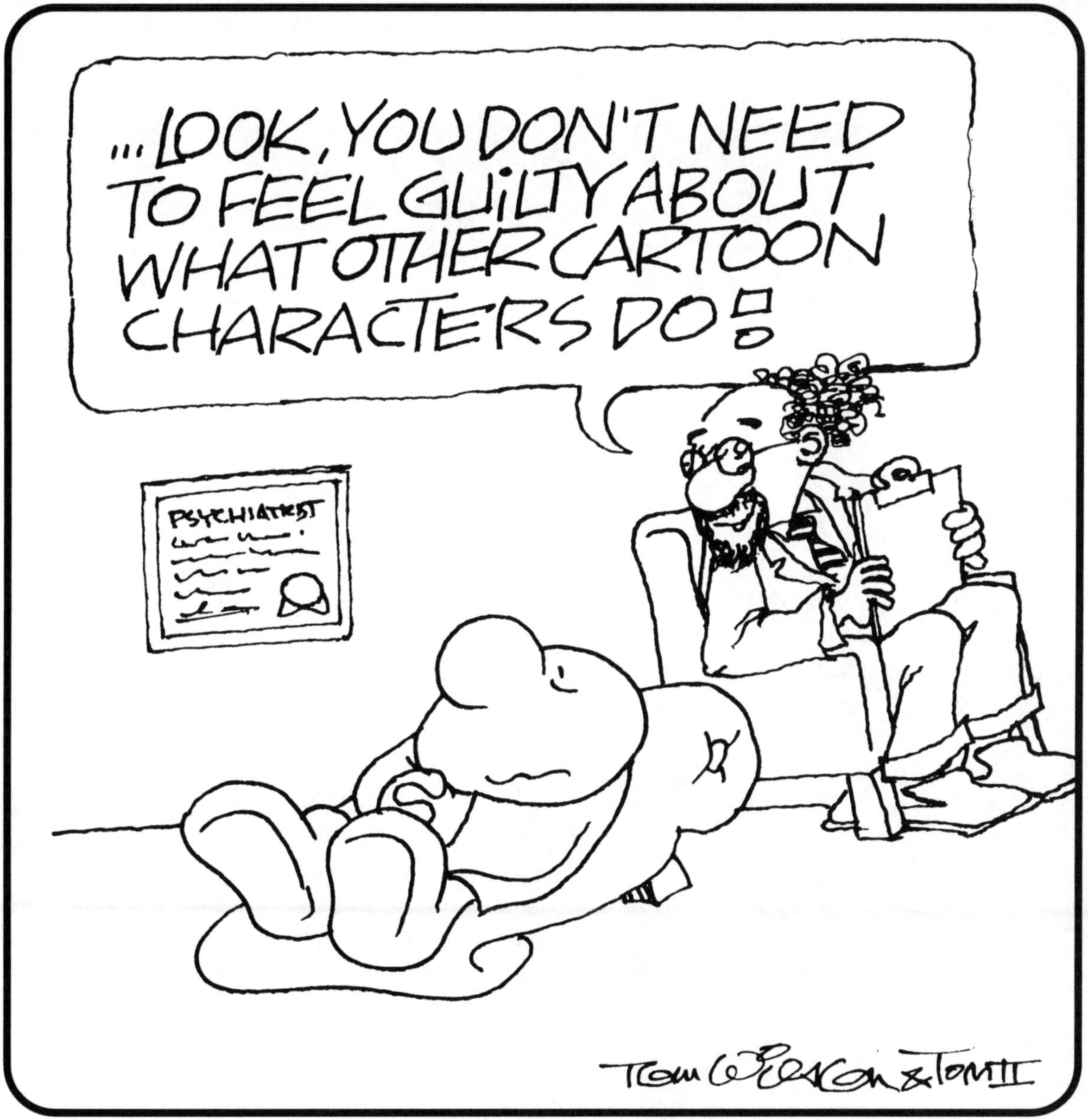
...LOOK, YOU DON'T NEED TO FEEL GUILTY ABOUT WHAT OTHER CARTOON CHARACTERS DO!!
PSYCHIATRIST
TOM WILSON & TOM II

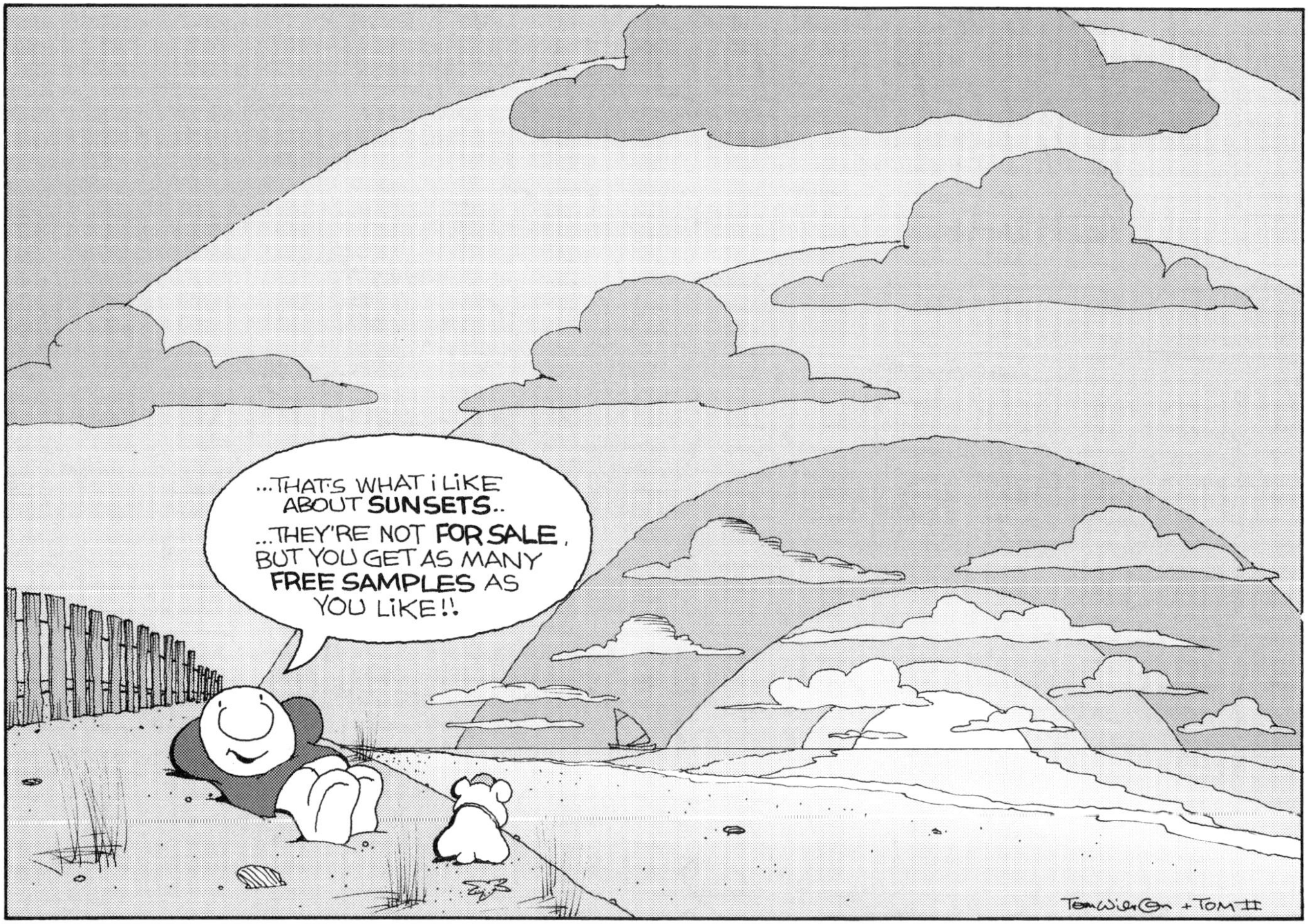
...THAT'S WHAT i LiKE ABOUT SUNSETS.. ...THEY'RE NOT FOR SALE, BUT YOU GET AS MANY FREE SAMPLES AS YOU LiKE!!
Tom Wilson + Tom II

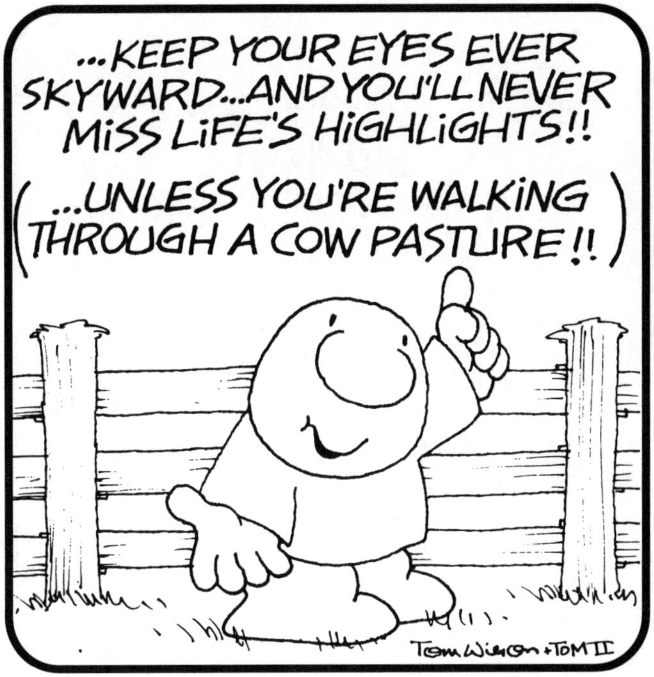
...KEEP YOUR EYES EVER SKYWARD...AND YOU'LL NEVER MISS LIFE'S HIGHLIGHTS!!
(...UNLESS YOU'RE WALKING THROUGH A COW PASTURE!!)
TOM WILSON + TOM II

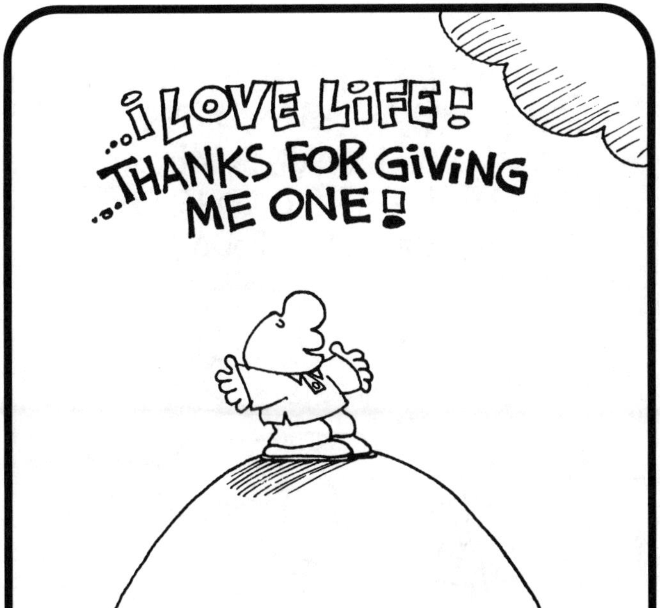
...I LOVE LIFE!
...THANKS FOR GIVING ME ONE!
TOM WILSON + TOM II

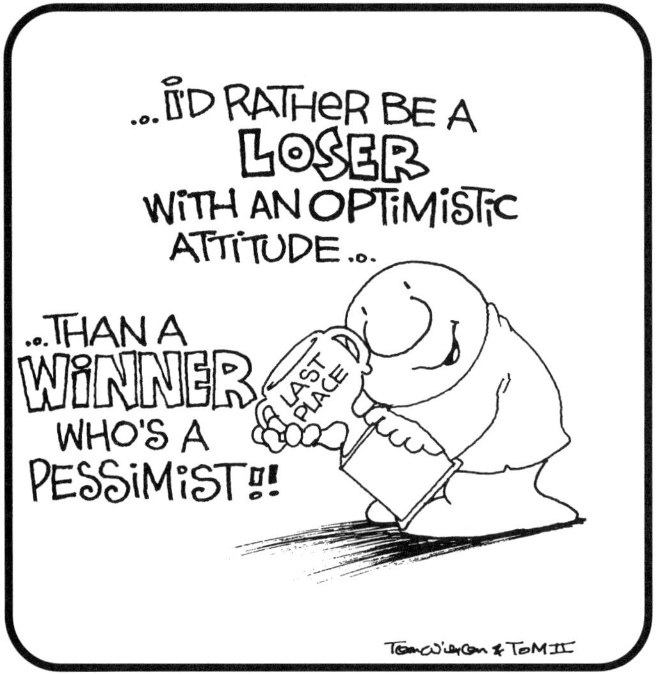
..I'D RATHER BE A
LOSER
WITH AN OPTIMISTIC
ATTITUDE ..
..THAN A
WINNER
WHO'S A
PESSIMIST!!
LAST PLACE

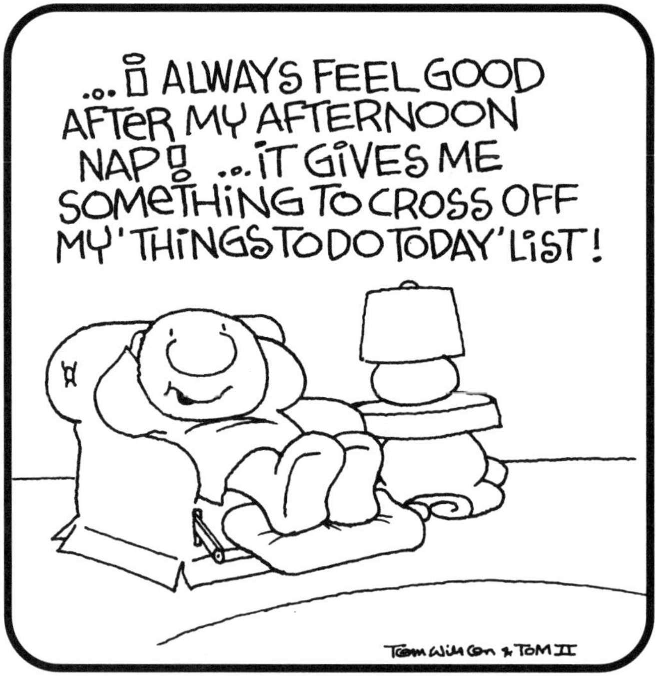
.. I ALWAYS FEEL GOOD
AFTER MY AFTERNOON
NAP! ..IT GIVES ME
SOMETHING TO CROSS OFF
MY 'THINGS TO DO TODAY' LIST!

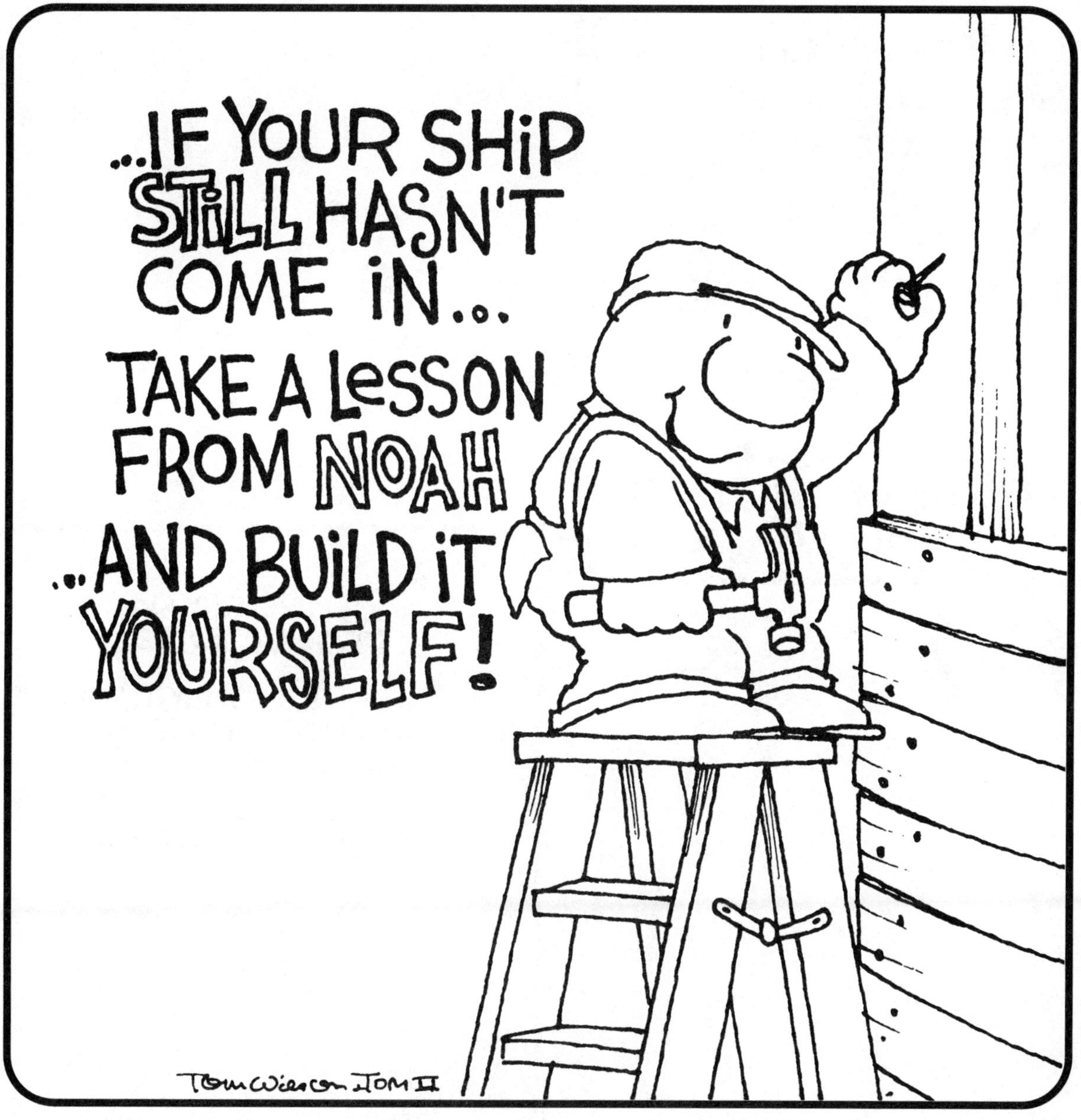
...IF YOUR SHIP STILL HASN'T COME IN...
TAKE A LESSON FROM NOAH
...AND BUILD IT YOURSELF!
TOM WILSON TOM II

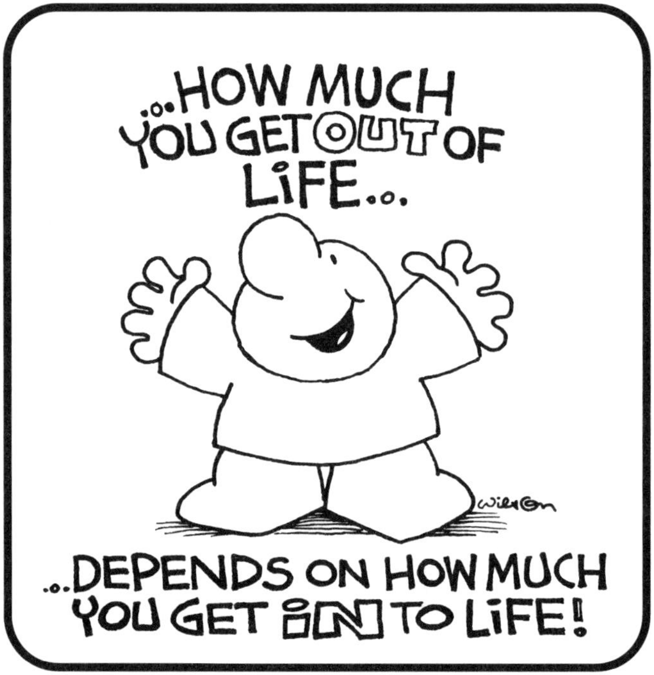
..o.HOW MUCH YOU GET OUT OF LIFE..o.
..o.DEPENDS ON HOW MUCH YOU GET IN TO LIFE!

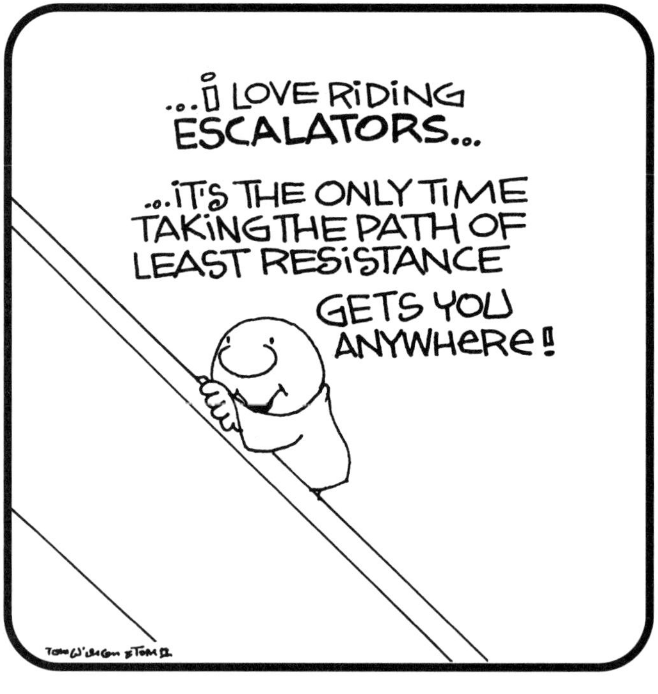
..o.I LOVE RIDING ESCALATORS..o.
..o.IT'S THE ONLY TIME TAKING THE PATH OF LEAST RESISTANCE GETS YOU ANYWHERE!

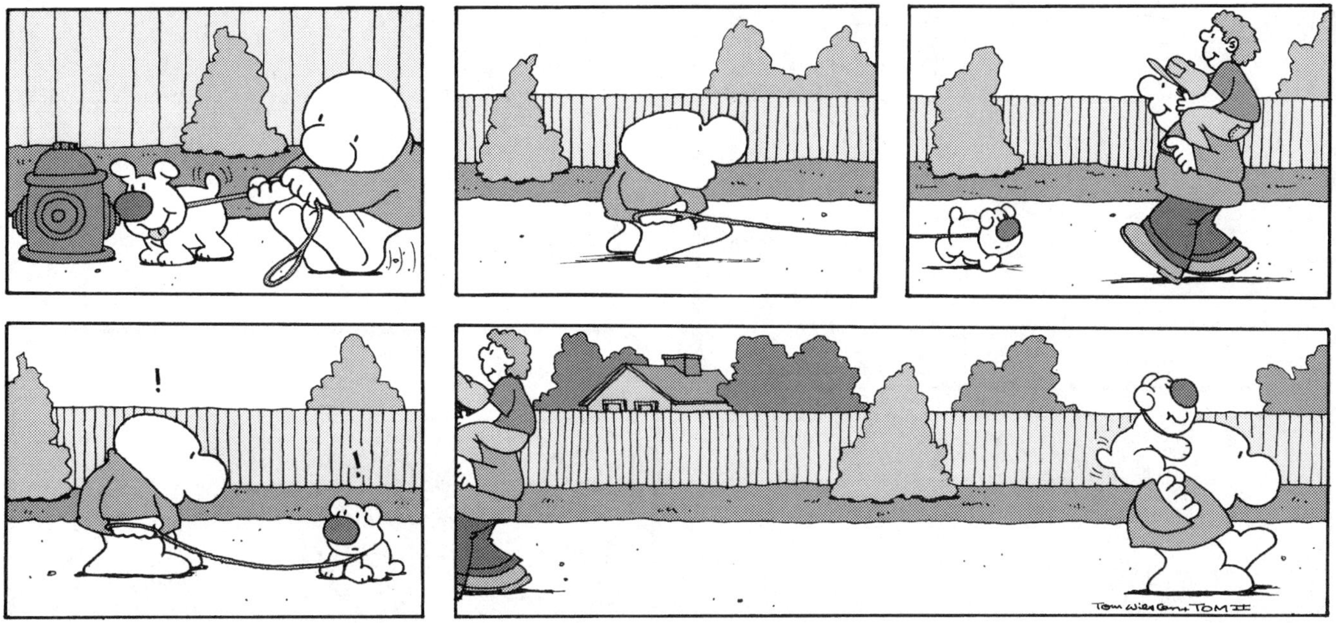
!
!
Tom Wilson & TOM II

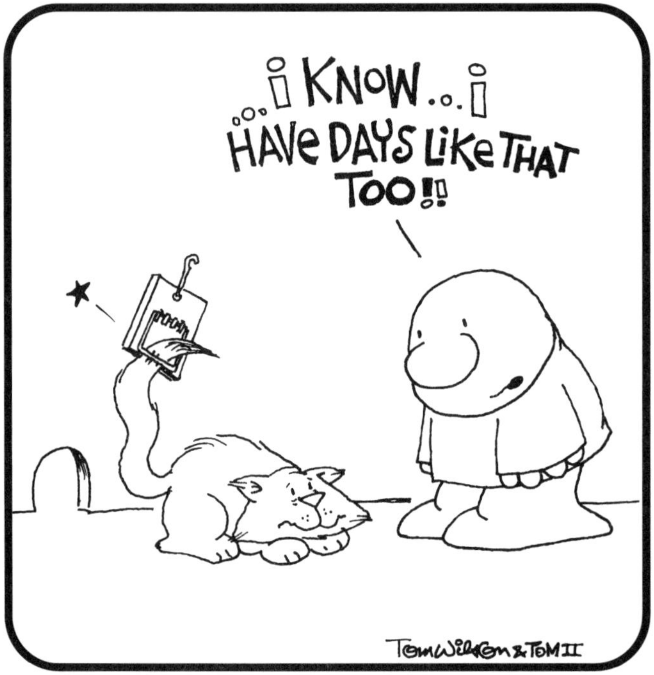
..o..i KNOW..o..i HAVE DAYS LIKE THAT TOO!!
TOM WILSON & TOM II

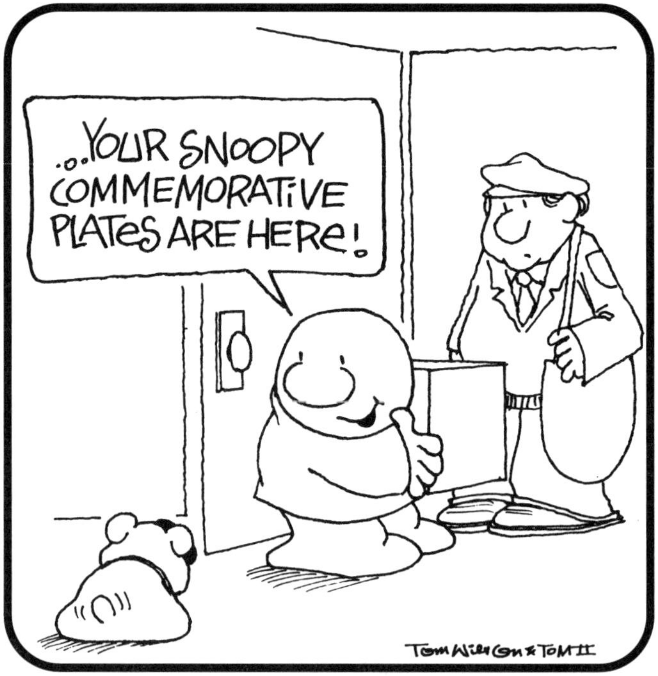
..o..YOUR SNOOPY COMMEMORATIVE PLATES ARE HERE!
TOM WILSON & TOM II

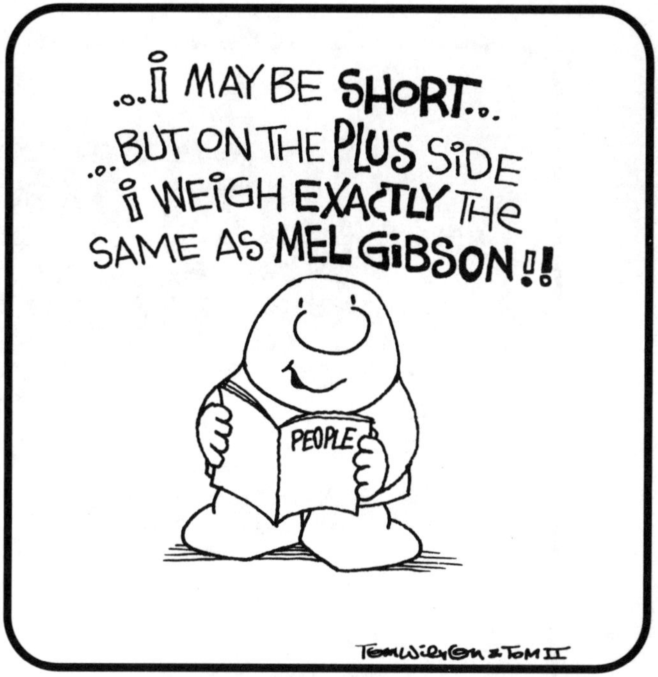
..I MAY BE SHORT...
..BUT ON THE PLUS SIDE I WEIGH EXACTLY THE SAME AS MEL GIBSON!!
PEOPLE
TOM WILSON & TOM II

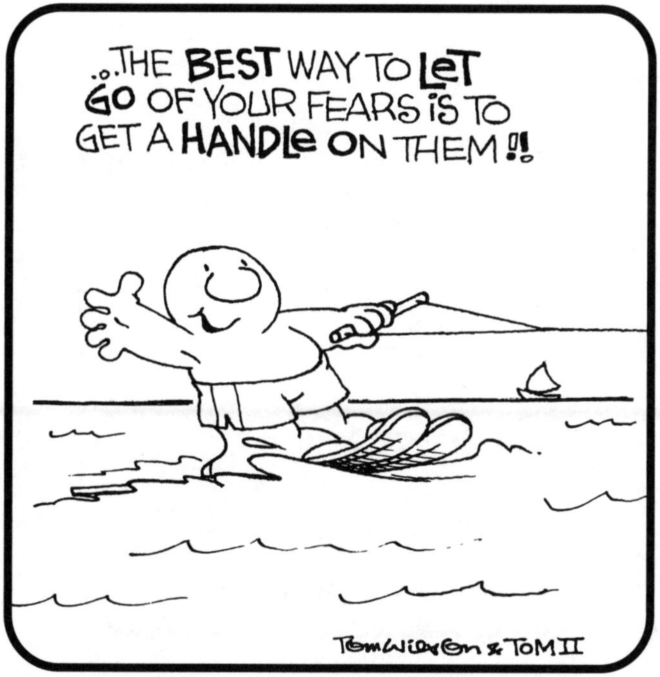
..THE BEST WAY TO LET GO OF YOUR FEARS IS TO GET A HANDLE ON THEM!!
TOM WILSON & TOM II

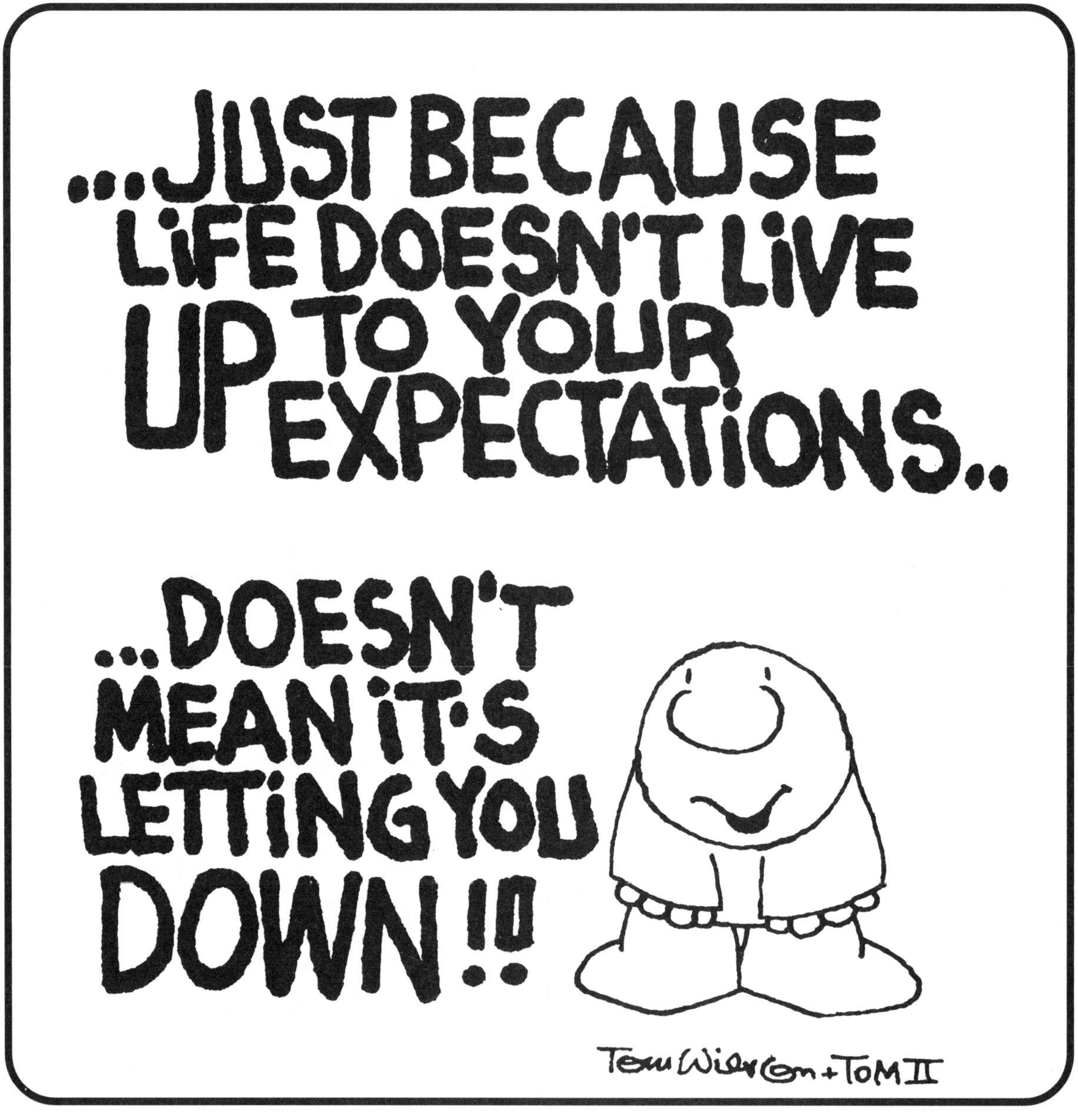
...JUST BECAUSE LIFE DOESN'T LIVE UP TO YOUR EXPECTATIONS..
...DOESN'T MEAN IT'S LETTING YOU DOWN!!
Tom Wilson + TOM II

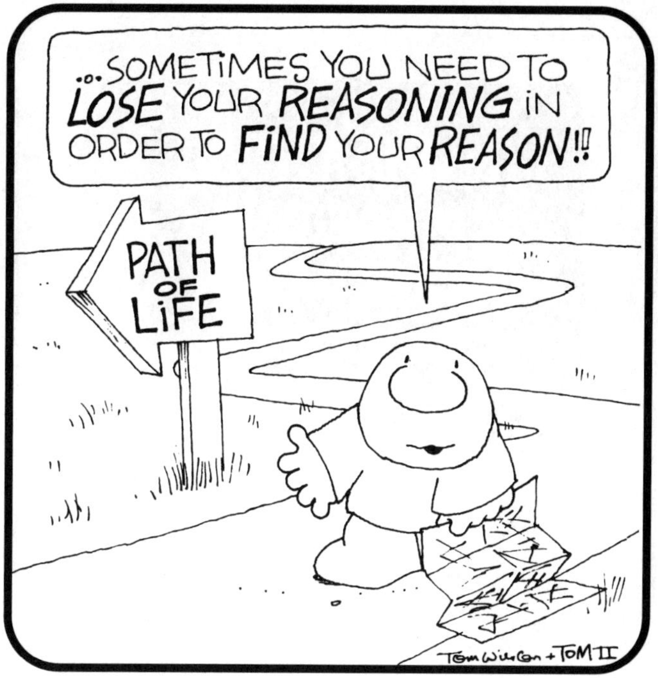
..SOMETIMES YOU NEED TO LOSE YOUR REASONING IN ORDER TO FIND YOUR REASON!!
PATH OF LIFE
Tom Wilson + TOM II

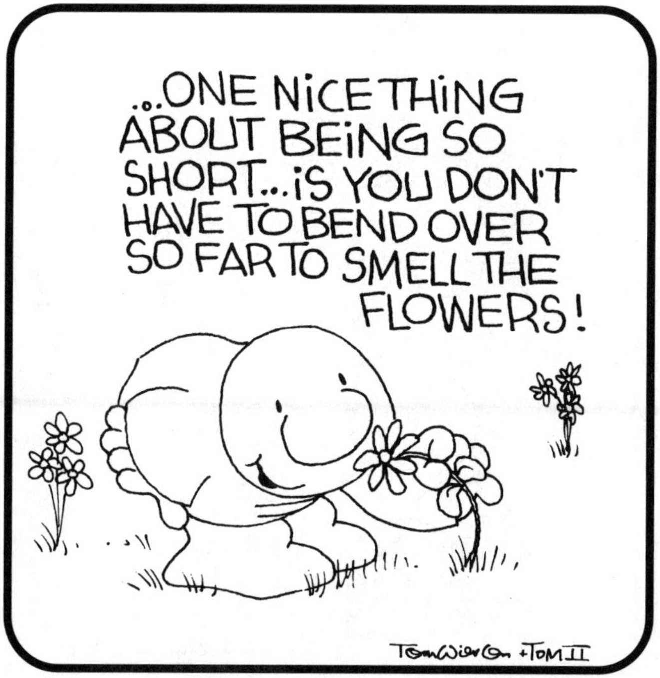
..ONE NICE THING ABOUT BEING SO SHORT...IS YOU DON'T HAVE TO BEND OVER SO FAR TO SMELL THE FLOWERS!
Tom Wilson + TOM II

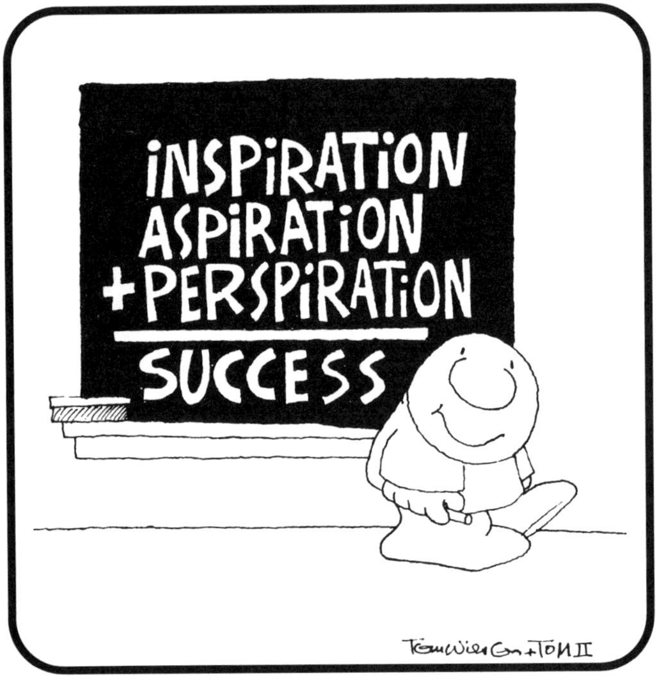
INSPIRATION
ASPIRATION
+PERSPIRATION
SUCCESS

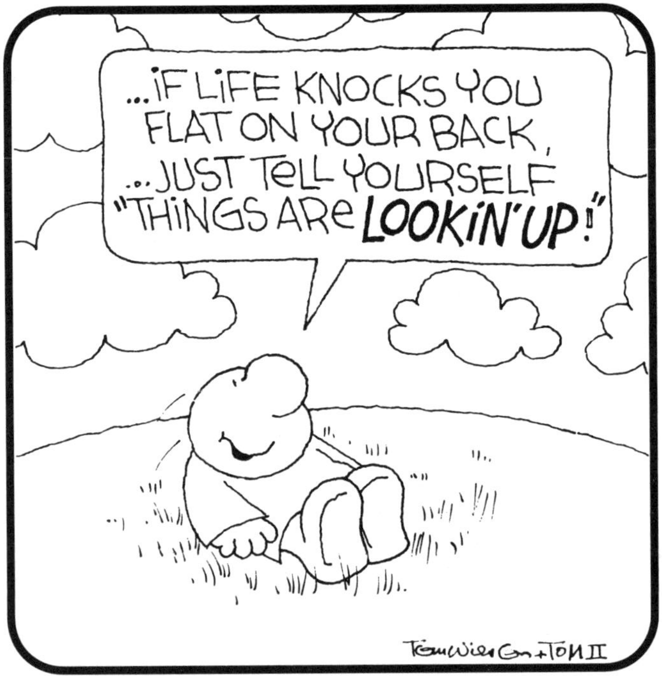
...IF LIFE KNOCKS YOU FLAT ON YOUR BACK, ...JUST TELL YOURSELF "THINGS ARE LOOKIN' UP!"

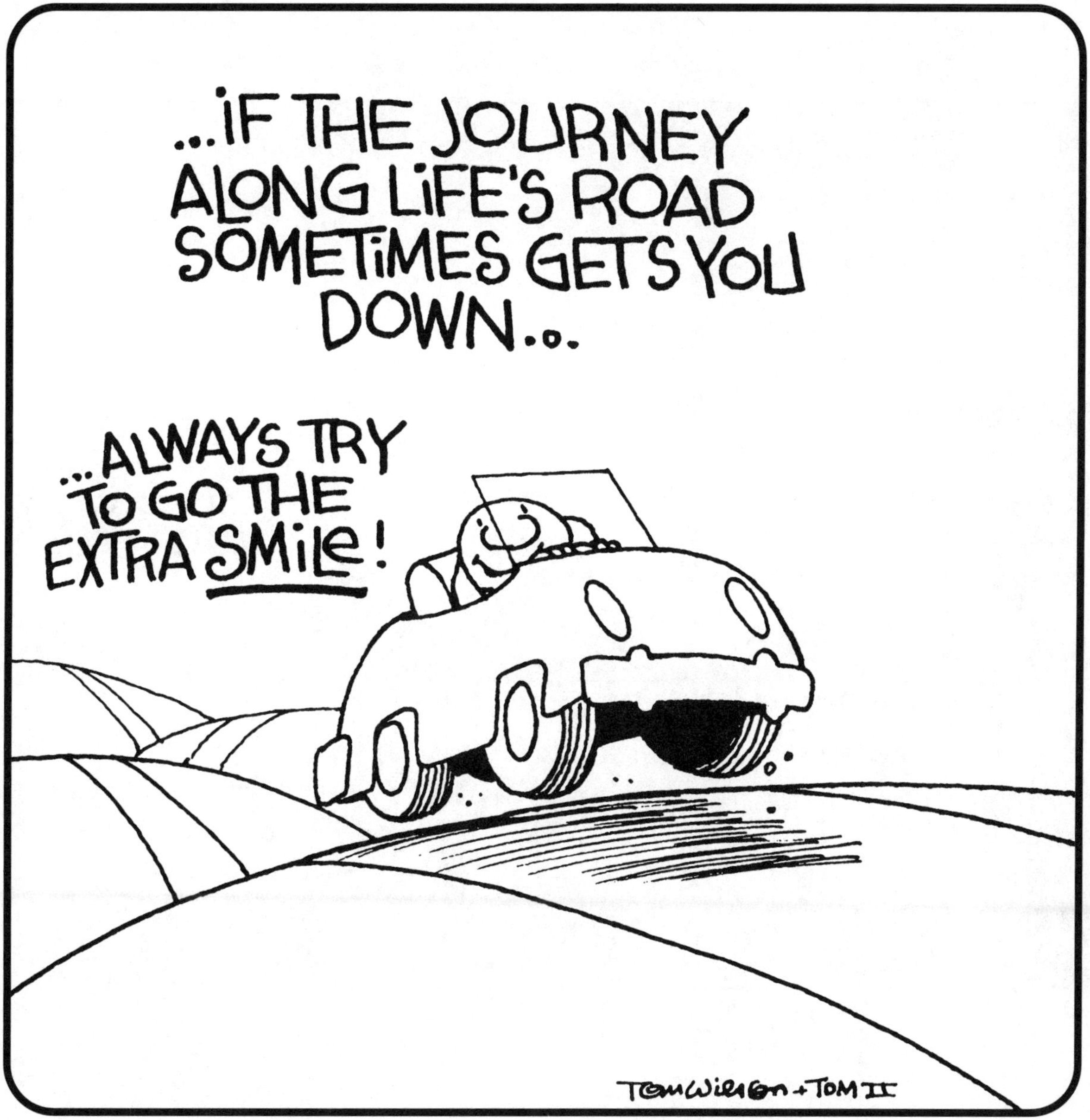
...IF THE JOURNEY ALONG LIFE'S ROAD SOMETIMES GETS YOU DOWN...
...ALWAYS TRY TO GO THE EXTRA SMILE!
TOM WILSON + TOM II

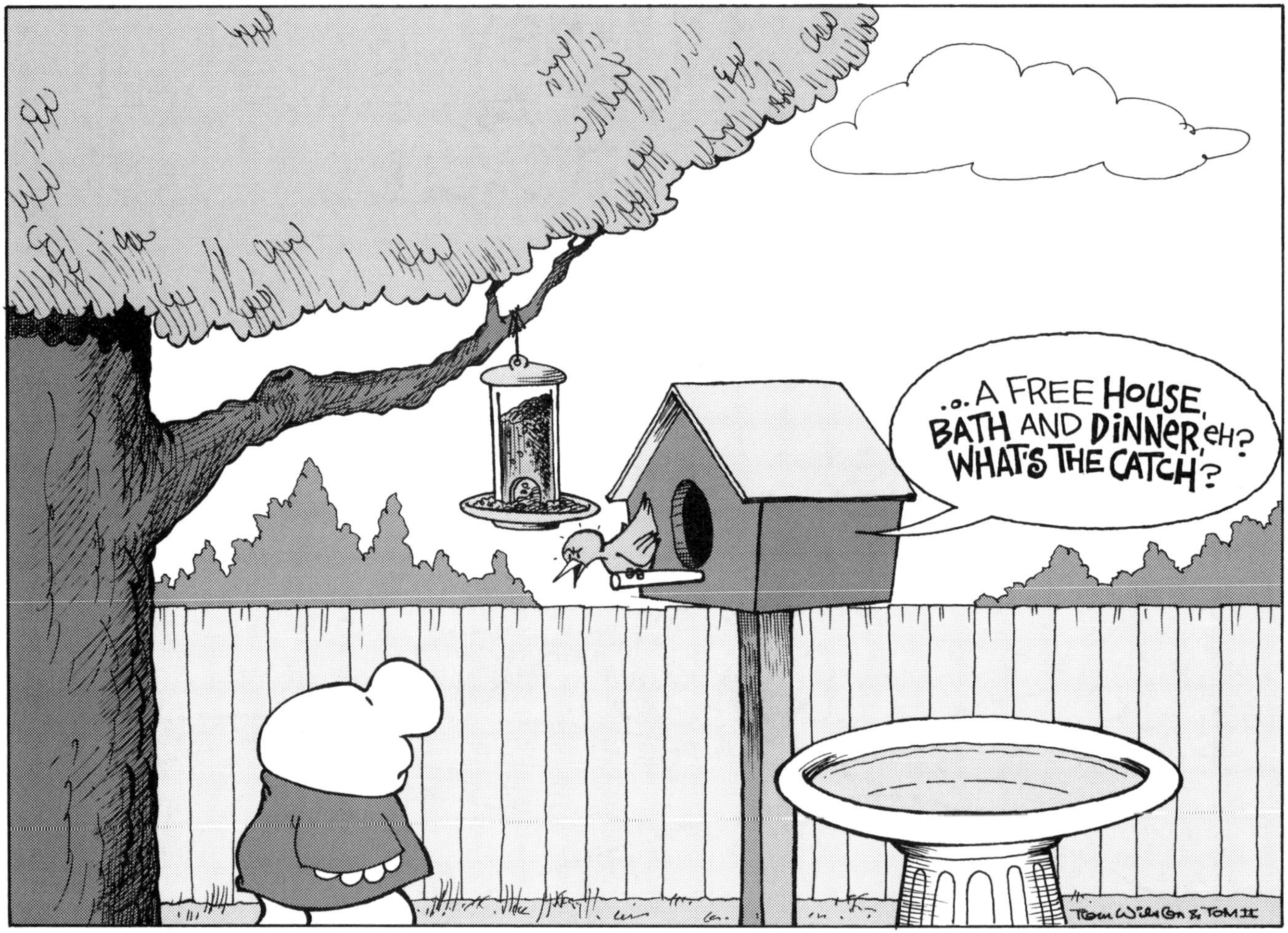
..o. A FREE HOUSE, BATH AND DINNER, EH? WHAT'S THE CATCH?
TOM WILSON & TOM II

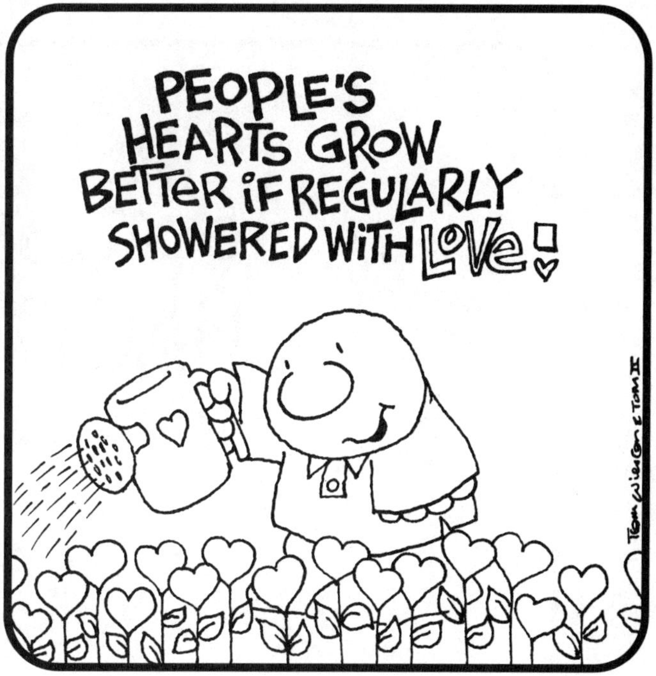
PEOPLE'S HEARTS GROW BETTER iF REGULARLY SHOWERED WITH LOVE!
TOM WILSON & TOM II

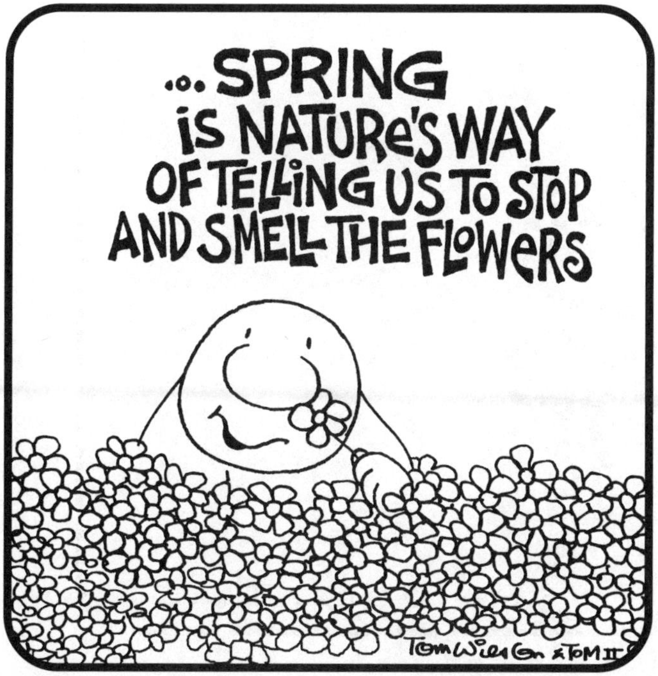
...SPRING is NATURE'S WAY OF TELLING US TO STOP AND SMELL THE FLOWERS
TOM WILSON & TOM II

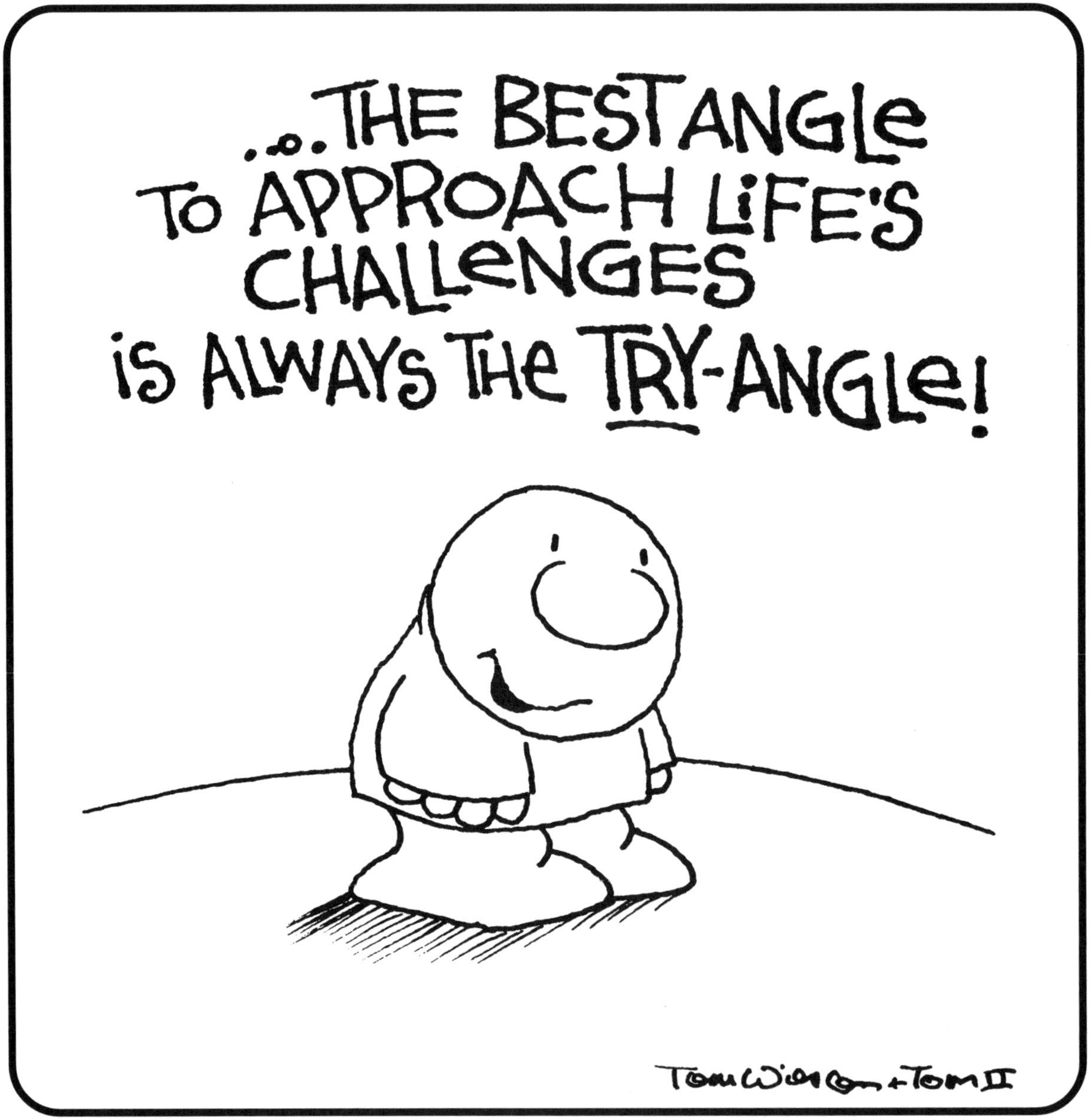
...THE BEST ANGLE
TO APPROACH LIFE'S
CHALLENGES
IS ALWAYS THE TRY-ANGLE!
Tom Wilson + Tom II

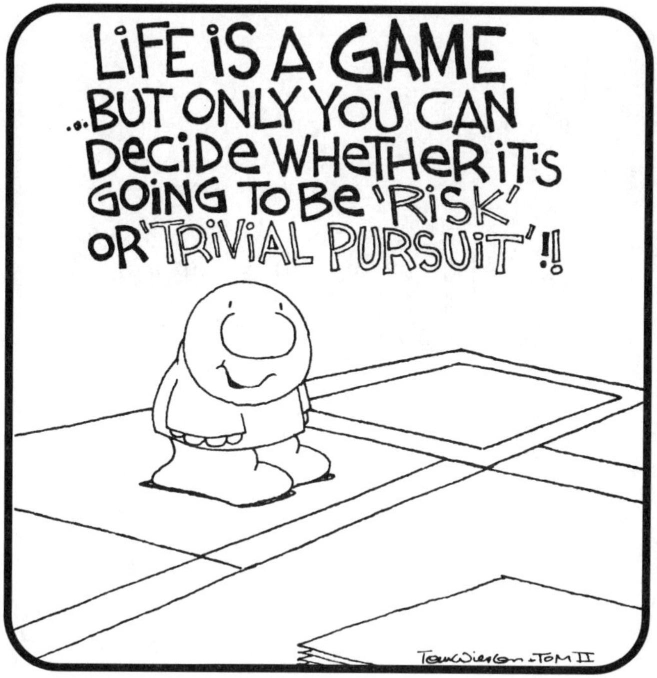
LIFE IS A GAME
..BUT ONLY YOU CAN DECIDE WHETHER IT'S GOING TO BE 'RISK' OR 'TRIVIAL PURSUIT'!!
TOM WILSON + TOM II

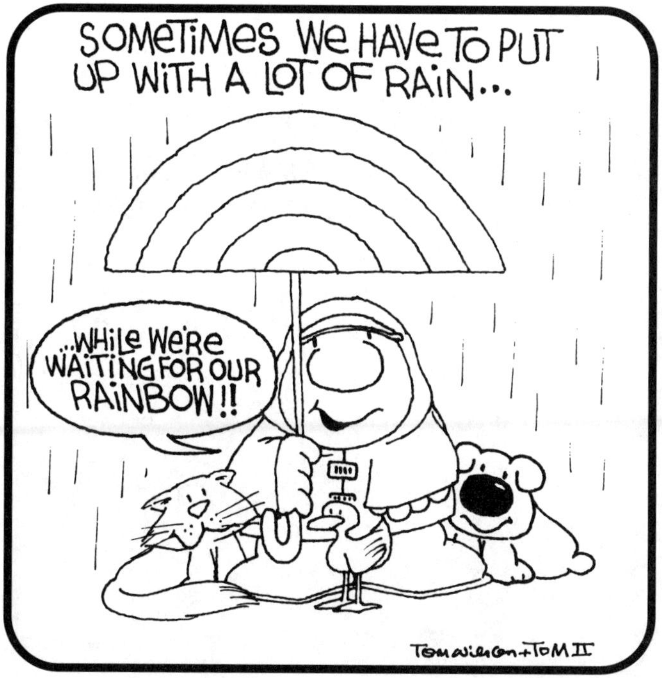
SOMETIMES WE HAVE TO PUT UP WITH A LOT OF RAIN...
...WHILE WE'RE WAITING FOR OUR RAINBOW!!
TOM WILSON + TOM II

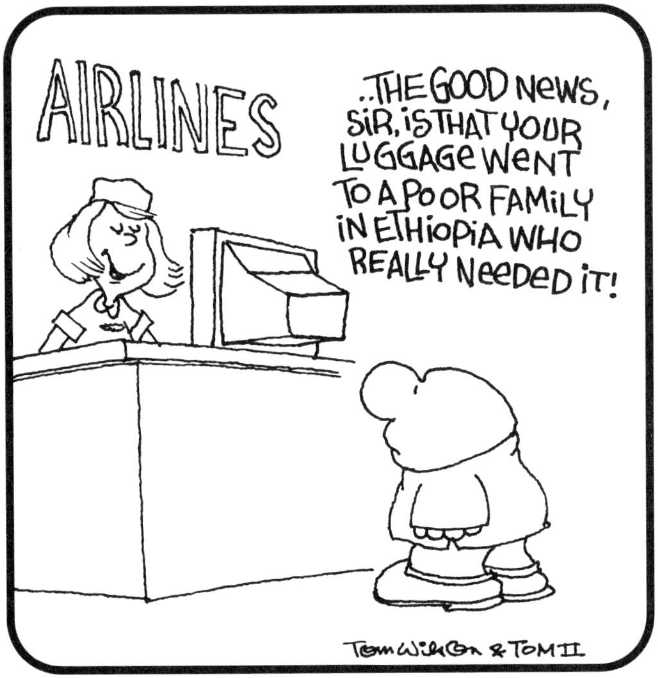
AIRLINES
..THE GOOD NEWS, SIR, IS THAT YOUR LUGGAGE WENT TO A POOR FAMILY IN ETHIOPIA WHO REALLY NEEDED IT!
Tom Wilson & TOM II

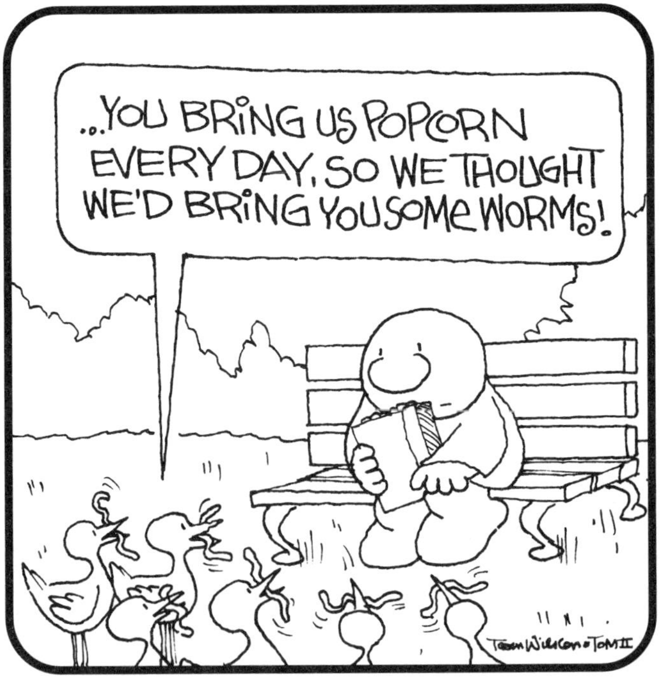
...YOU BRING US POPCORN EVERY DAY, SO WE THOUGHT WE'D BRING YOU SOME WORMS!
Tom Wilson & Tom II

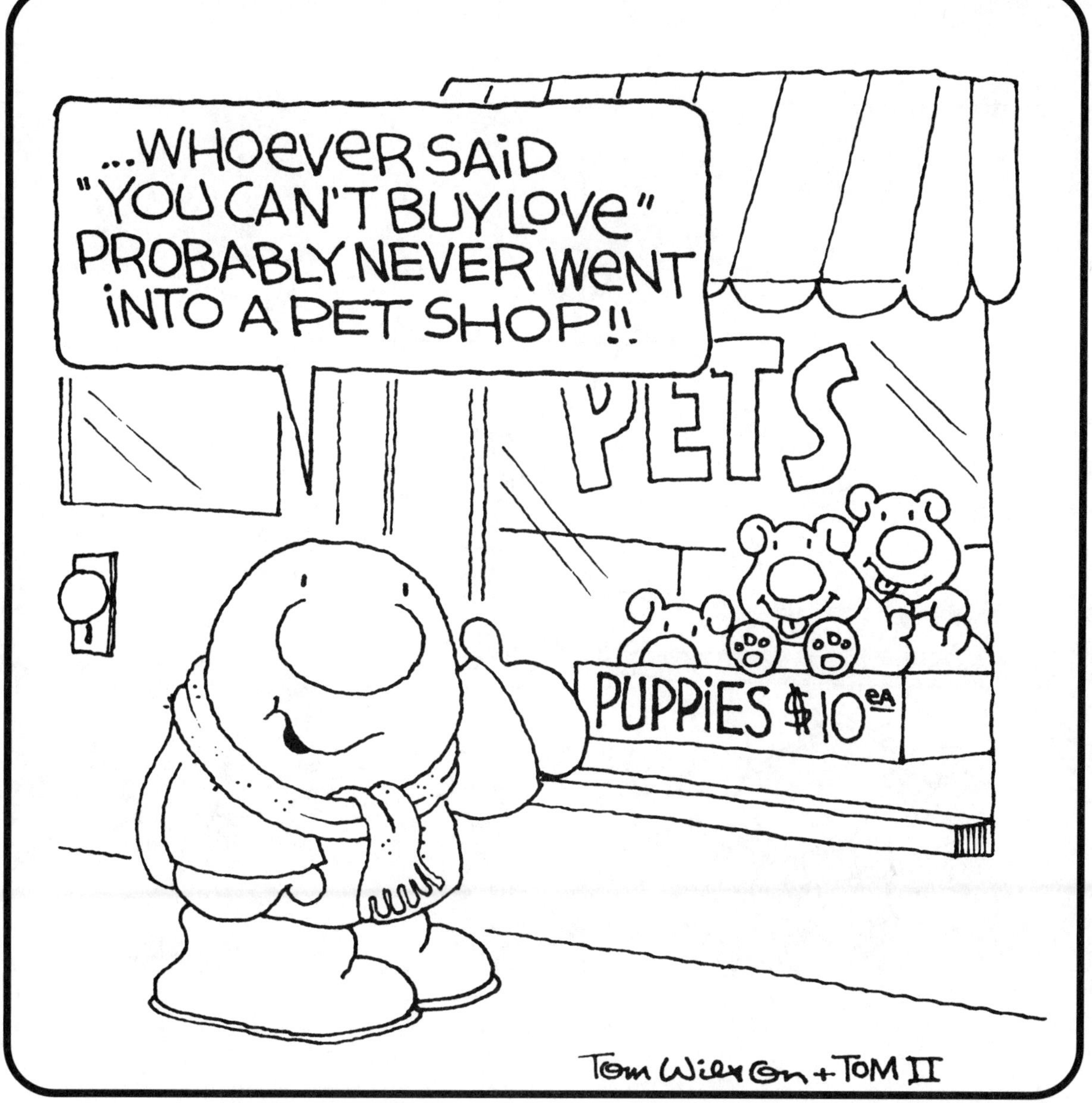
...WHOEVER SAID "YOU CAN'T BUY LOVE" PROBABLY NEVER WENT INTO A PET SHOP!!
PETS
PUPPIES $10 EA
Tom Wilson + TOM II

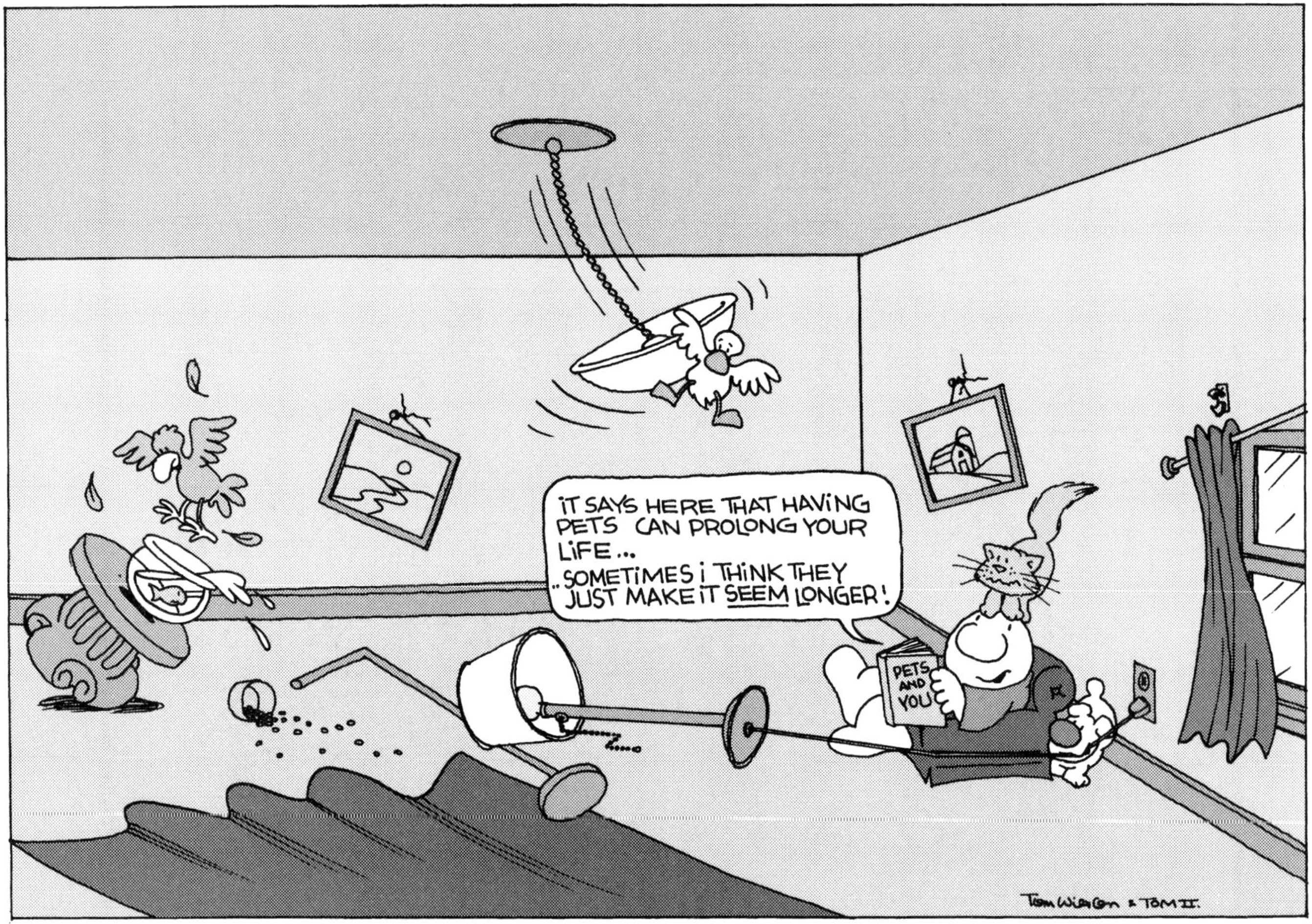
IT SAYS HERE THAT HAVING PETS CAN PROLONG YOUR LIFE...
"SOMETIMES I THINK THEY JUST MAKE IT SEEM LONGER!
PETS AND YOU
Tom Wilson & TOM II.

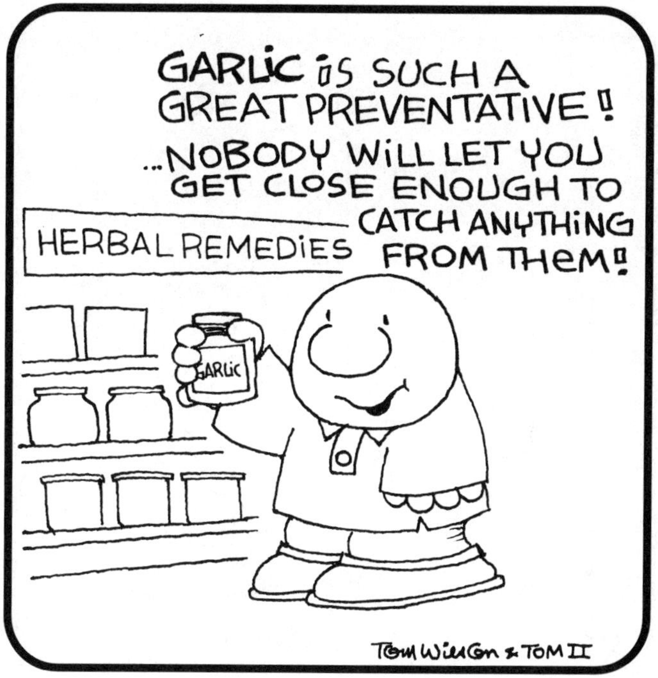
GARLIC IS SUCH A GREAT PREVENTATIVE! ...NOBODY WILL LET YOU GET CLOSE ENOUGH TO CATCH ANYTHING FROM THEM!
HERBAL REMEDIES
GARLIC
TOM WILSON & TOM II

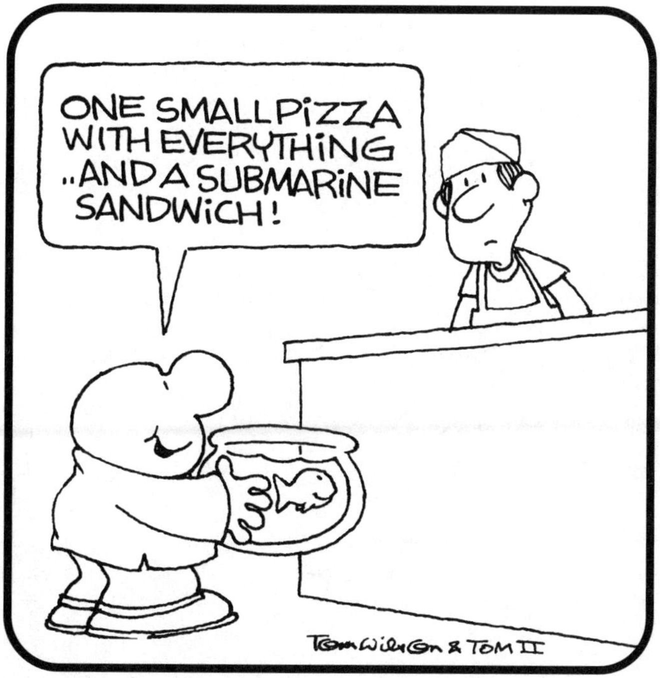
ONE SMALL PIZZA WITH EVERYTHING ..AND A SUBMARINE SANDWICH!
TOM WILSON & TOM II

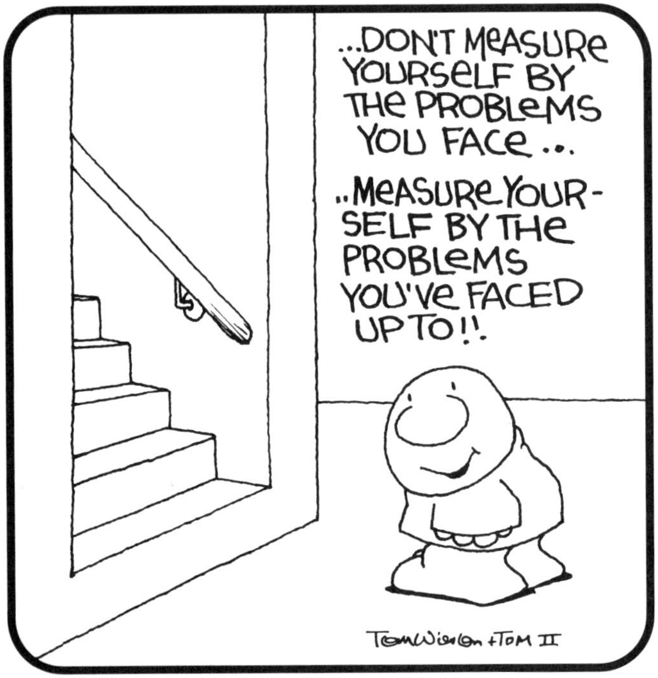
...DON'T MEASURE YOURSELF BY THE PROBLEMS YOU FACE...
..MEASURE YOURSELF BY THE PROBLEMS YOU'VE FACED UP TO!!
TOM WILSON + TOM II

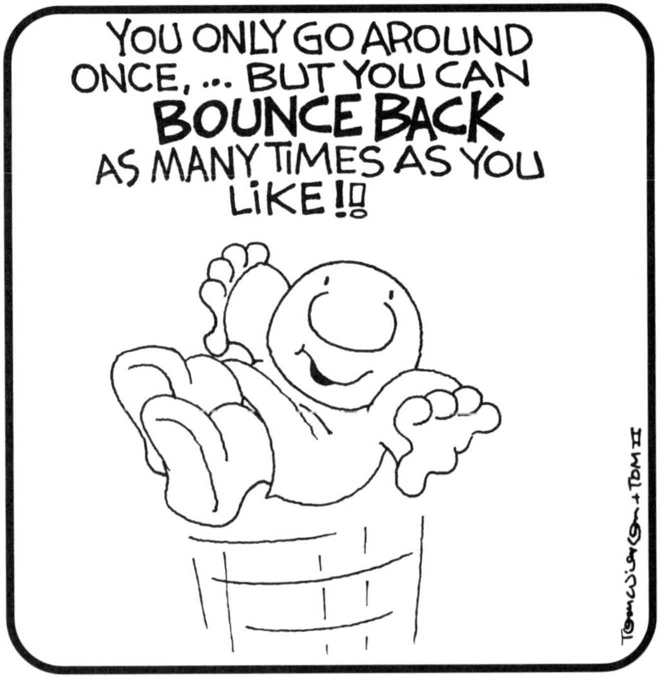
YOU ONLY GO AROUND ONCE, ... BUT YOU CAN BOUNCE BACK AS MANY TIMES AS YOU LIKE!!
TOM WILSON + TOM II

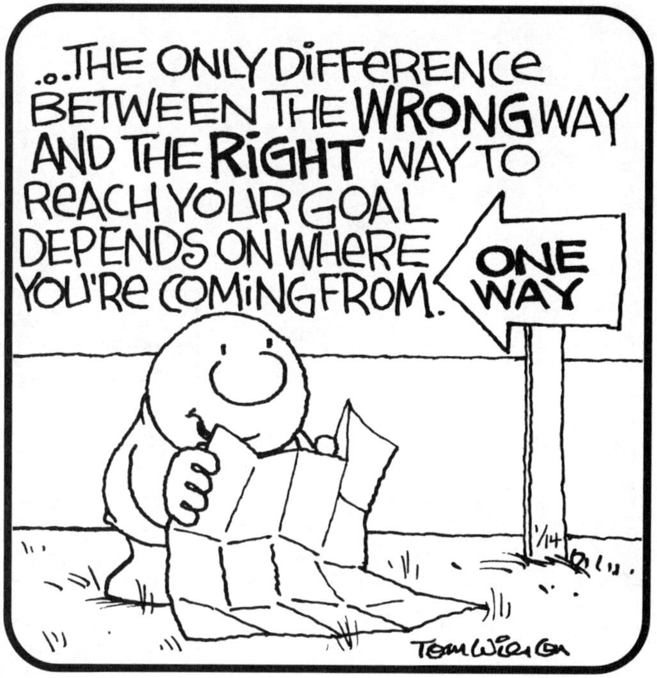
...THE ONLY DIFFERENCE BETWEEN THE WRONG WAY AND THE RIGHT WAY TO REACH YOUR GOAL DEPENDS ON WHERE YOU'RE COMING FROM.
ONE WAY

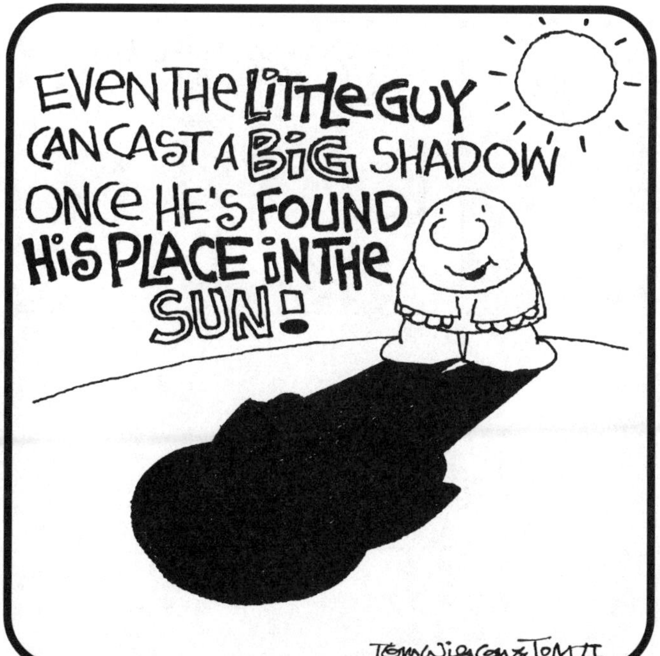
EVEN THE LITTLE GUY CAN CAST A BIG SHADOW ONCE HE'S FOUND HIS PLACE IN THE SUN!

SOMETIMES I THINK THAT IN LIFE'S JOURNEY SOME OF US GET SO LOST..

..BECAUSE DEEP DOWN INSIDE, SOME REALLY LIVE FOR THE SEARCH FOR WHO THEY REALLY ARE!

...AND THE MORE LOST THEY BECOME..

..THE MORE THEY GET TO SEARCH FOR THEIR TRUE SELVES!!

..SO BASICALLY, SOME OF US REALLY NEED TO BE LOST..

..IN ORDER TO FIND OURSELVES!!

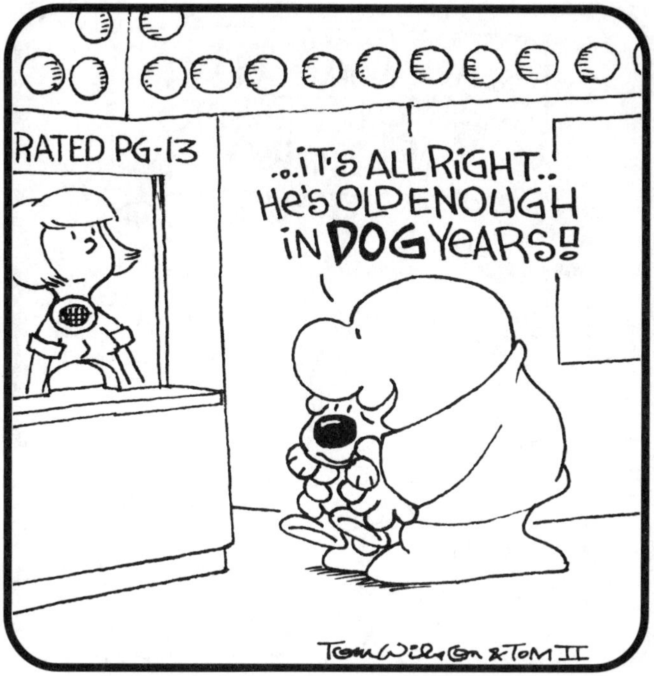
RATED PG-13
..iT'S ALL RiGHT.. He's OLD ENOUGH iN DOG YeARS!
Tom Wilson & Tom II

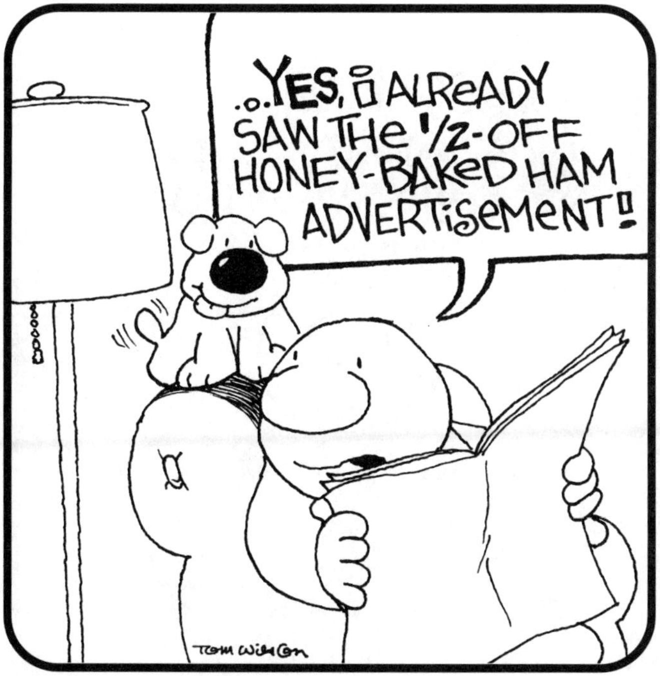
..o..YES, i ALReADY SAW THe 1/2-OFF HONEY-BAKeD HAM ADVERTiSeMENT!
Tom Wilson

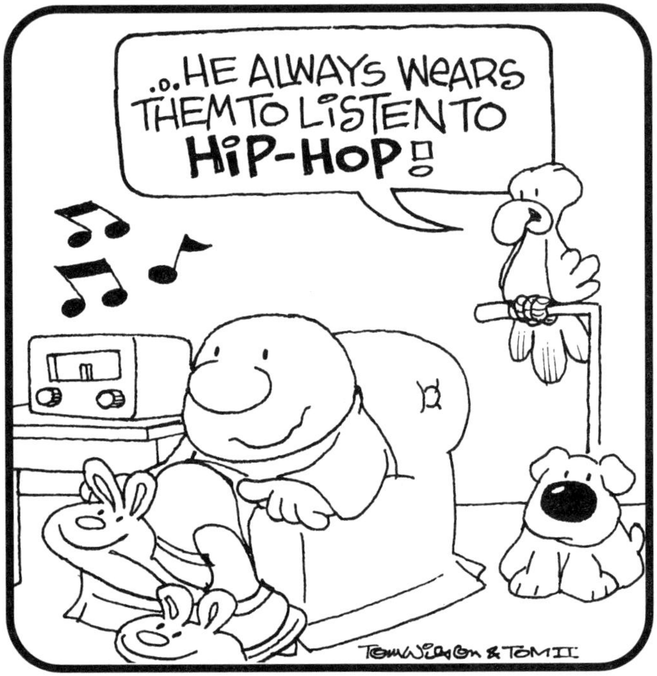
..o.HE ALWAYS WEARS THEM TO LISTEN TO HIP-HOP!!
TOM WILSON & TOM II

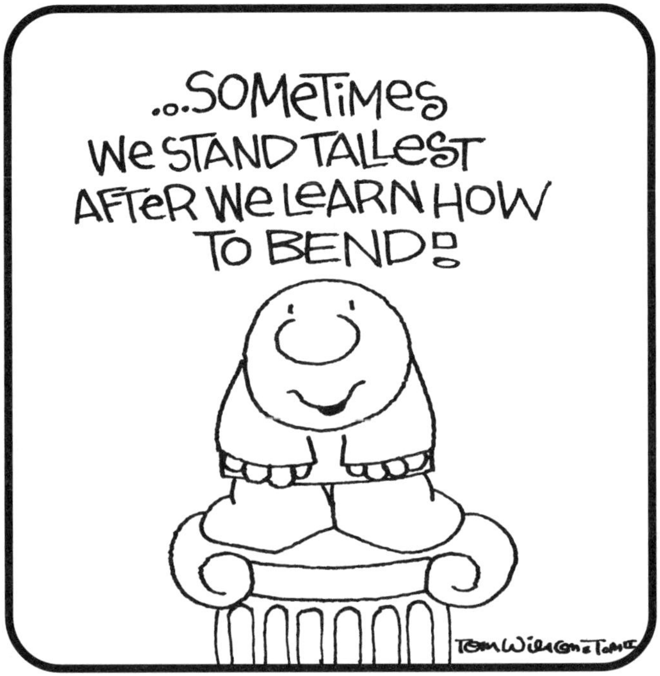
..o..SOMETIMES WE STAND TALLEST AFTER WE LEARN HOW TO BEND!!

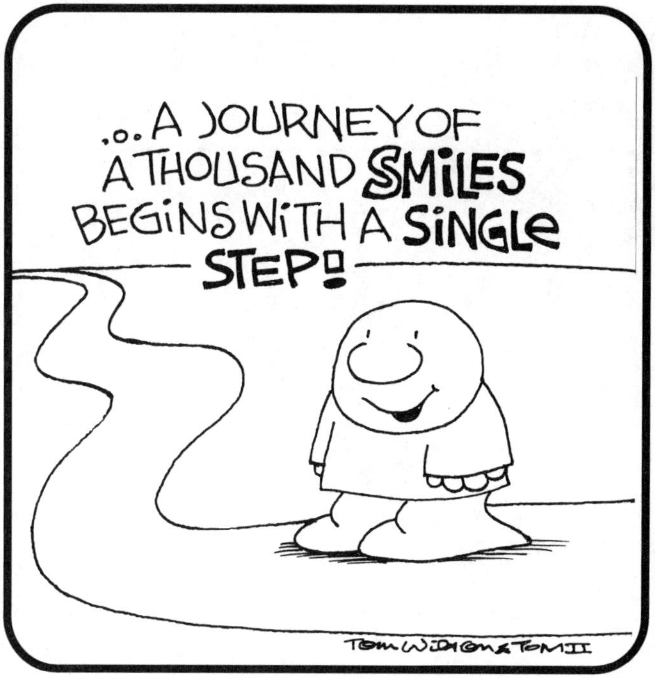
..o.. A JOURNEY OF A THOUSAND SMILES BEGINS WITH A SINGLE STEP!
TOM WILSON & TOM II

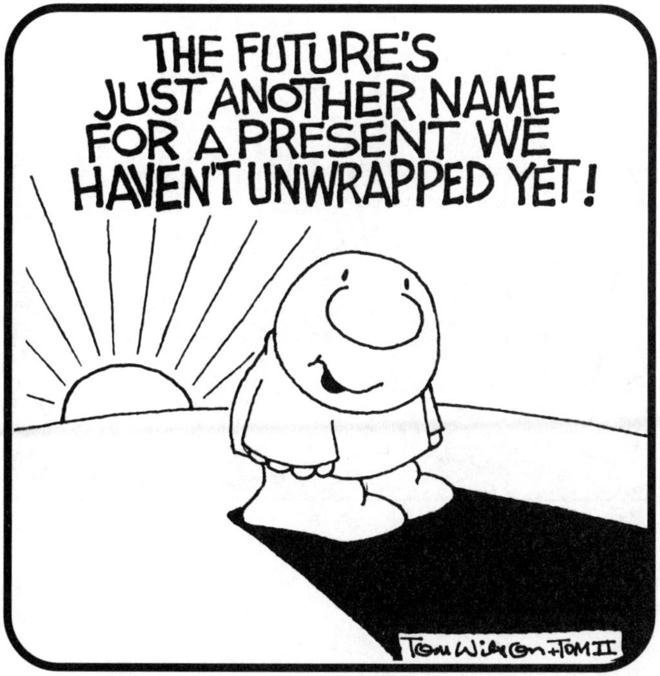
THE FUTURE'S JUST ANOTHER NAME FOR A PRESENT WE HAVEN'T UNWRAPPED YET!
TOM WILSON + TOM II

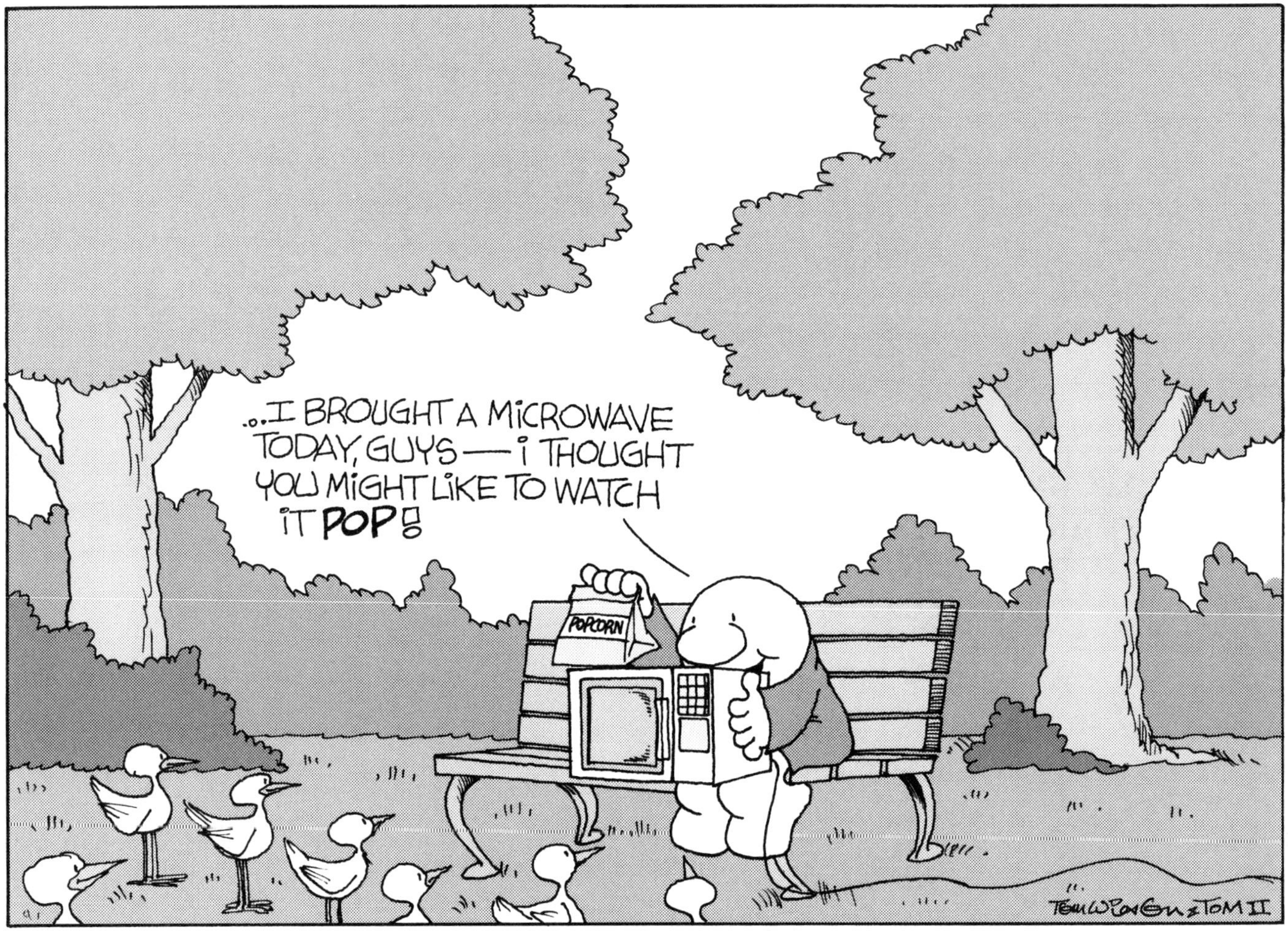
...I BROUGHT A MICROWAVE TODAY, GUYS — I THOUGHT YOU MIGHT LIKE TO WATCH IT **POP**!!
POPCORN
TOM WILSON & TOM II

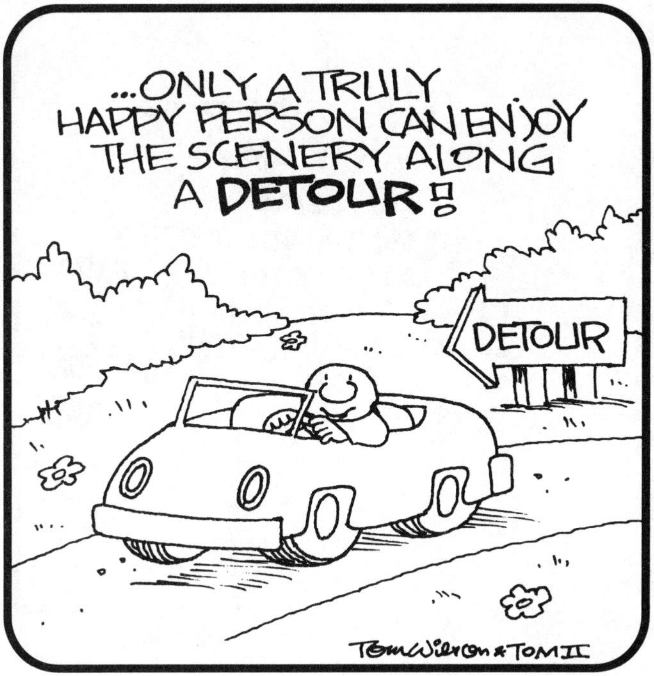
...ONLY A TRULY HAPPY PERSON CAN ENJOY THE SCENERY ALONG A DETOUR!
DETOUR
TOM WILSON & TOM II

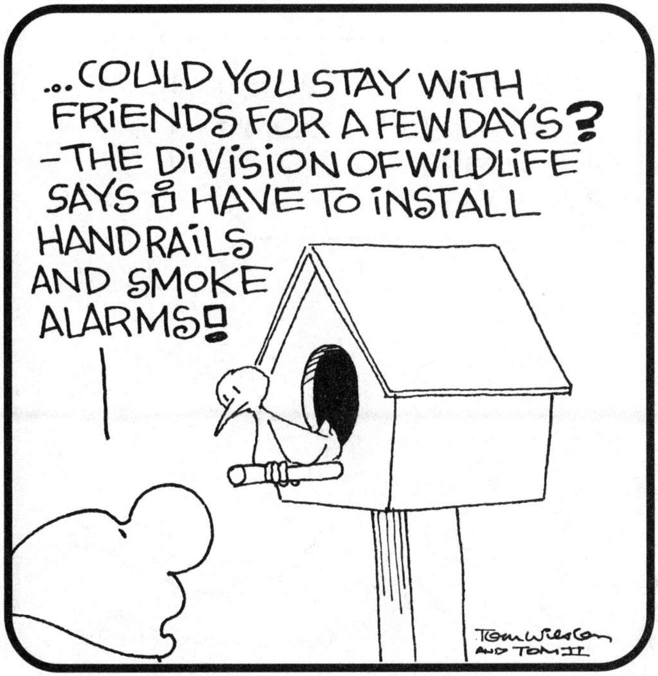
...COULD YOU STAY WITH FRIENDS FOR A FEW DAYS? -THE DIVISION OF WILDLIFE SAYS I HAVE TO INSTALL HANDRAILS AND SMOKE ALARMS!
TOM WILSON AND TOM II

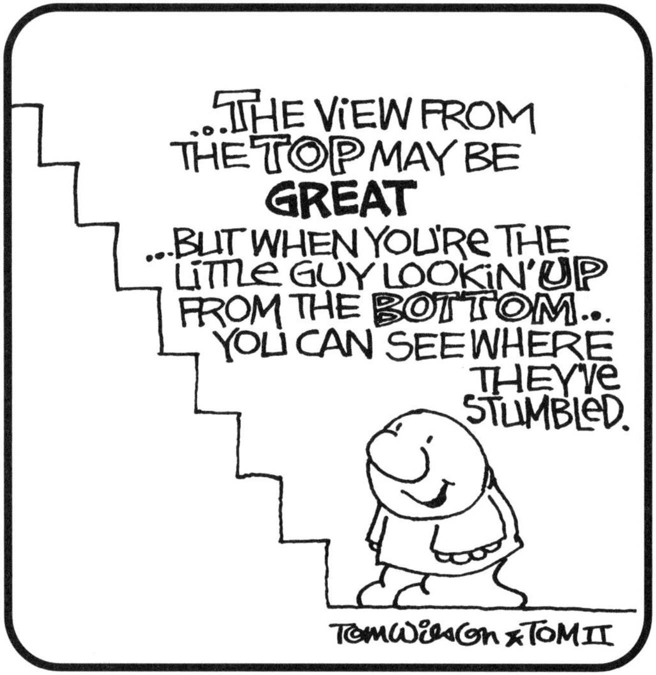
...THE VIEW FROM THE TOP MAY BE GREAT ...BUT WHEN YOU'RE THE LITTLE GUY LOOKIN' UP FROM THE BOTTOM... YOU CAN SEE WHERE THEY'VE STUMBLED.
Tom Wilson & TOM II

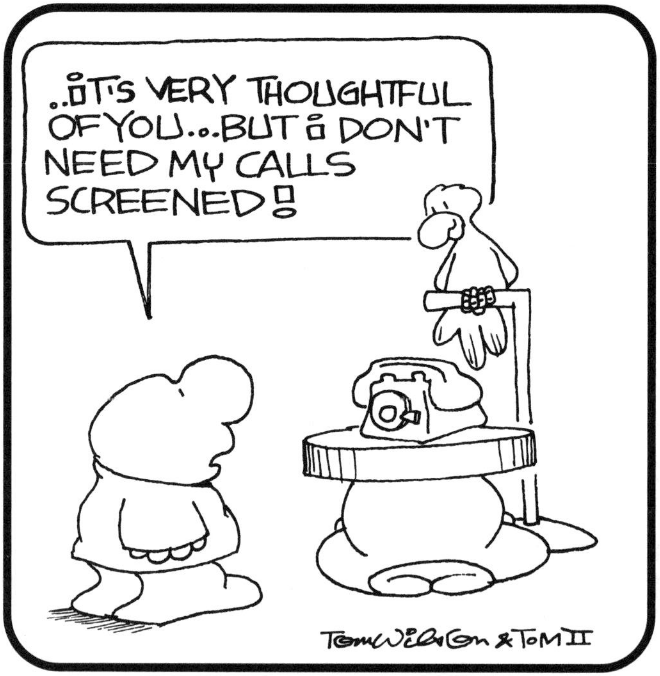
..IT'S VERY THOUGHTFUL OF YOU...BUT I DON'T NEED MY CALLS SCREENED!
Tom Wilson & TOM II

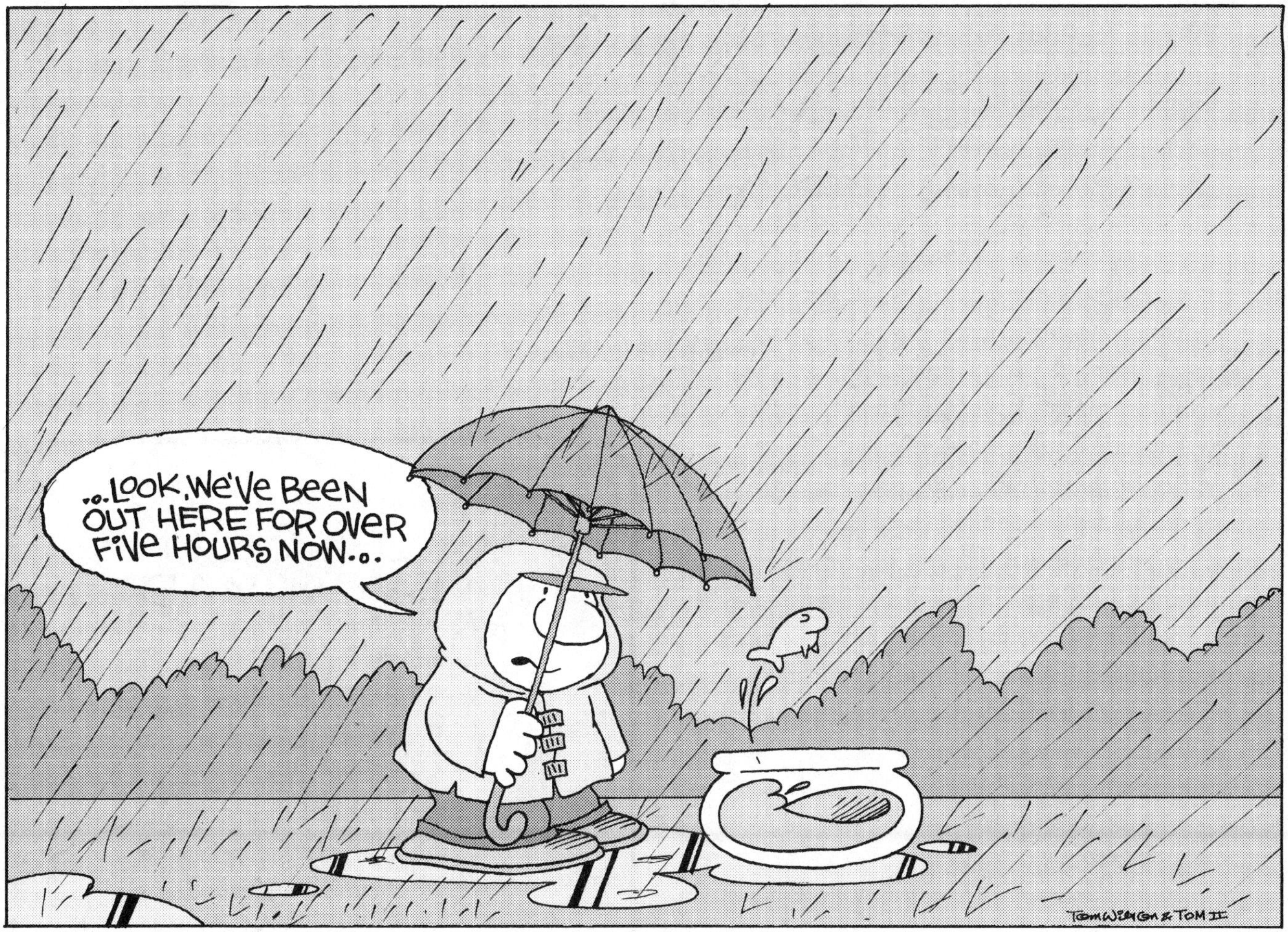
..LOOK, WE'VE BEEN OUT HERE FOR OVER FIVE HOURS NOW..
TOM WILSON & TOM II

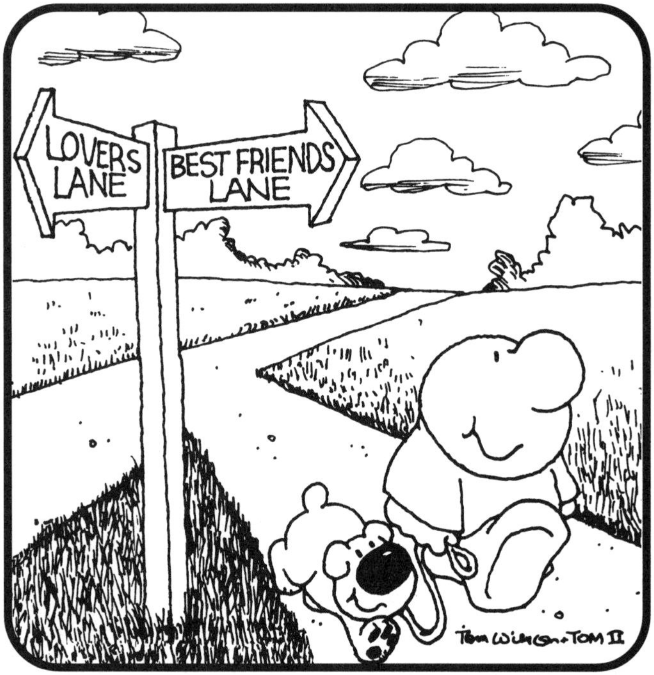
LOVERS LANE
BEST FRIENDS LANE
Tom Wilson + TOM II

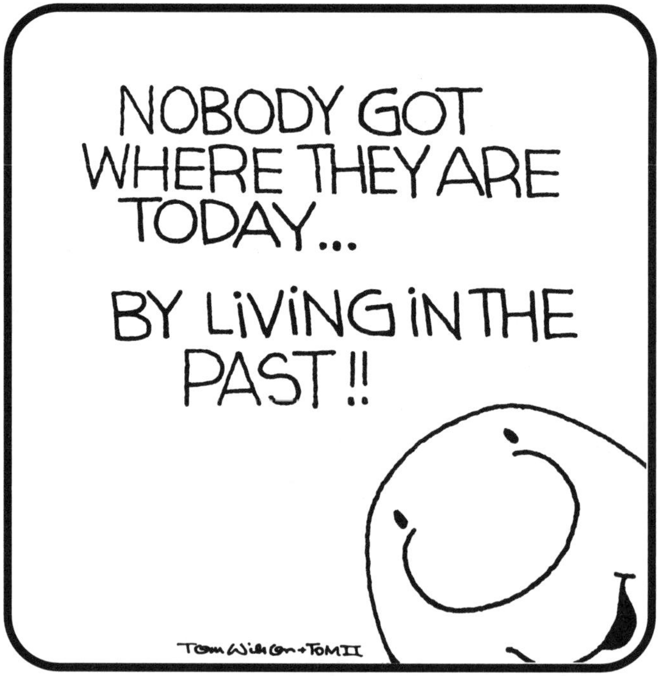
NOBODY GOT WHERE THEY ARE TODAY...
BY LiViNG iN THE PAST!!
Tom Wilson + TOM II

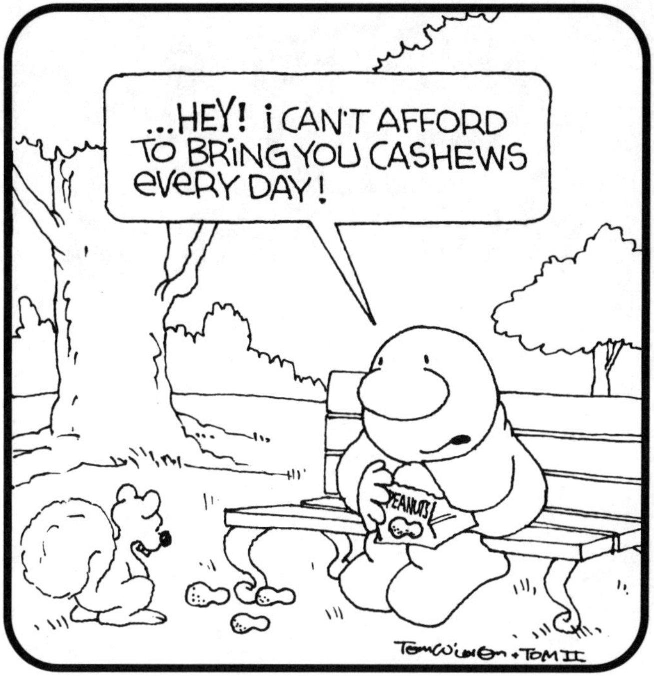
...HEY! I CAN'T AFFORD TO BRING YOU CASHEWS EVERY DAY!
PEANUTS!
TOM WILSON + TOM II

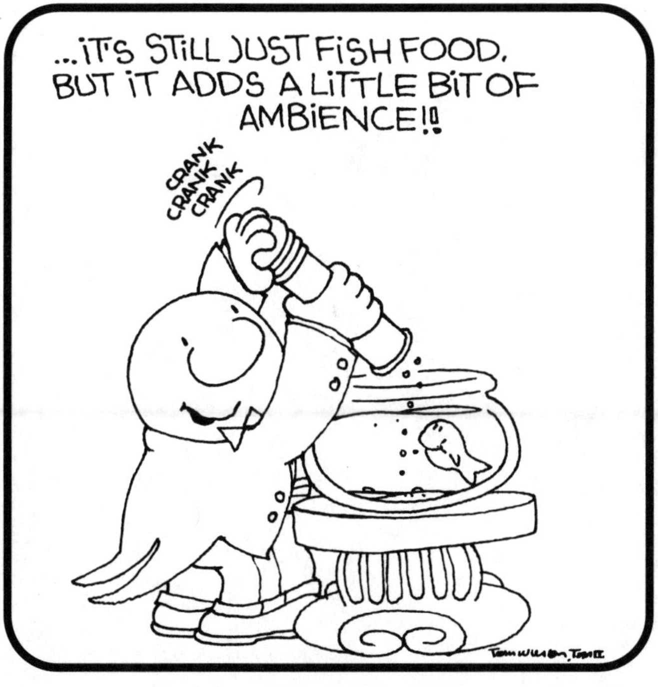
...IT'S STILL JUST FISH FOOD, BUT IT ADDS A LITTLE BIT OF AMBIENCE!!
CRANK CRANK CRANK
TOM WILSON, TOM II

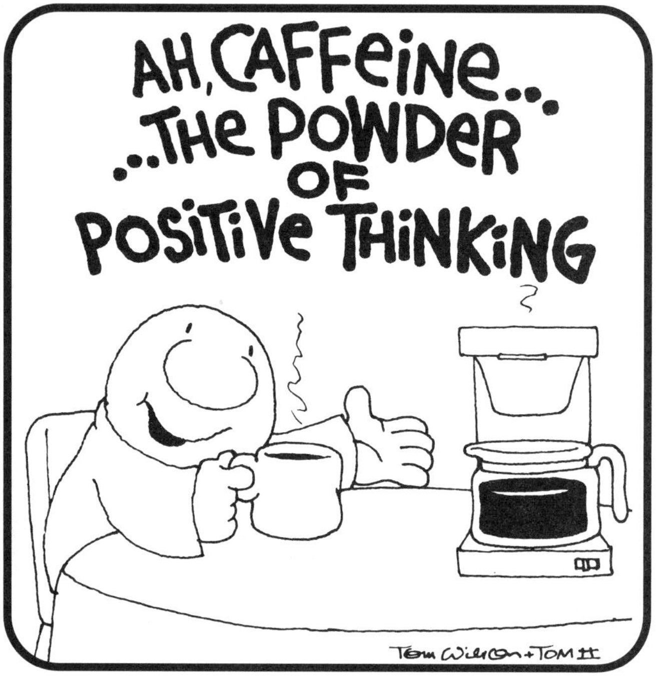
AH, CAFFeiNe... ...THe POWDeR OF POSITiVe THiNKiNG
Tom Wilson + TOM II

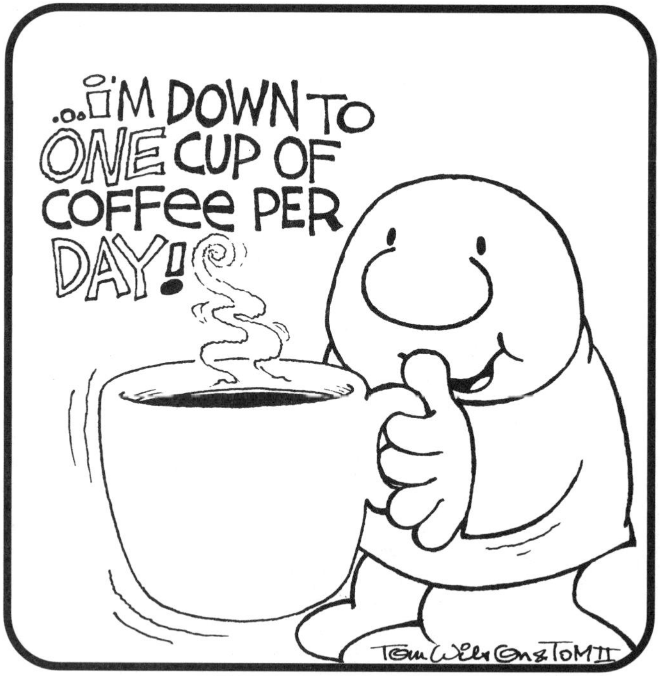
...I'M DOWN TO ONE CUP OF COFFee PER DAY!
Tom Wilson & TOM II

..DO YOU REALIZE THAT WE'VE BEEN OUT HERE FOR 3 HOURS AND YOU HAVEN'T HAD A SINGLE BITE ?
..THAT'S BECAUSE I'M NOT USING ANY BAIT!!
HUH?
..SOMETIMES IT'S THE FISH I'M AFTER..
..AND SOMETIMES IT'S JUST THE FISHING!

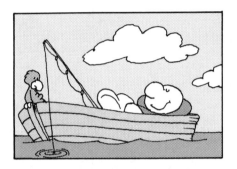

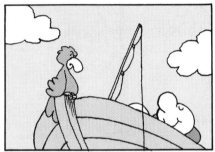

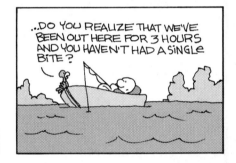

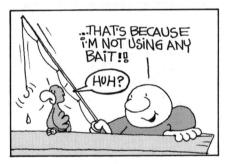

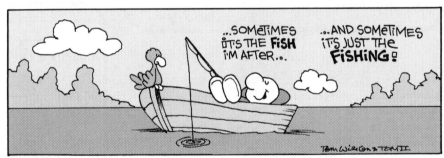

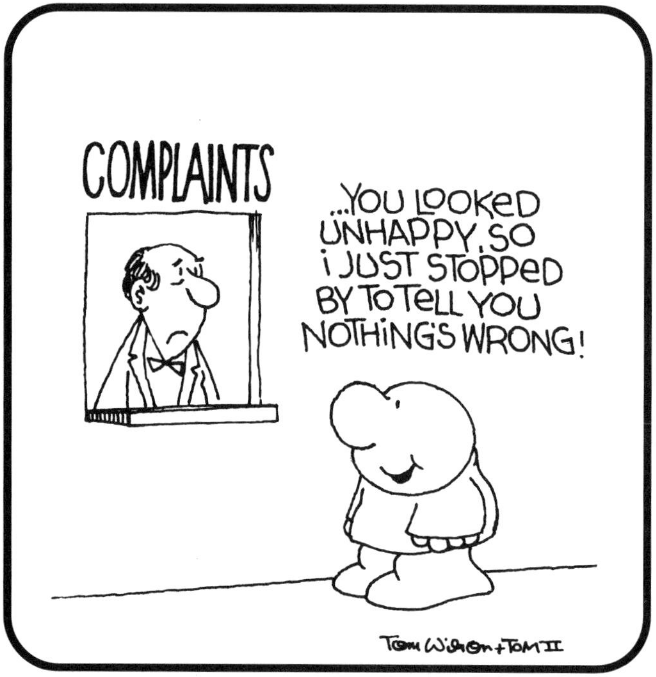
COMPLAINTS
...YOU LOOKED UNHAPPY, SO I JUST STOPPED BY TO TELL YOU NOTHING'S WRONG!
Tom Wilson + Tom II

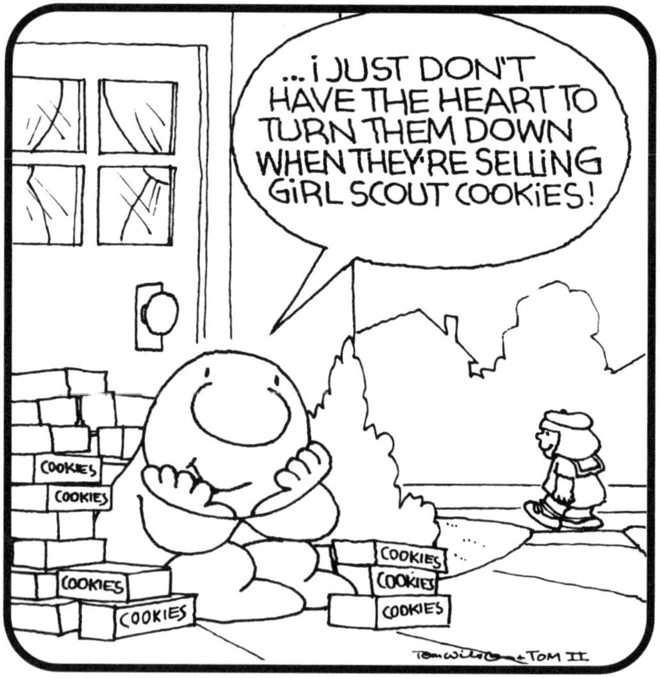
...I JUST DON'T HAVE THE HEART TO TURN THEM DOWN WHEN THEY'RE SELLING GIRL SCOUT COOKIES!
COOKIES
COOKIES
COOKIES
COOKIES
COOKIES
COOKIES
COOKIES
TOM II

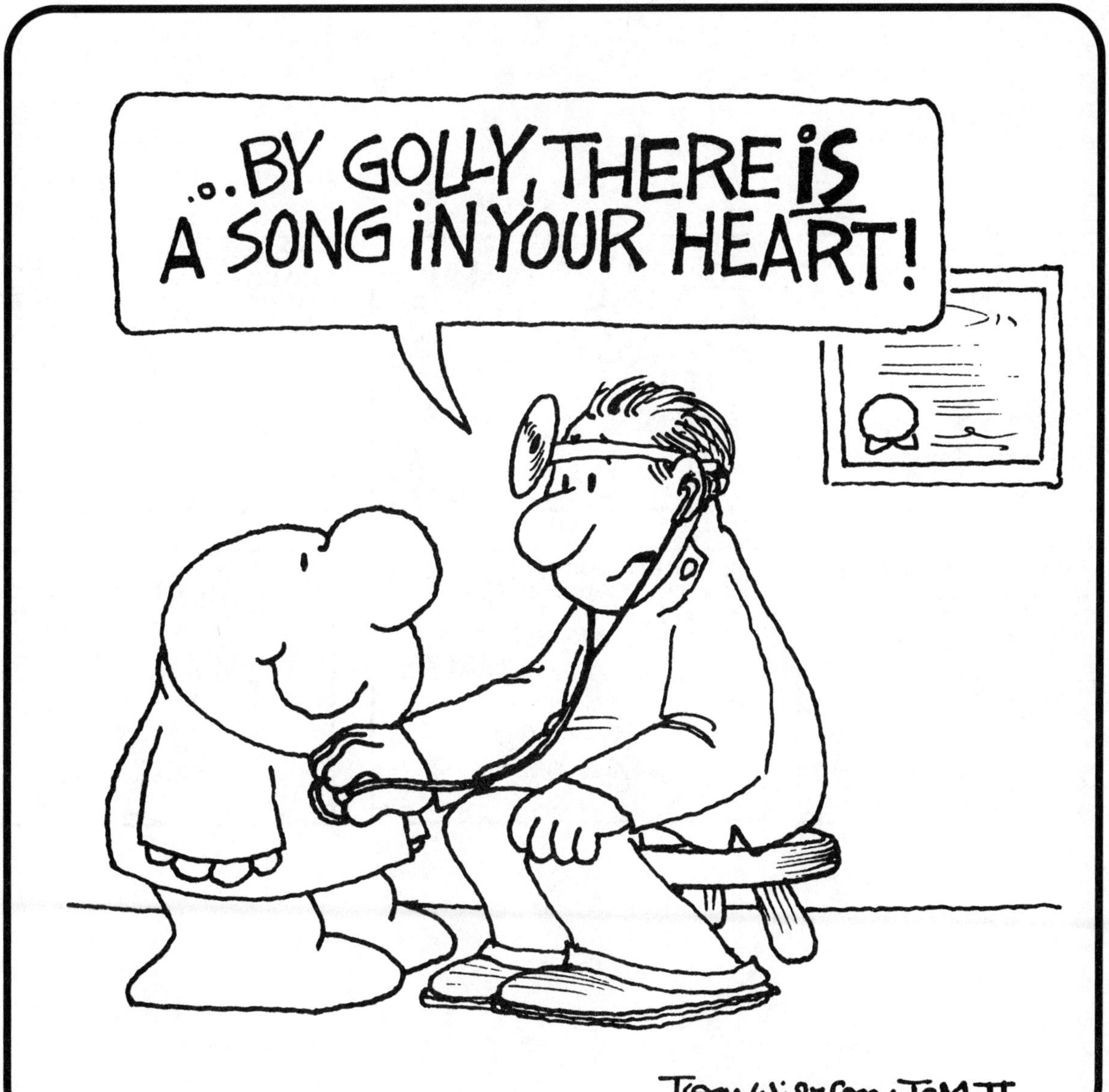
...BY GOLLY, THERE IS A SONG IN YOUR HEART!
TOM WILSON + TOM II

THERE HAVE BEEN SO MANY BOOKS WRITTEN ABOUT HOW TO WIN AT THE GAME OF LOVE!
WIN AT LOVE
LOVE PLAY
...WE CALL LOVE A 'GAME' BECAUSE ALL OF US FEAR WHAT WE DON'T UNDERSTAND, BUT WE DO UNDERSTAND THAT WE ALL NEED LOVE!
SO WE TRY TO MAKE LOVE FAMILIAR BY CALLING LOVE A GAME, WITH MOVES, RULES, WITH PLAYERS, WINNERS & LOSERS...
WHAT'S AMAZING IS THAT FOR THOUSANDS OF YEARS, HISTORY'S GREATEST WRITERS & THINKERS SPEAK OF THE GAME OF LOVE...
...BUT STILL HAVEN'T FIGURED OUT HOW TO WIN & WHAT IT'S ALL ABOUT!..SO MAYBE LOVE ISN'T A GAME WE PLAY...
MAYBE...
LOVE PLAYS US!

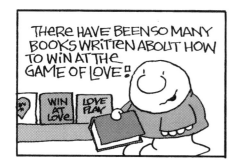

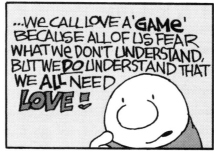

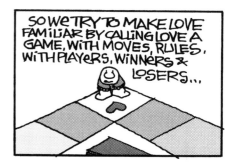

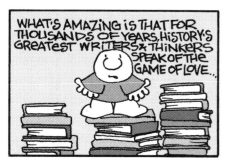

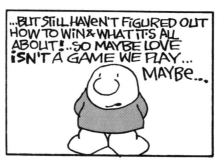

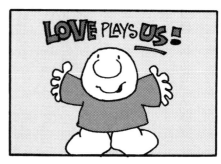

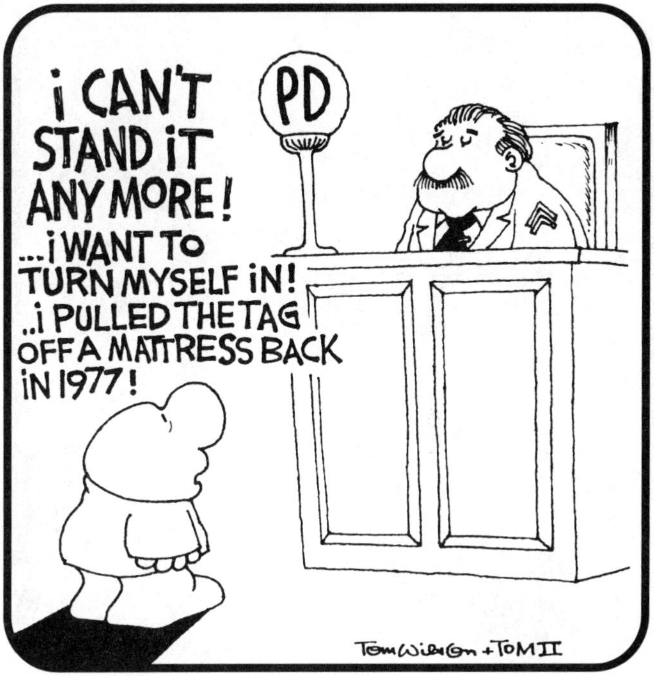
i CAN'T STAND iT ANY MORE! ...i WANT TO TURN MYSELF iN! ..i PULLED THE TAG OFF A MATTRESS BACK iN 1977!
PD
Tom Wilson + TOM II

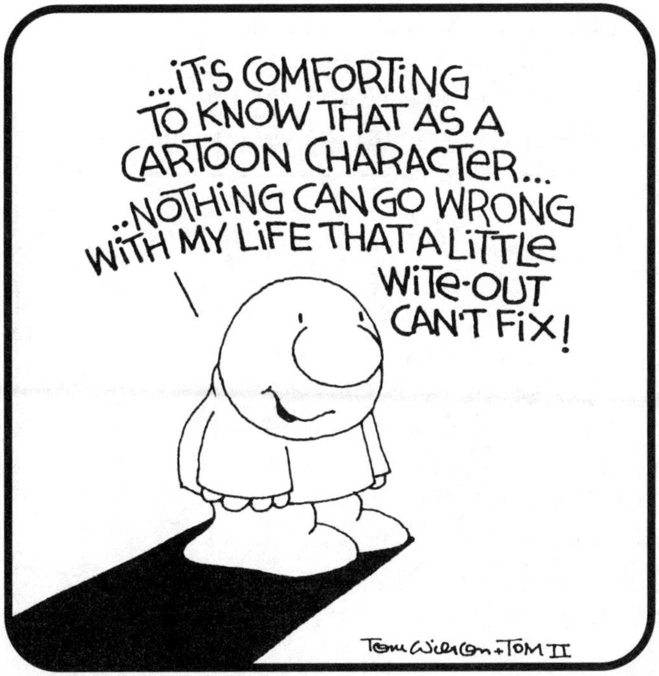
...iT'S COMFORTiNG TO KNOW THAT AS A CARTOON CHARACTER... ..NOTHiNG CAN GO WRONG WiTH MY LiFE THAT A LiTTLE WiTE-OUT CAN'T FiX!
Tom Wilson + TOM II

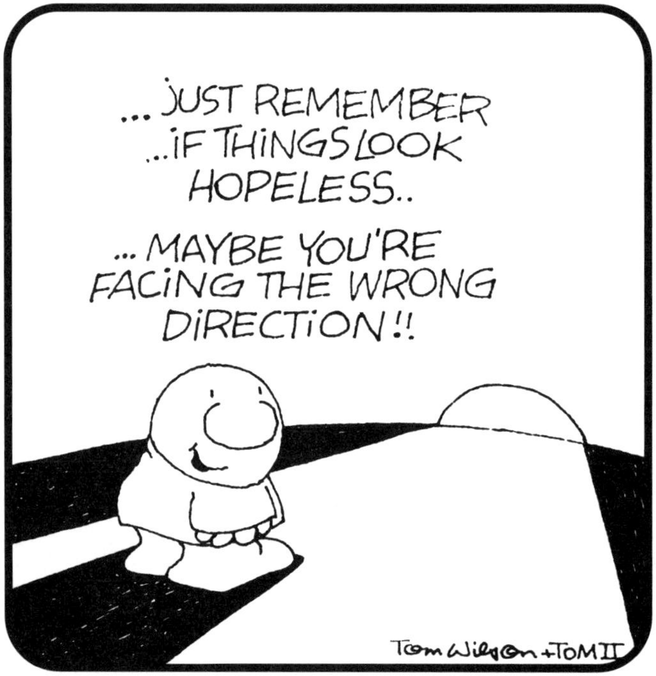
...JUST REMEMBER ...IF THINGS LOOK HOPELESS..
...MAYBE YOU'RE FACING THE WRONG DIRECTION!!
Tom Wilson + TOM II

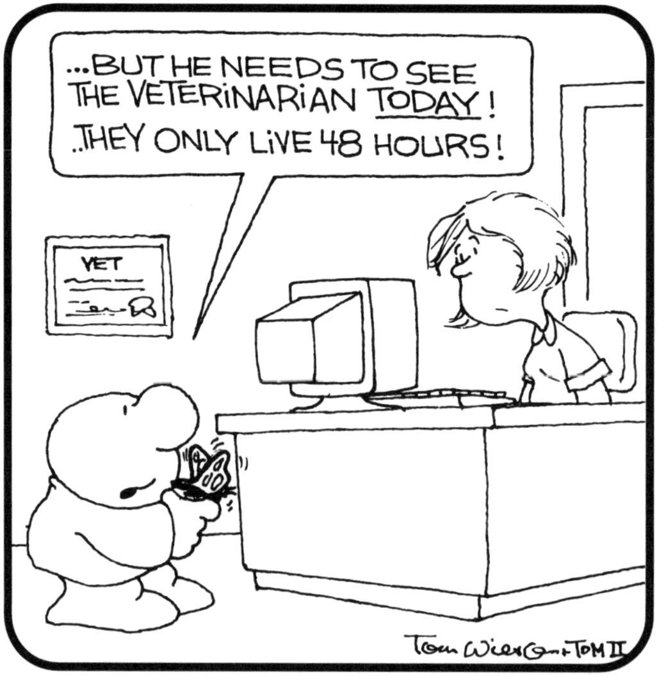
...BUT HE NEEDS TO SEE THE VETERINARIAN TODAY! ..THEY ONLY LIVE 48 HOURS!
VET
Tom Wilson + TOM II

HELP!
—I'VE FALLEN AND I CAN'T GET UP!
HELP!
...I'VE FALLEN... I CAN'T GET UP!
!
TOM WILSON & TOM II

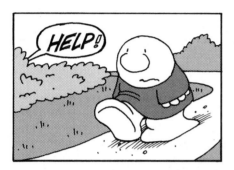

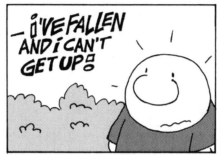

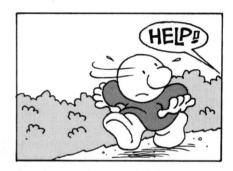

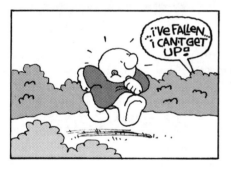

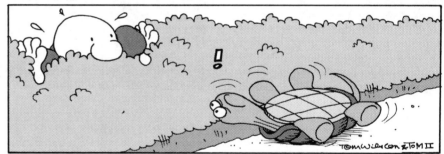

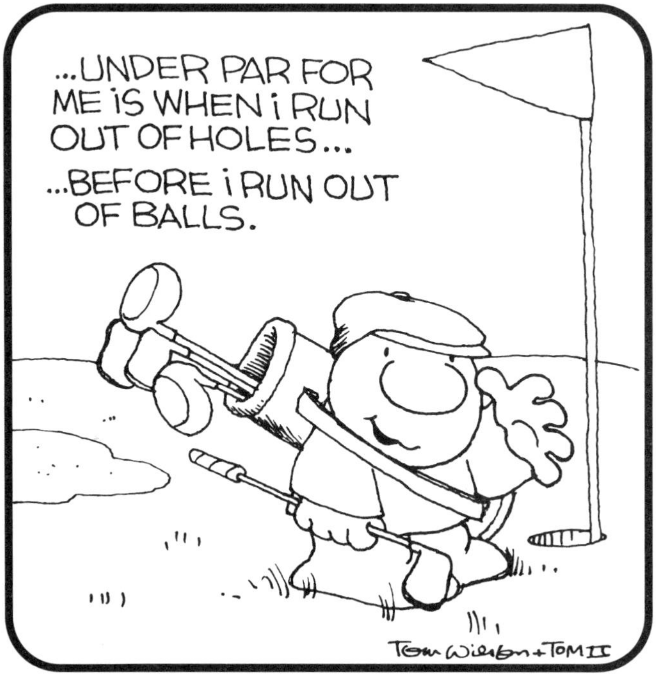
...UNDER PAR FOR ME iS WHEN i RUN OUT OF HOLES...
...BEFORE i RUN OUT OF BALLS.
Tom Wilson + TOM II

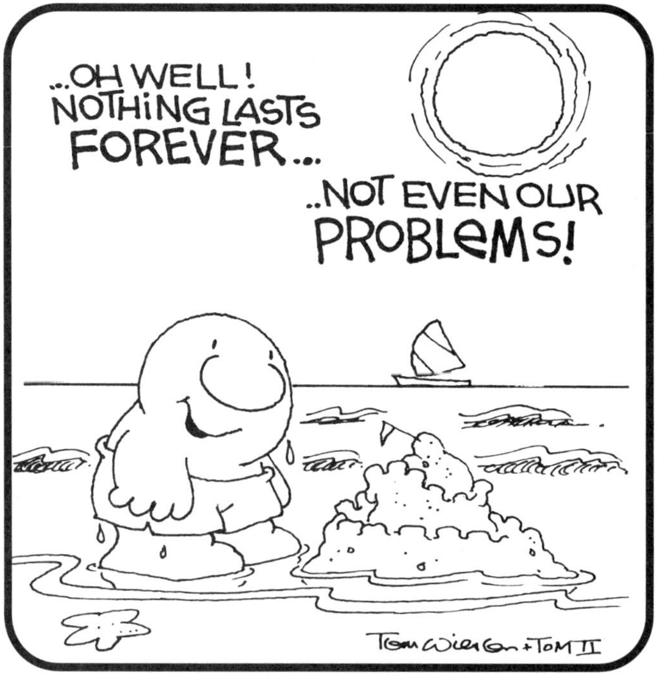
...OH WELL! NOTHiNG LASTS FOREVER...
..NOT EVEN OUR PROBLEMS!
Tom Wilson + TOM II

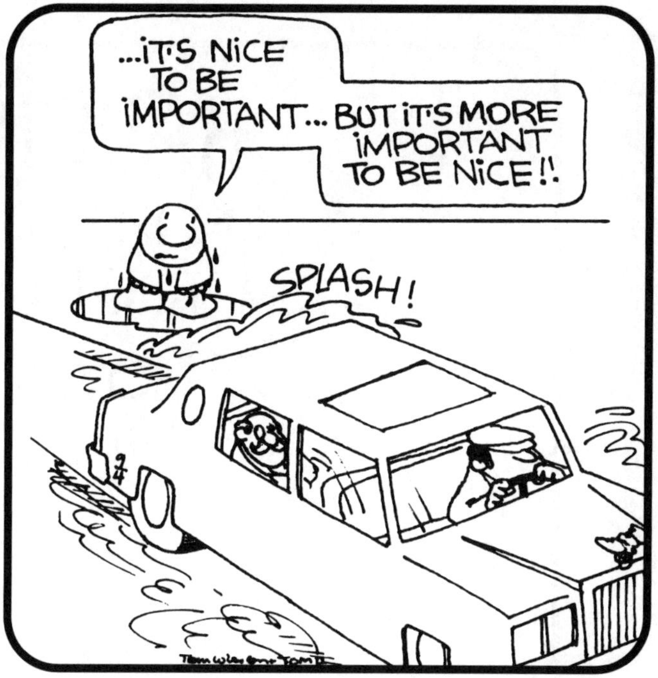
...IT'S NICE TO BE IMPORTANT... BUT IT'S MORE IMPORTANT TO BE NICE!!
SPLASH!

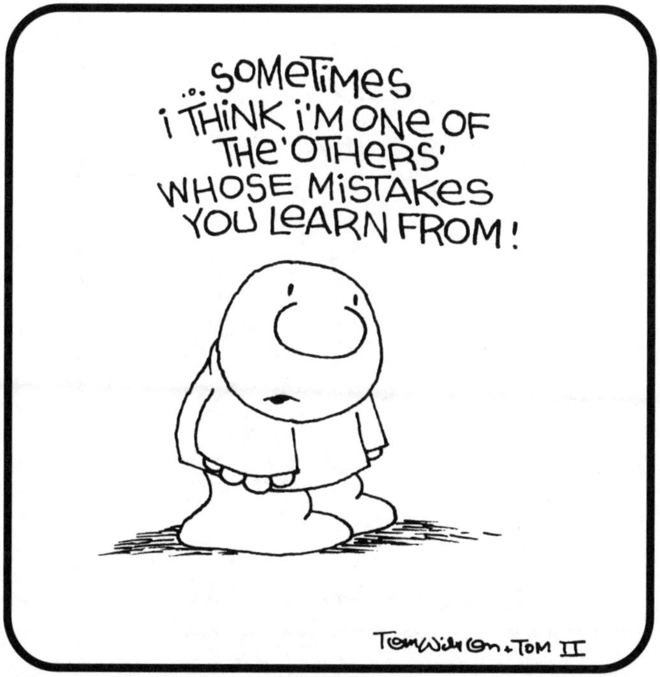
... SOMETIMES I THINK I'M ONE OF THE 'OTHERS' WHOSE MISTAKES YOU LEARN FROM!

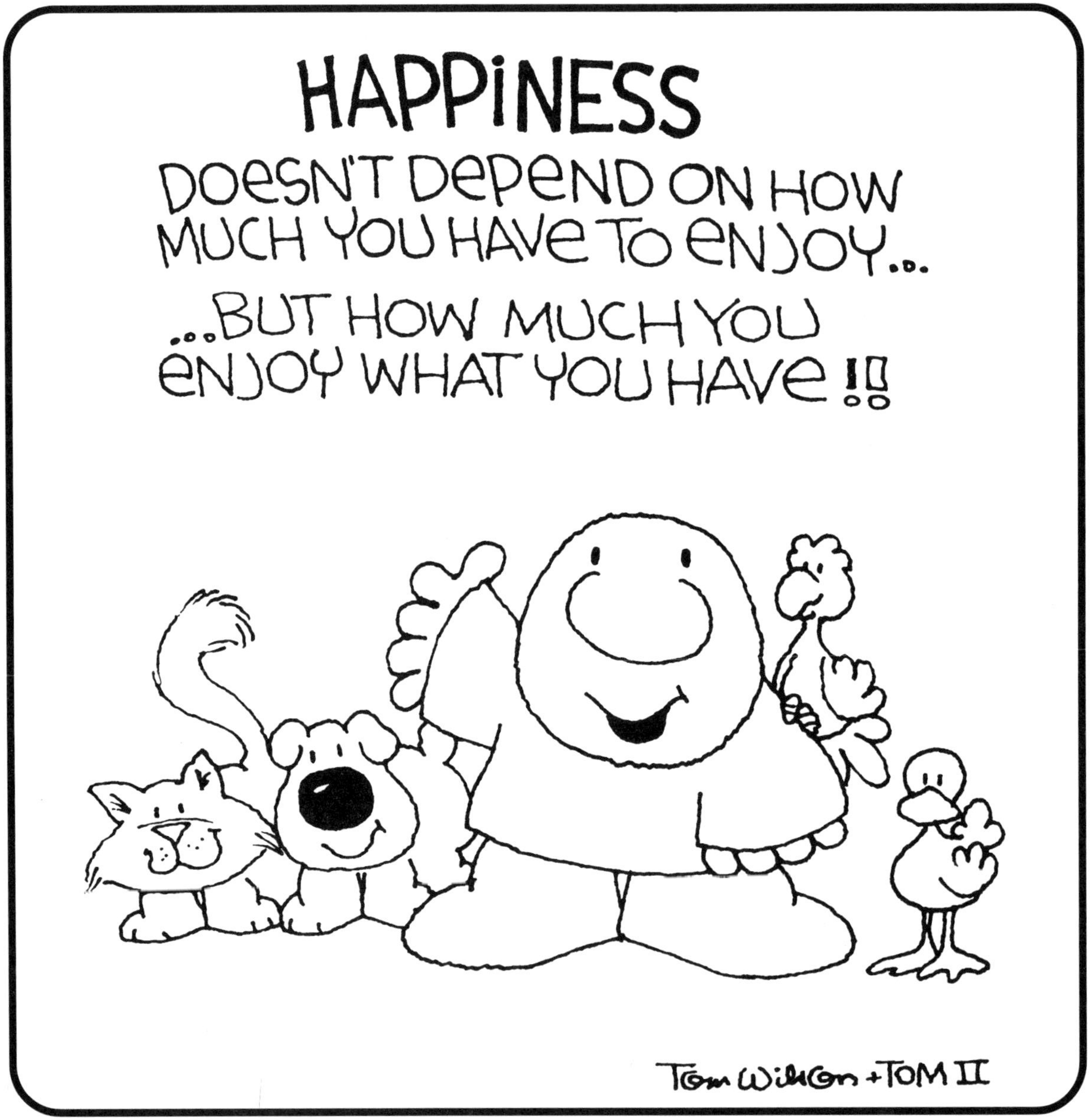
HAPPINESS
DOESN'T DEPEND ON HOW MUCH YOU HAVE TO ENJOY...
...BUT HOW MUCH YOU ENJOY WHAT YOU HAVE!!
Tom Wilson + TOM II

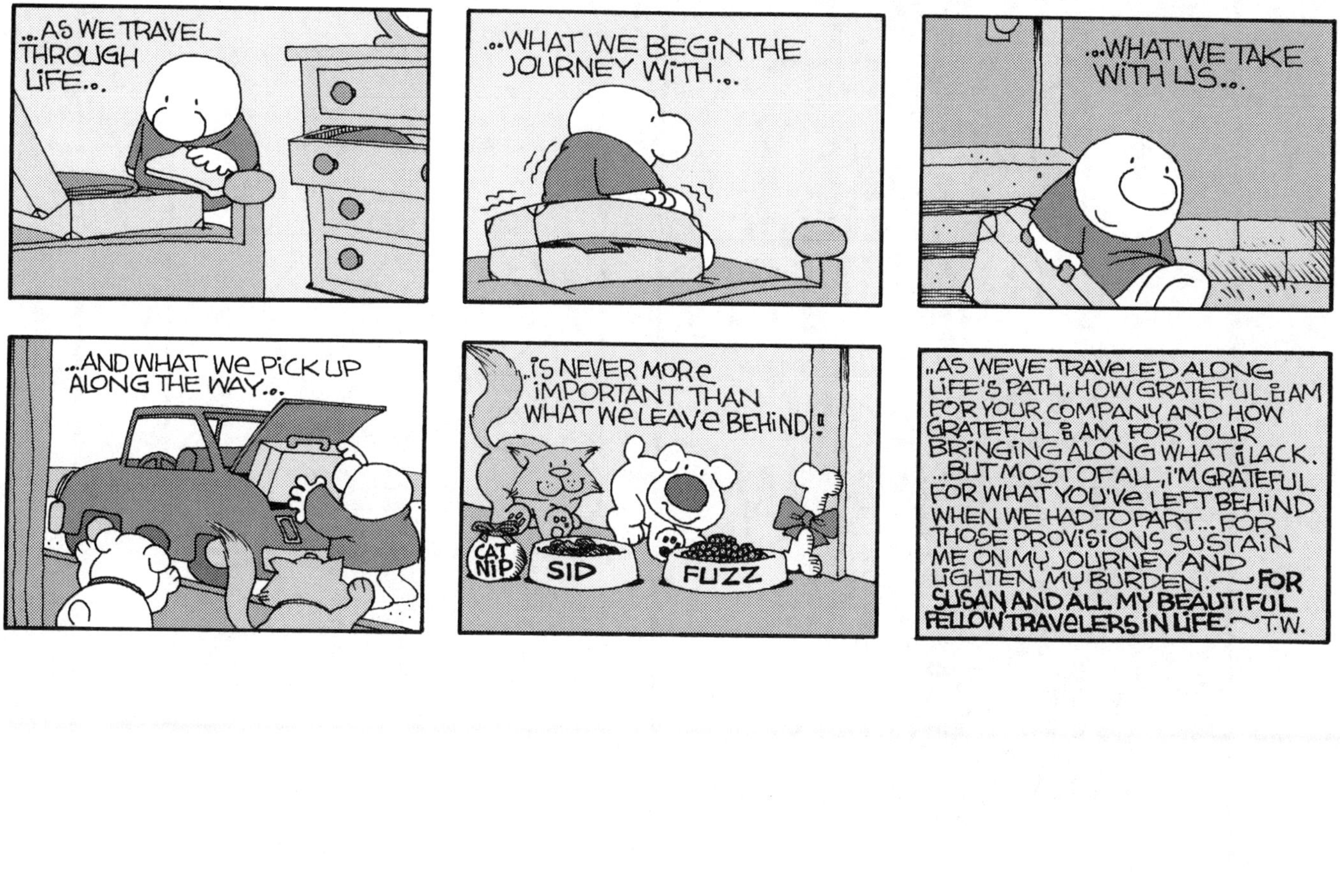
...AS WE TRAVEL THROUGH LIFE...
...WHAT WE BEGIN THE JOURNEY WITH...
...WHAT WE TAKE WITH US...
...AND WHAT WE PICK UP ALONG THE WAY...
...IS NEVER MORE IMPORTANT THAN WHAT WE LEAVE BEHIND!
CAT NIP
SID
FUZZ
..AS WE'VE TRAVELED ALONG LIFE'S PATH, HOW GRATEFUL I AM FOR YOUR COMPANY AND HOW GRATEFUL I AM FOR YOUR BRINGING ALONG WHAT I LACK. ...BUT MOST OF ALL, I'M GRATEFUL FOR WHAT YOU'VE LEFT BEHIND WHEN WE HAD TO PART... FOR THOSE PROVISIONS SUSTAIN ME ON MY JOURNEY AND LIGHTEN MY BURDEN. ~ FOR SUSAN AND ALL MY BEAUTIFUL FELLOW TRAVELERS IN LIFE. ~ T.W.

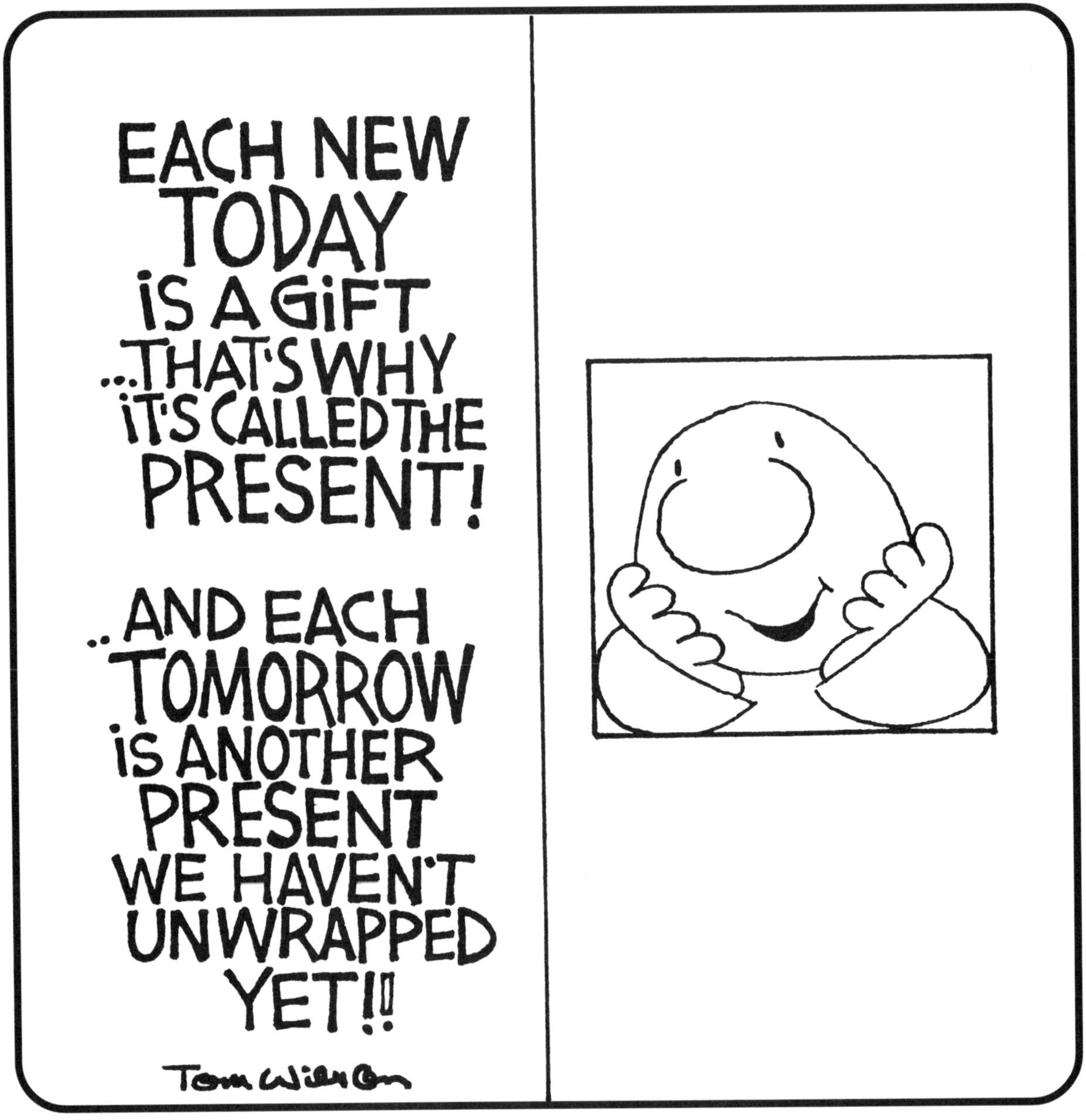
EACH NEW TODAY IS A GIFT ...THAT'S WHY IT'S CALLED THE PRESENT!
..AND EACH TOMORROW IS ANOTHER PRESENT WE HAVEN'T UNWRAPPED YET!!
Tom Wilson

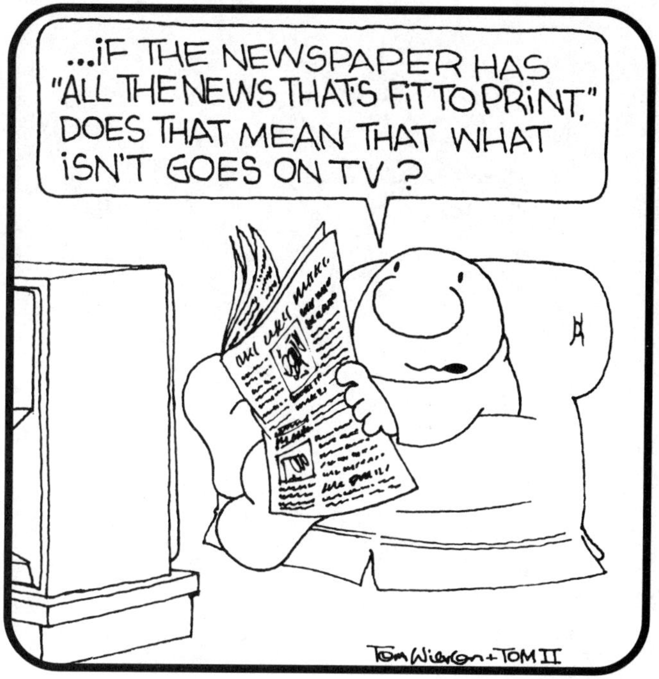
...IF THE NEWSPAPER HAS "ALL THE NEWS THAT'S FIT TO PRINT," DOES THAT MEAN THAT WHAT ISN'T GOES ON TV ?
Tom Wilson + TOM II

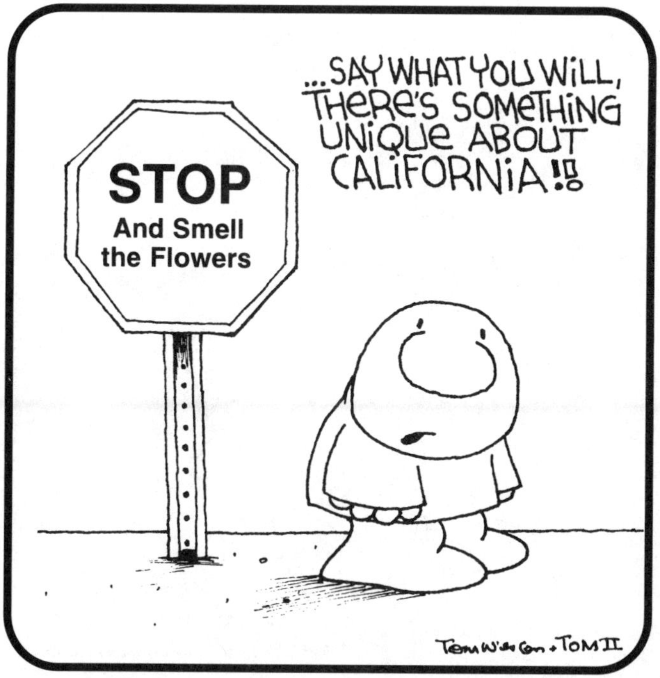
STOP
And Smell the Flowers
...SAY WHAT YOU WILL, THERE'S SOMETHING UNIQUE ABOUT CALIFORNIA!!
Tom Wilson + TOM II

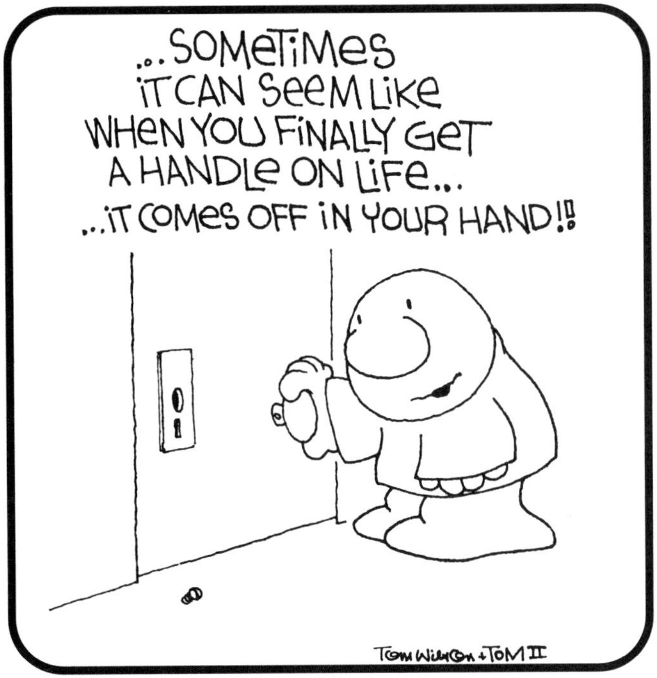
...SOMETIMES
IT CAN SEEM LIKE
WHEN YOU FINALLY GET
A HANDLE ON LIFE...
...IT COMES OFF IN YOUR HAND!!
Tom Wilson + Tom II

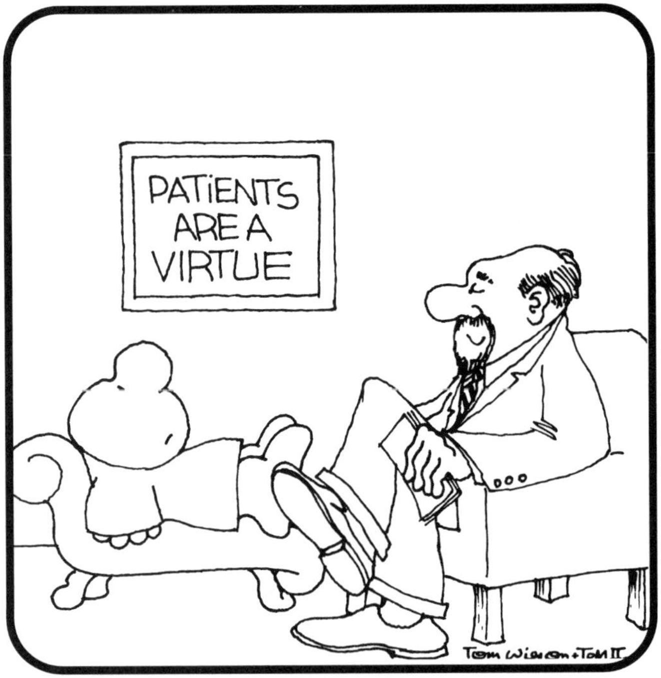
PATIENTS
ARE A
VIRTUE
Tom Wilson + Tom II

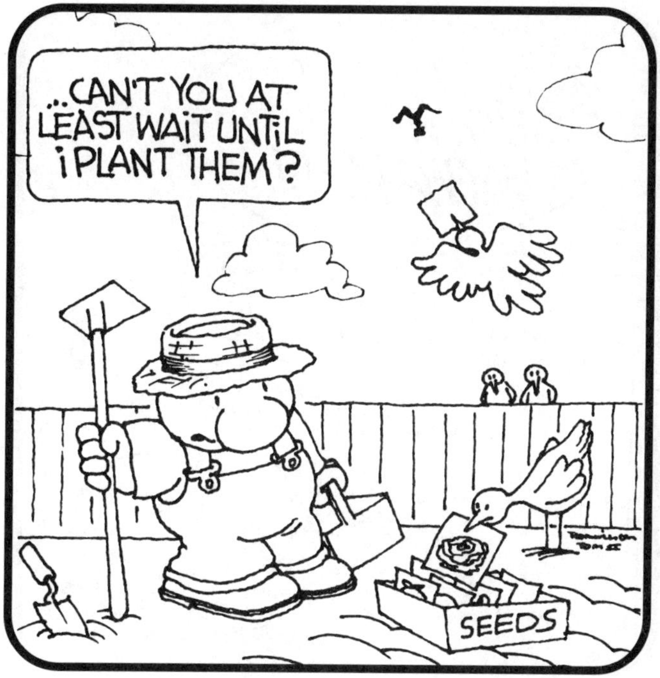
...CAN'T YOU AT LEAST WAIT UNTIL I PLANT THEM?
SEEDS

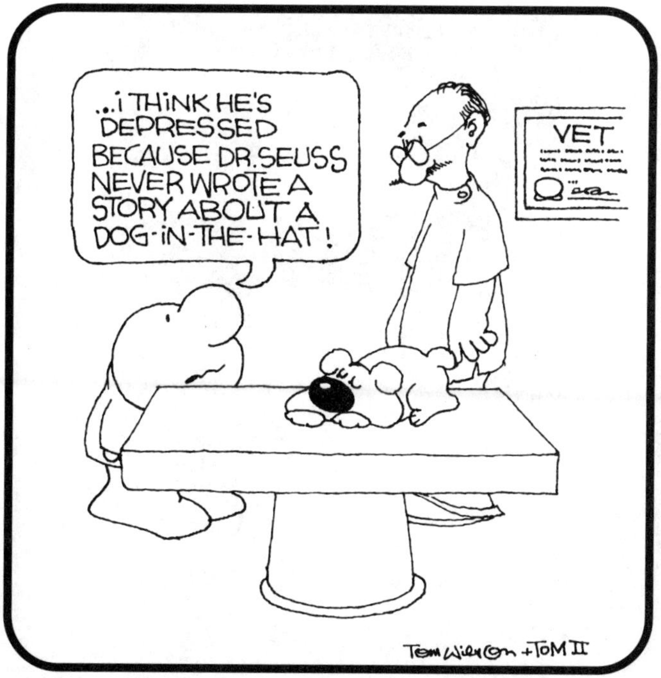
...I THINK HE'S DEPRESSED BECAUSE DR. SEUSS NEVER WROTE A STORY ABOUT A DOG-IN-THE-HAT!
VET
Tom Wilson + TOM II

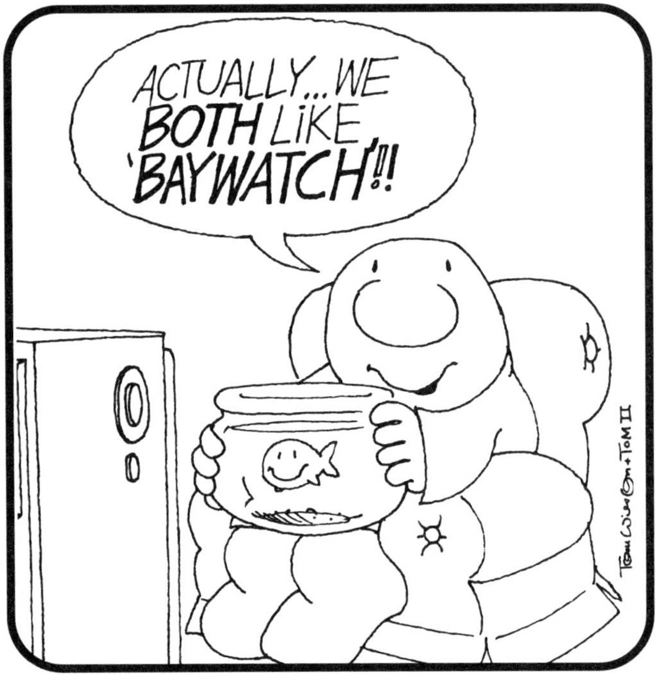
ACTUALLY...WE BOTH LIKE 'BAYWATCH'!!
TOM WILSON + TOM II

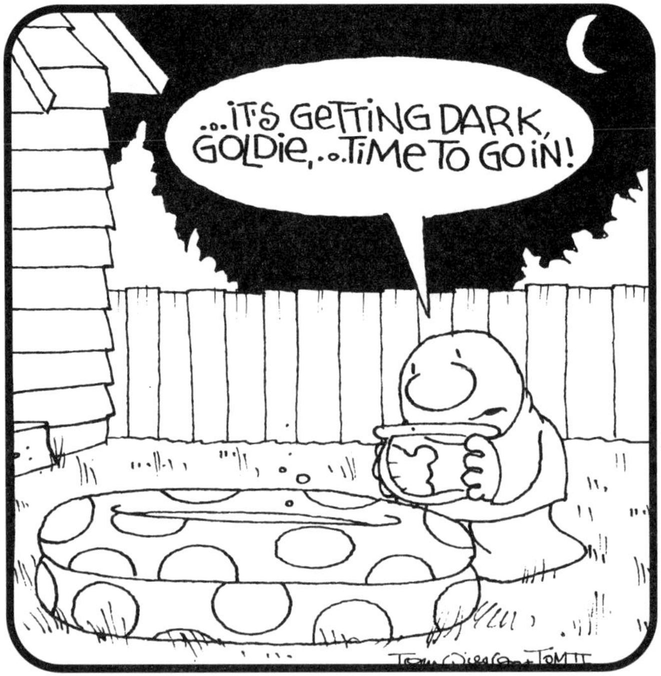
...IT'S GETTING DARK, GOLDIE,...TIME TO GO IN!

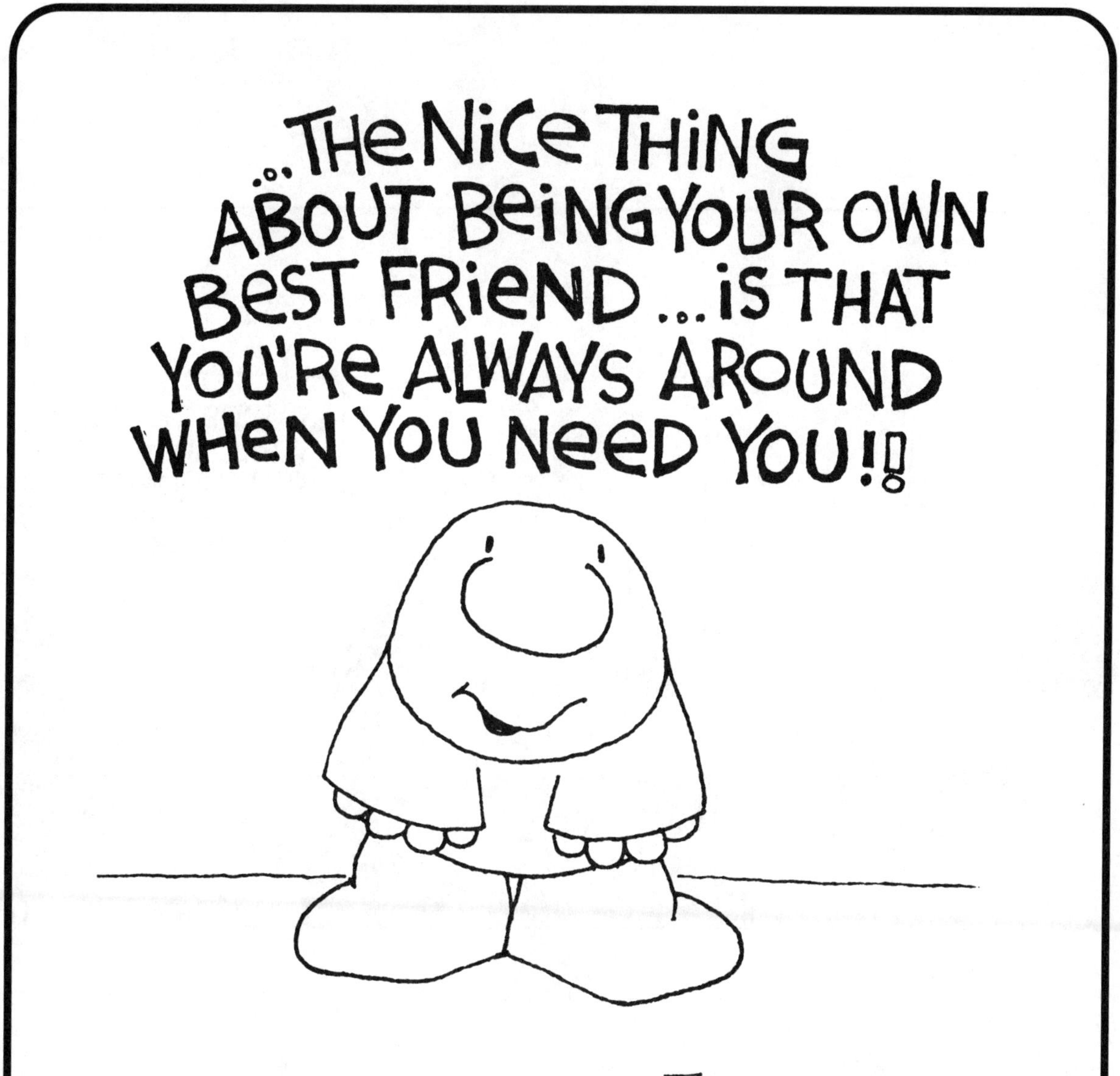
...THE NICE THING ABOUT BEING YOUR OWN BEST FRIEND ... IS THAT YOU'RE ALWAYS AROUND WHEN YOU NEED YOU!!
Tom Wilson + Tom II

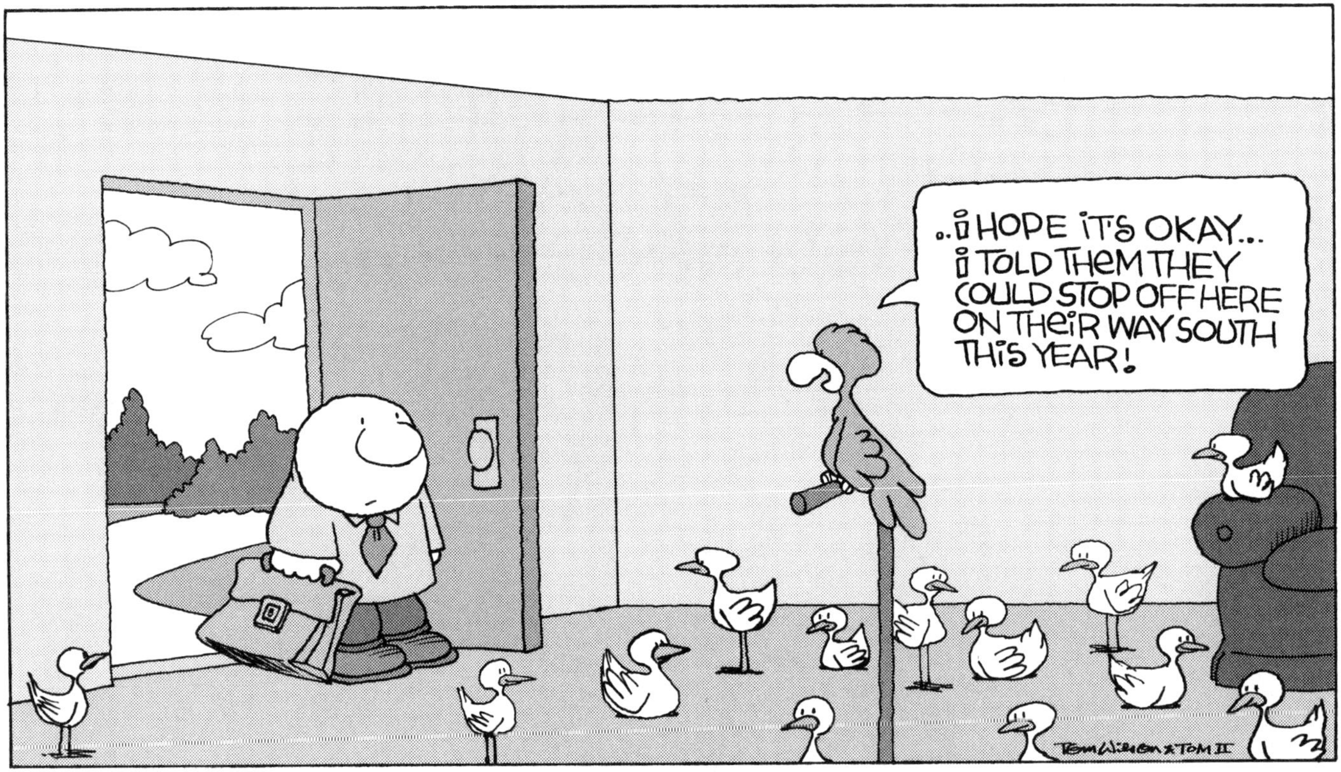
..I HOPE IT'S OKAY...
I TOLD THEM THEY
COULD STOP OFF HERE
ON THEIR WAY SOUTH
THIS YEAR!
Tom Wilson & TOM II

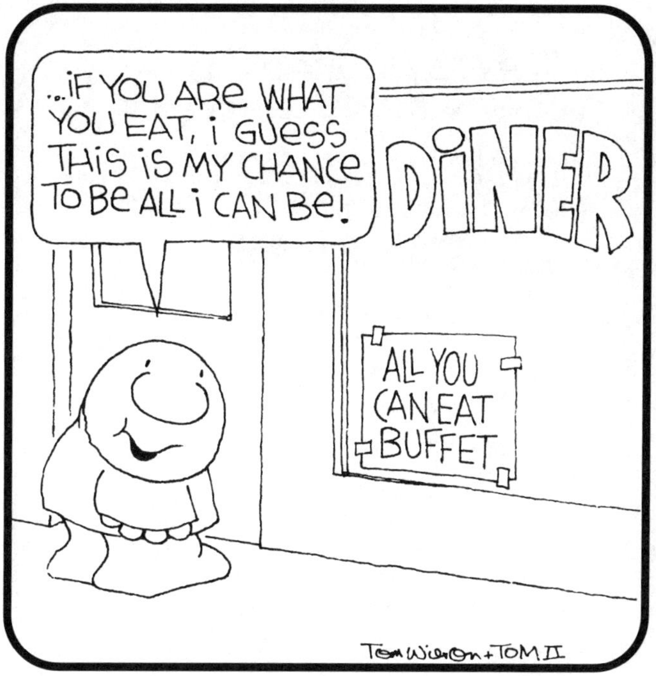
...IF YOU ARE WHAT YOU EAT, I GUESS THIS IS MY CHANCE TO BE ALL I CAN BE!
DINER
ALL YOU CAN EAT BUFFET
TOM WILSON + TOM II

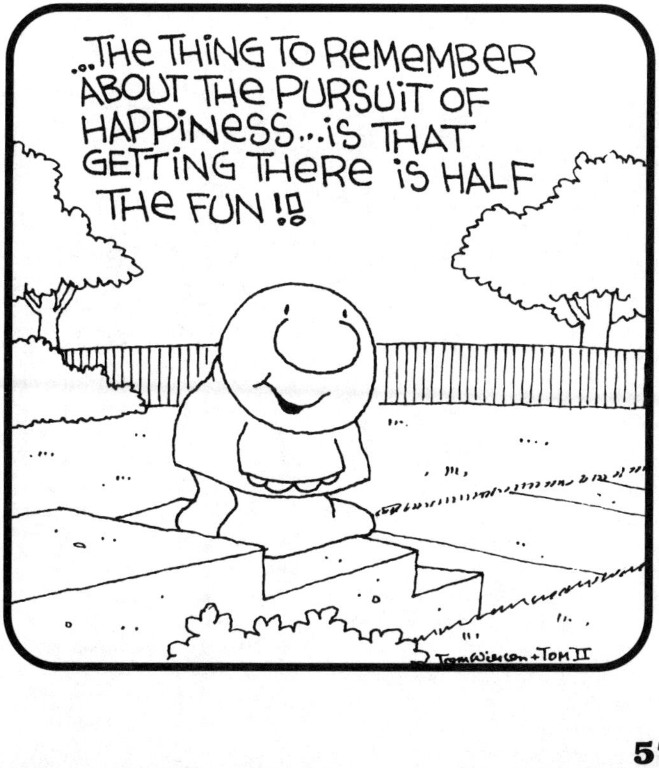
...THE THING TO REMEMBER ABOUT THE PURSUIT OF HAPPINESS...IS THAT GETTING THERE IS HALF THE FUN!!
TOM WILSON + TOM II

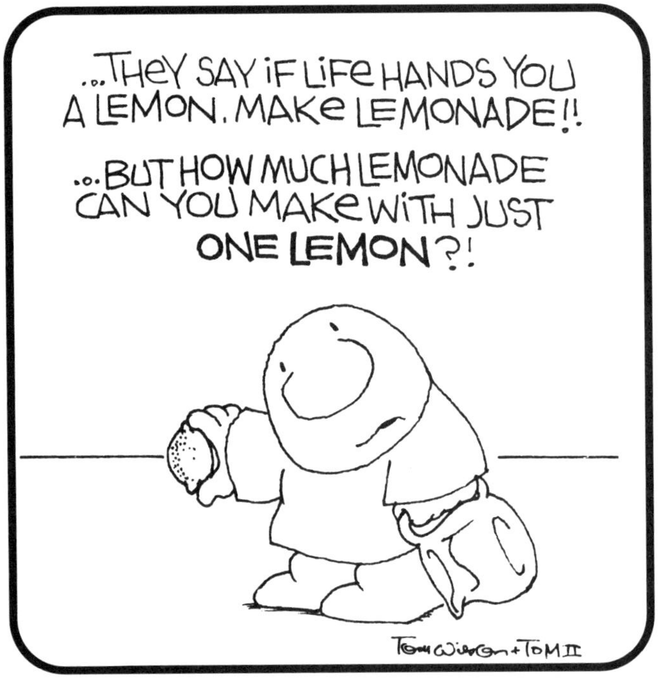
...THEY SAY IF LIFE HANDS YOU A LEMON, MAKE LEMONADE!!
...BUT HOW MUCH LEMONADE CAN YOU MAKE WITH JUST **ONE LEMON**?!
Tom Wilson + Tom II

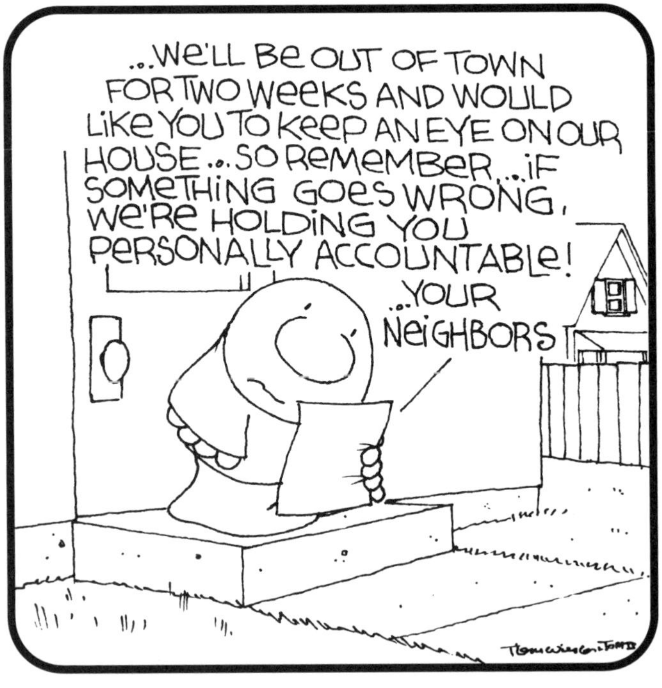
...WE'LL BE OUT OF TOWN FOR TWO WEEKS AND WOULD LIKE YOU TO KEEP AN EYE ON OUR HOUSE... SO REMEMBER... IF SOMETHING GOES WRONG, WE'RE HOLDING YOU PERSONALLY ACCOUNTABLE!
...YOUR NEIGHBORS
Tom Wilson + Tom II

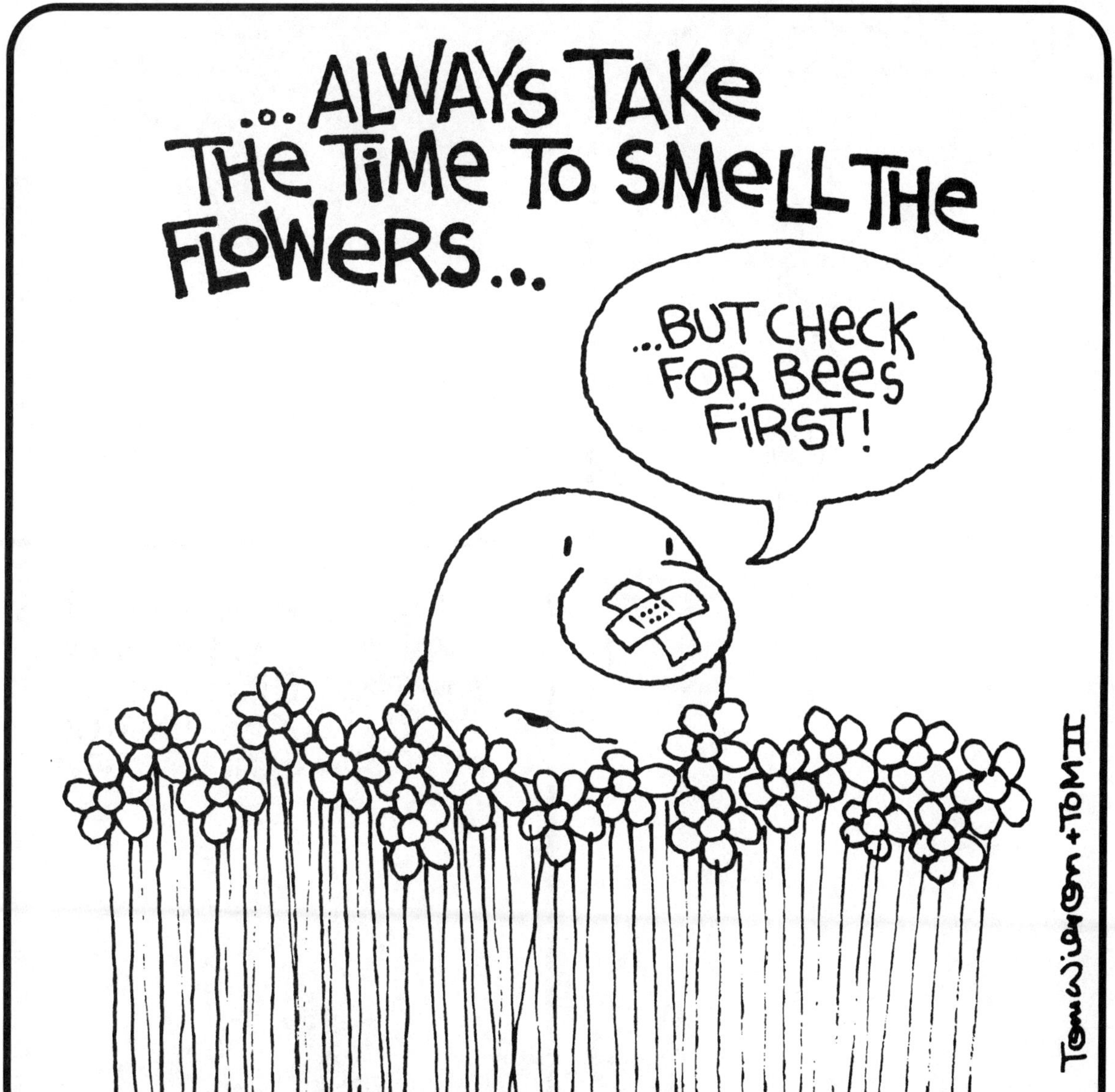
...ALWAYS TAKE THE TIME TO SMELL THE FLOWERS...
...BUT CHECK FOR BEES FIRST!
TOM WILSON + TOM II

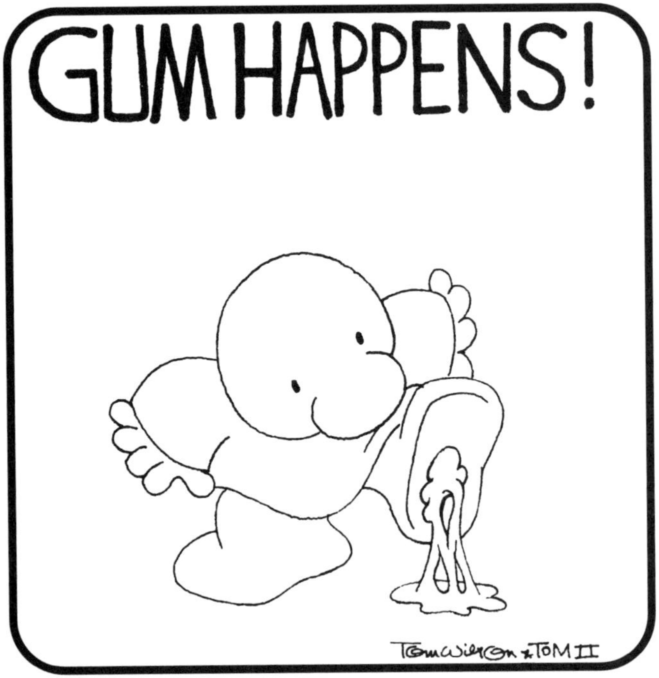
GUM HAPPENS!
Tom Wilson & TOM II

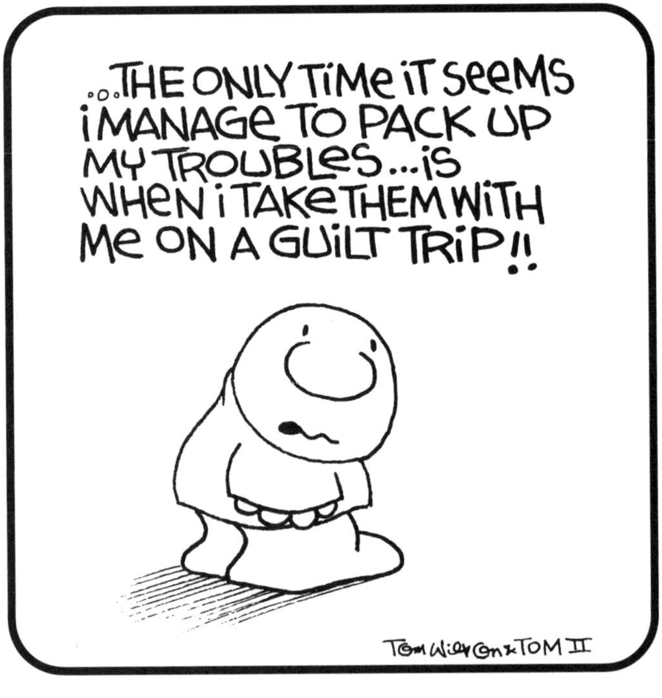
...THE ONLY TIME IT SEEMS I MANAGE TO PACK UP MY TROUBLES...IS WHEN I TAKE THEM WITH ME ON A GUILT TRIP!!
Tom Wilson & TOM II

STARLIGHT, STAR BRIGHT, FIRST STAR I SEE TONIGHT. I WISH I MAY, I WISH I MIGHT ...HAVE THE WISH I MAKE TONIGHT...
...FIRST OFF, I WISH FOR WORLD PEACE, ...AN END TO WORLD HUNGER, ...AN END TO ALL POLLUTION... BRING BACK "SEINFELD."...
WHOA... BACK UP A BIT, PAL!!
...I'M ONLY A DWARF STAR!
...HOW ABOUT WISHING FOR SOMETHING SMALL, ...LIKE A HAMBURGER AND FRIES?

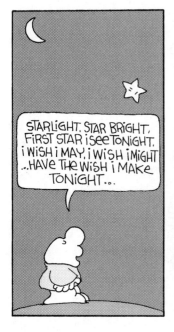

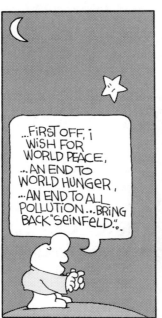

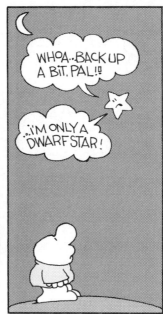

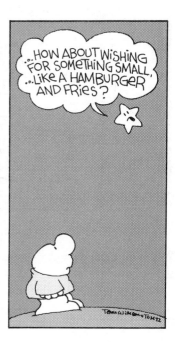

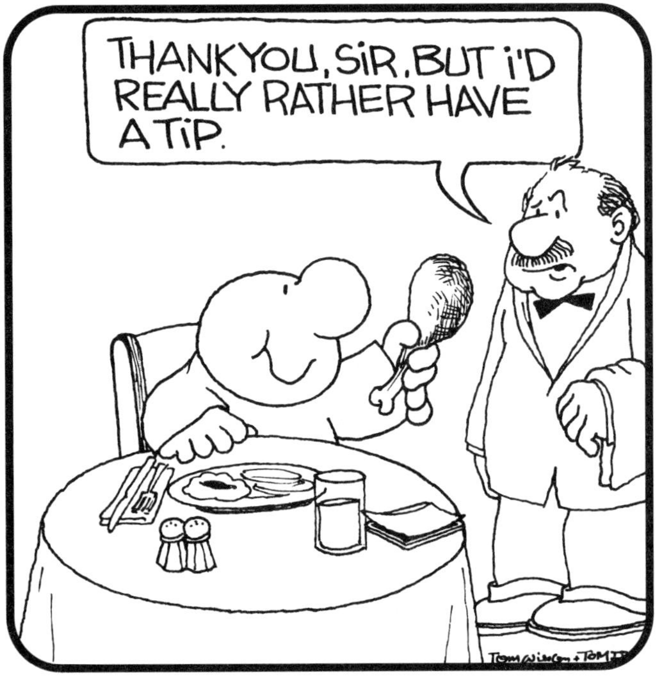
THANK YOU, SIR, BUT I'D REALLY RATHER HAVE A TIP.

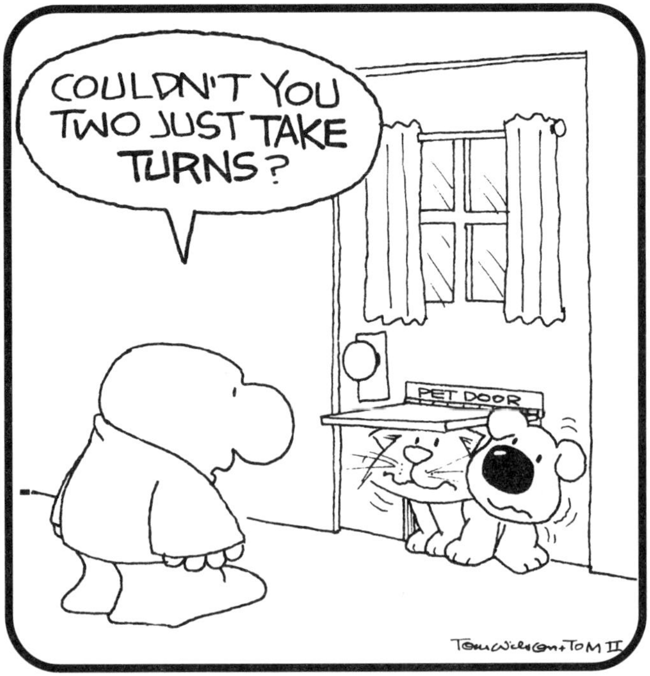
COULDN'T YOU TWO JUST TAKE TURNS?
PET DOOR

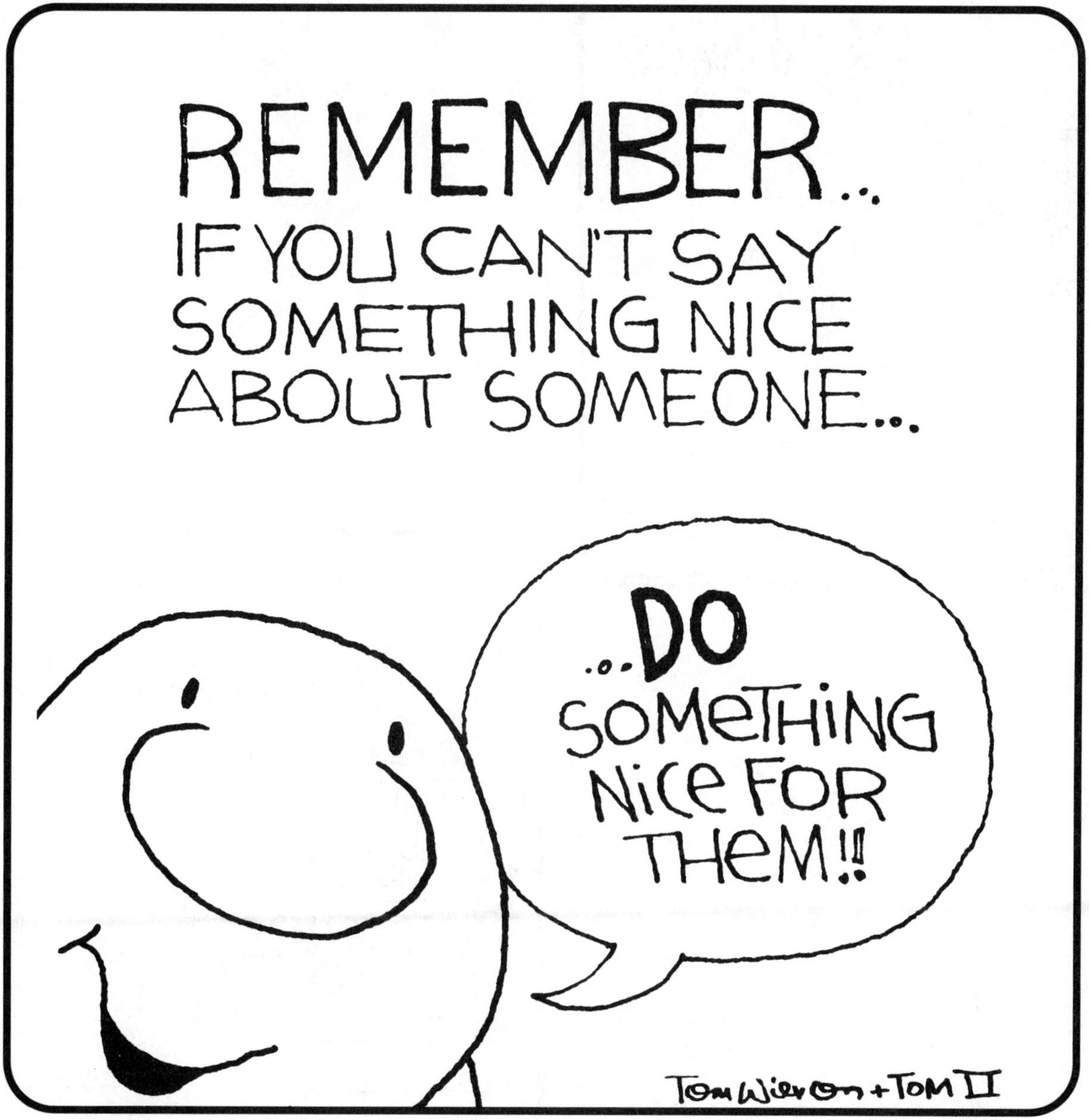
REMEMBER... IF YOU CAN'T SAY SOMETHING NICE ABOUT SOMEONE...
...DO SOMETHING NICE FOR THEM!!
Tom Wilson + TOM II

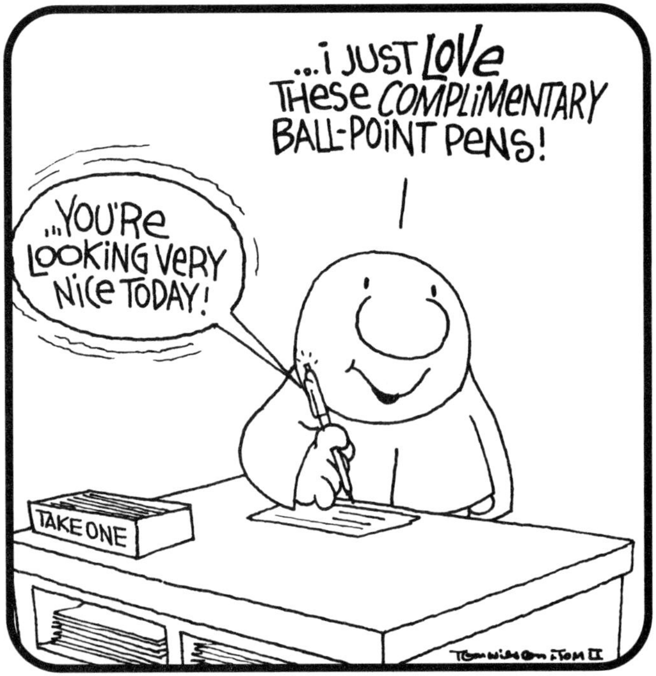
...i JUST LOVE THESE COMPLIMENTARY BALL-POINT PENS!
...YOU'RE LOOKING VERY NICE TODAY!
TAKE ONE
TOM WILSON & TOM II

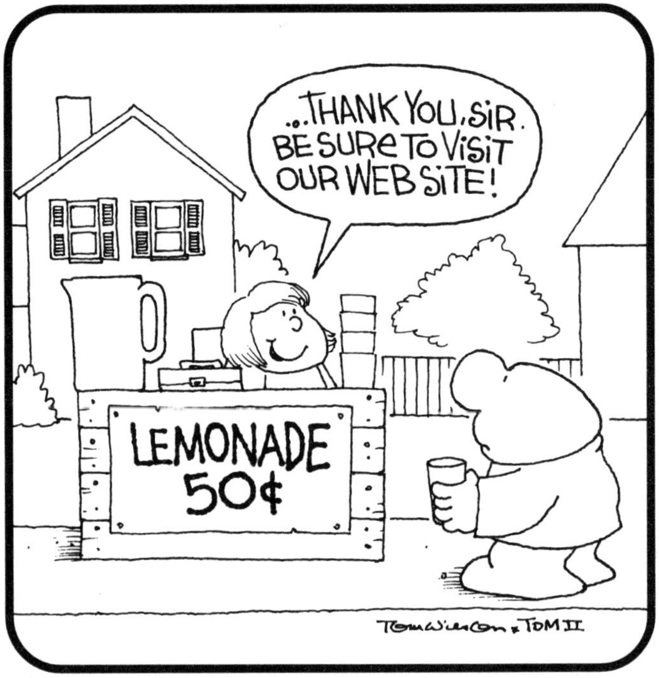
...THANK YOU, SIR. BE SURE TO VISIT OUR WEB SITE!
LEMONADE 50¢
TOM WILSON & TOM II

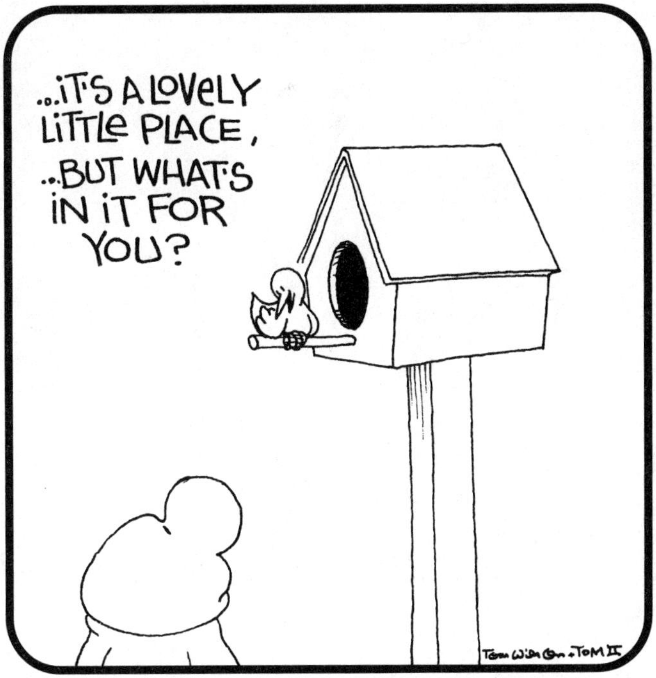
..IT'S A LOVELY LITTLE PLACE, ..BUT WHAT'S IN IT FOR YOU?
TOM WILSON & TOM II

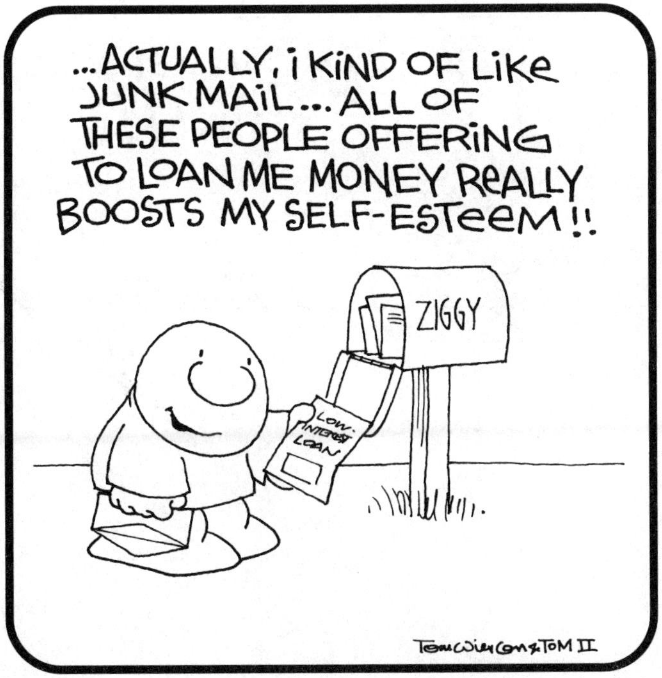
...ACTUALLY, I KIND OF LIKE JUNK MAIL... ALL OF THESE PEOPLE OFFERING TO LOAN ME MONEY REALLY BOOSTS MY SELF-ESTEEM!!
ZIGGY
LOW-INTEREST LOAN
TOM WILSON & TOM II

MEN'S ROOM
RETURNS
TAKE A NUMBER
NUMBER THREE!
437
...IF GETTING AHEAD IN LIFE IS YOUR AIM..
LIFE
...THEN SIMPLY SHOWING UP IS THE MAIN PART OF THE GAME!!
—FOR OLIVIA W/THANKS!
TOM WILSON & TOM II

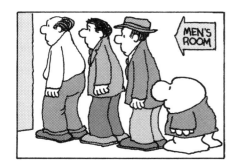

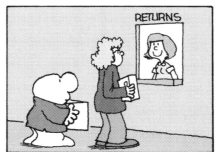

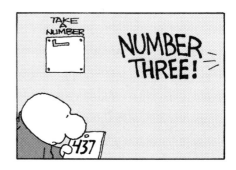

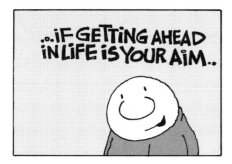

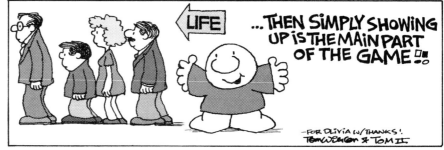

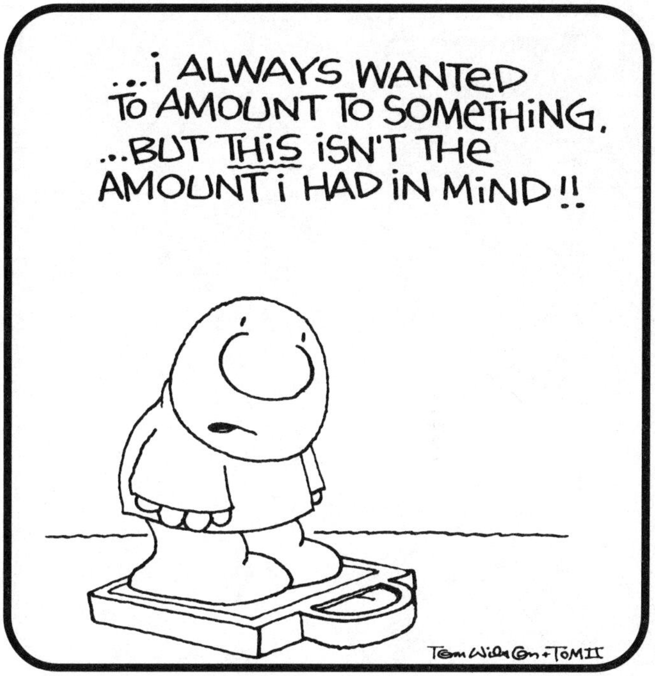
...i ALWAYS WANTED TO AMOUNT TO SOMETHING. ...BUT THIS ISN'T THE AMOUNT i HAD iN MiND!!
Tom Wilson + TOM II

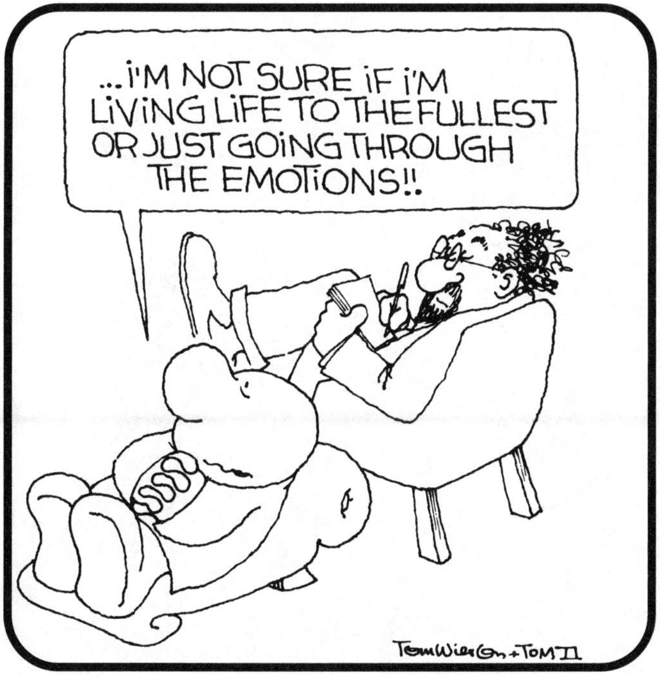
...i'M NOT SURE iF i'M LiViNG LiFE TO THE FULLEST OR JUST GOiNG THROUGH THE EMOTiONS!!
Tom Wilson + TOM II

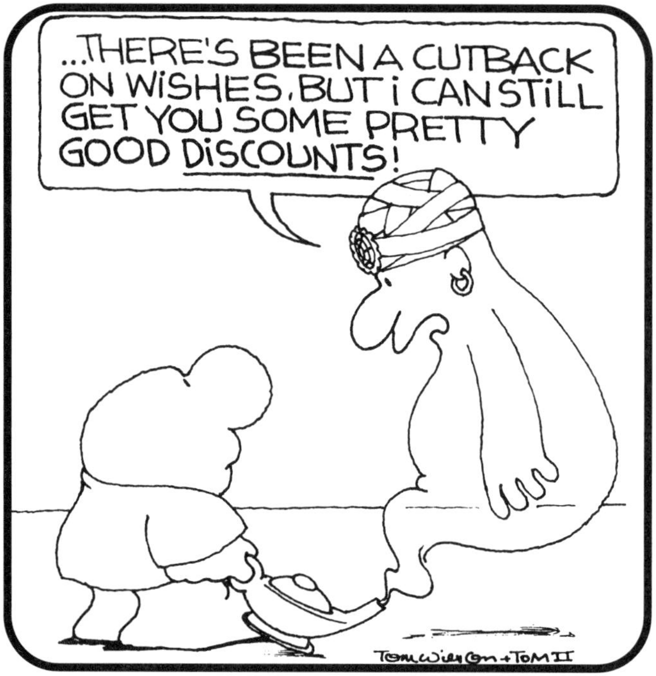
...THERE'S BEEN A CUTBACK ON WISHES, BUT I CAN STILL GET YOU SOME PRETTY GOOD DISCOUNTS!
TOM WILSON + TOM II

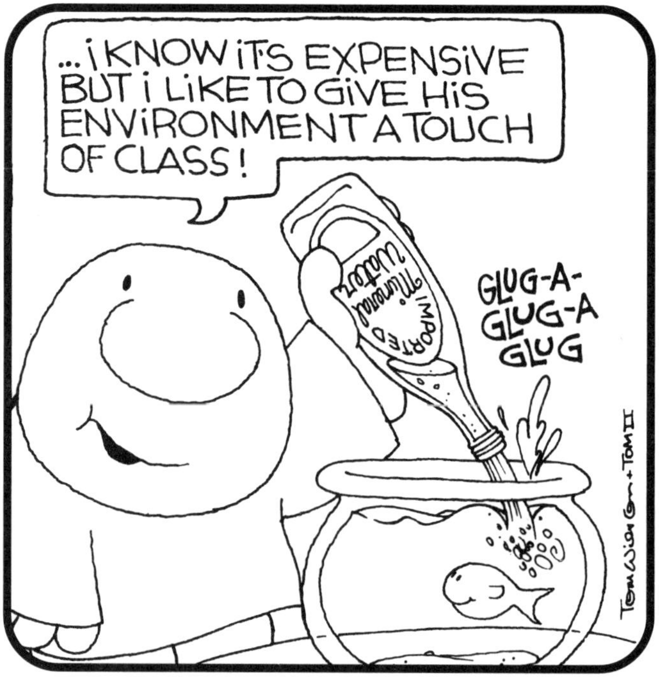
...I KNOW IT'S EXPENSIVE BUT I LIKE TO GIVE HIS ENVIRONMENT A TOUCH OF CLASS!
IMPORTED Mineral Water
GLUG-A-GLUG-A GLUG
TOM WILSON + TOM II

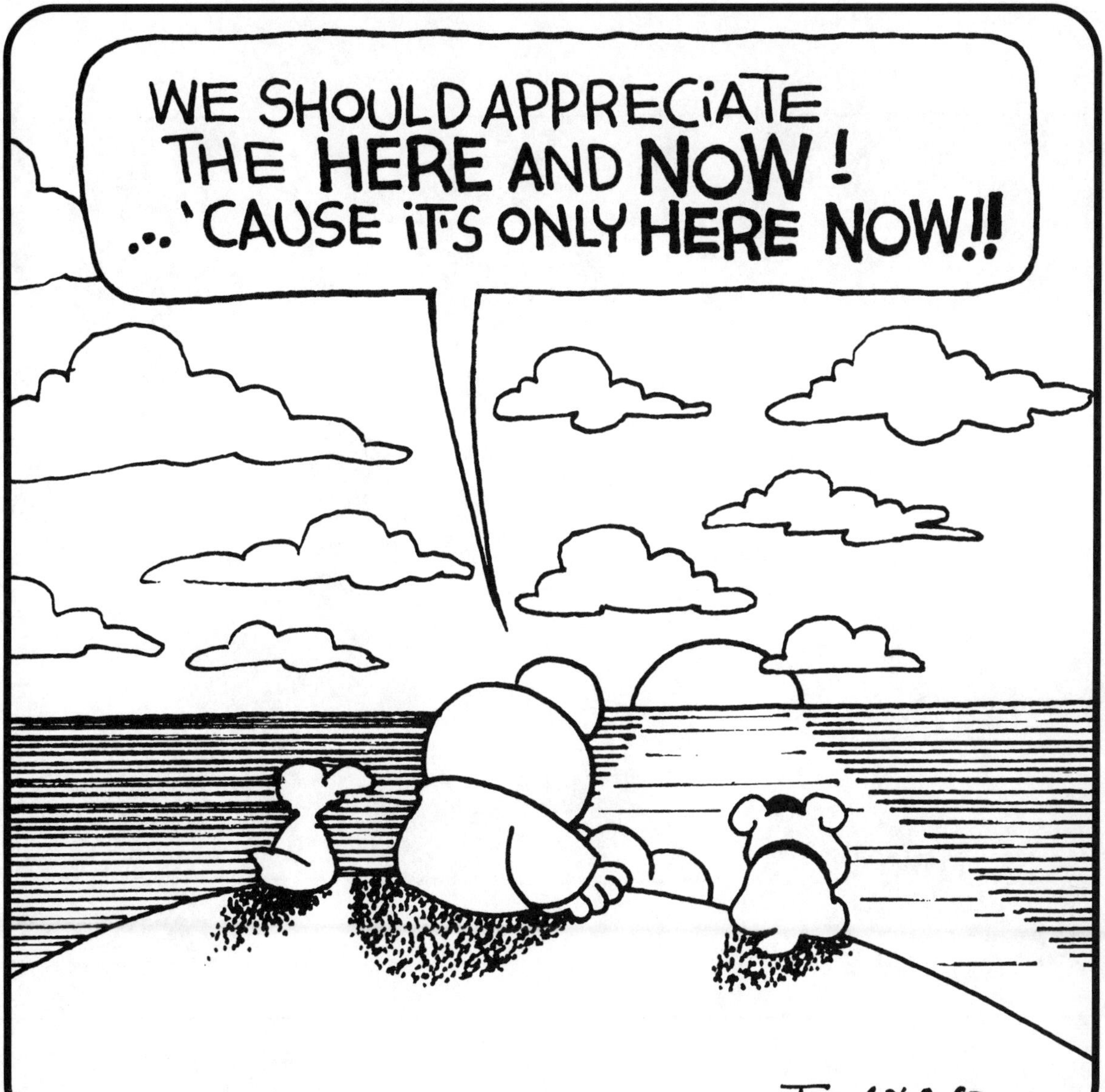
WE SHOULD APPRECIATE THE HERE AND NOW! ...'CAUSE IT'S ONLY HERE NOW!!
Tom Wilson

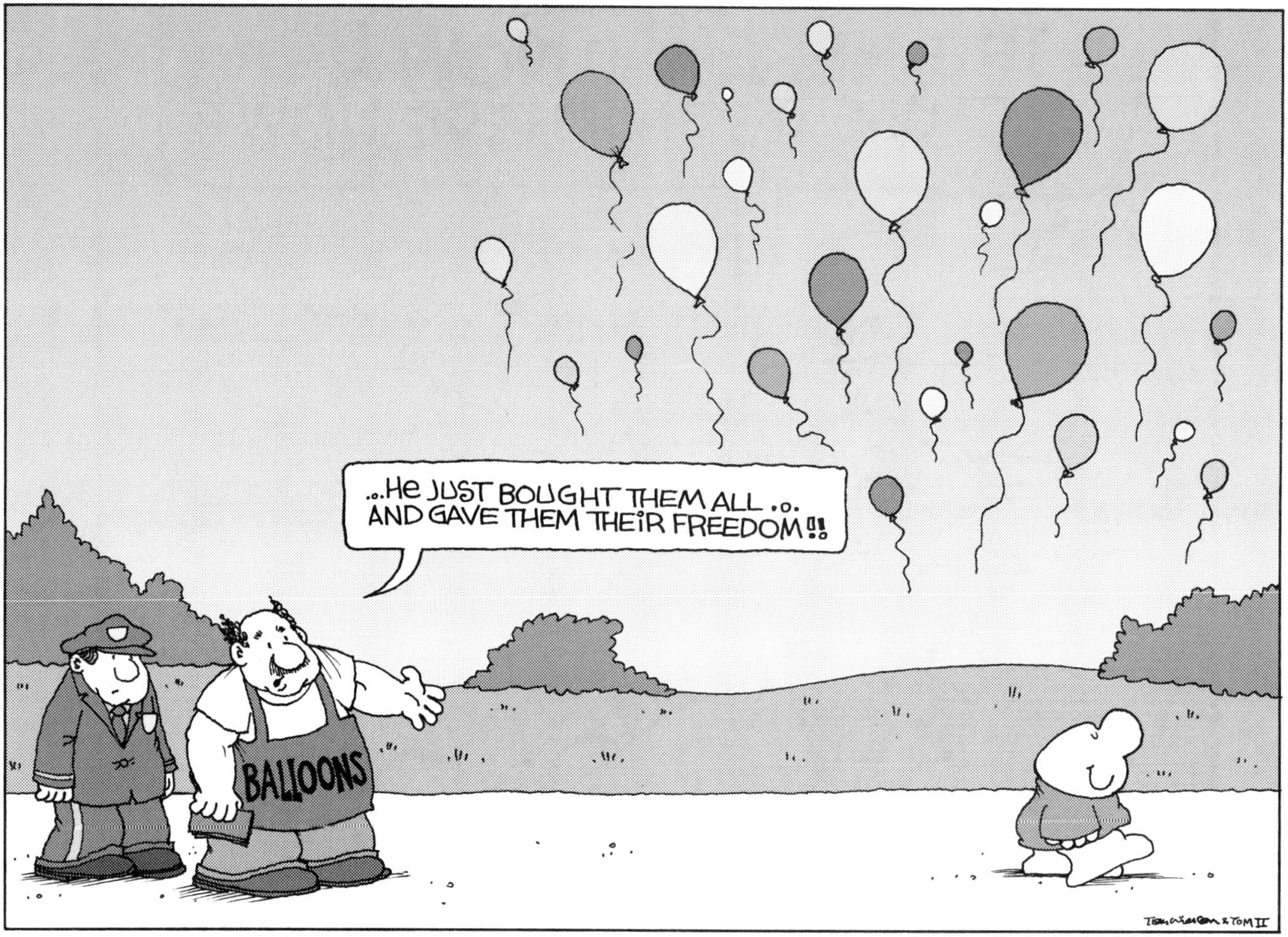
..He JUST BOUGHT THEM ALL ... AND GAVE THEM THEIR FREEDOM!!
BALLOONS

POP!
FOOSH!!
..THANKS. BUT NEXT TIME, LET ME OPEN MY OWN POTATO CHIP BAG!

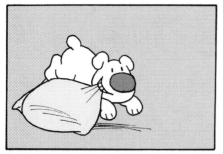

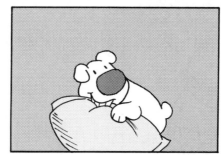

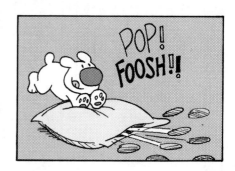

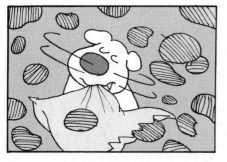

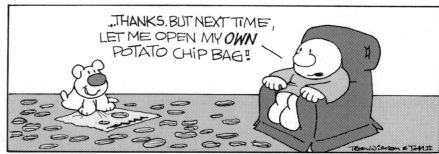

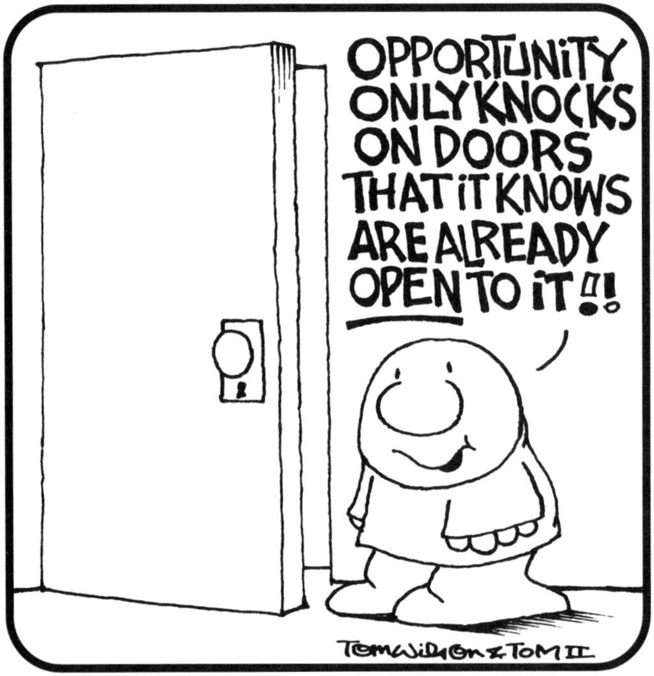
OPPORTUNITY ONLY KNOCKS ON DOORS THAT IT KNOWS ARE ALREADY OPEN TO IT!!
TOM WILSON & TOM II

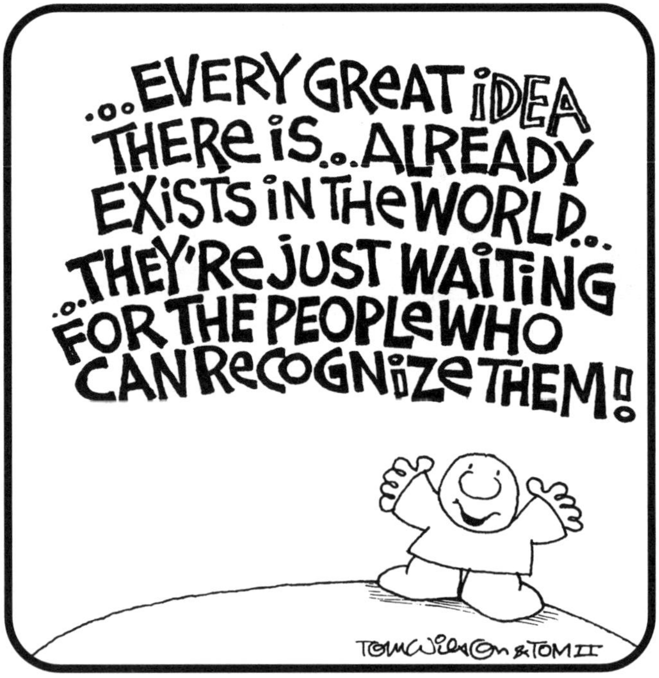
...EVERY GREAT IDEA THERE IS...ALREADY EXISTS IN THE WORLD... ...THEY'RE JUST WAITING FOR THE PEOPLE WHO CAN RECOGNIZE THEM!
TOM WILSON & TOM II

...LIFE GETS COMPARED TO A HIGHWAY FOR A LOT OF REASONS.
KEEP RIGHT
KEEP LEFT
...BOTH CAN SEEM LIKE ONE CONFUSING SIGN AFTER ANOTHER!
...AND WHEN YOU'RE IN A RUT, IT'S LIKE BEING STUCK IN TRAFFIC!!
...AND WE ALL GO THROUGH STRETCHES WHEN IT FEELS LIKE WE'RE STRUGGLING UPHILL.
...THE BIG DIFFERENCE IS THAT IN LIFE, THE JOURNEY IS ALWAYS MORE IMPORTANT THAN THE DESTINATION!!
...AND YOU NEVER HAVE TO WORRY ABOUT MISSING YOUR EXIT!
ALL TRAFFIC NEXT RIGHT

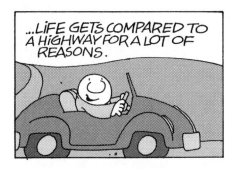

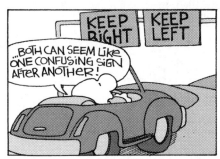

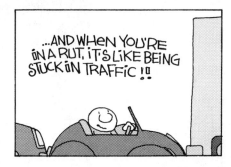

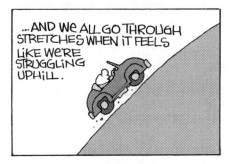

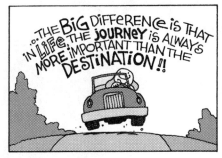

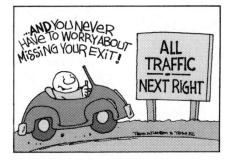

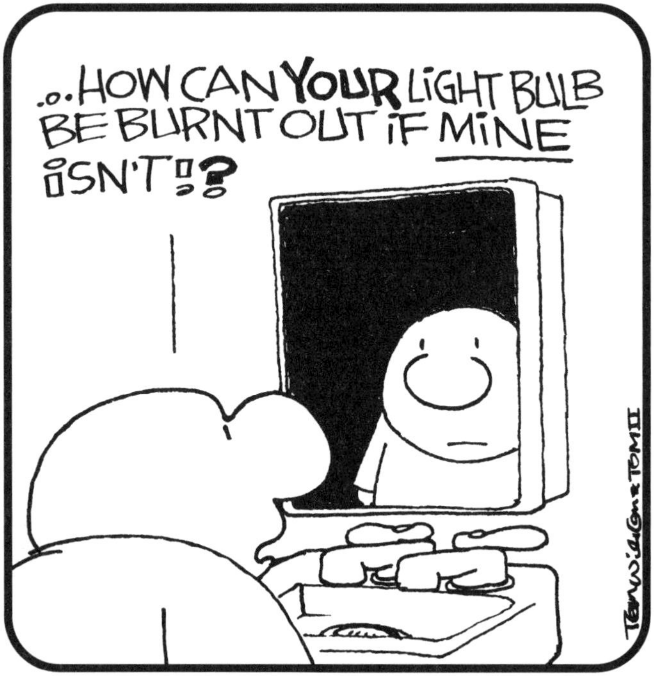
..HOW CAN YOUR LIGHT BULB BE BURNT OUT IF MINE ISN'T!?

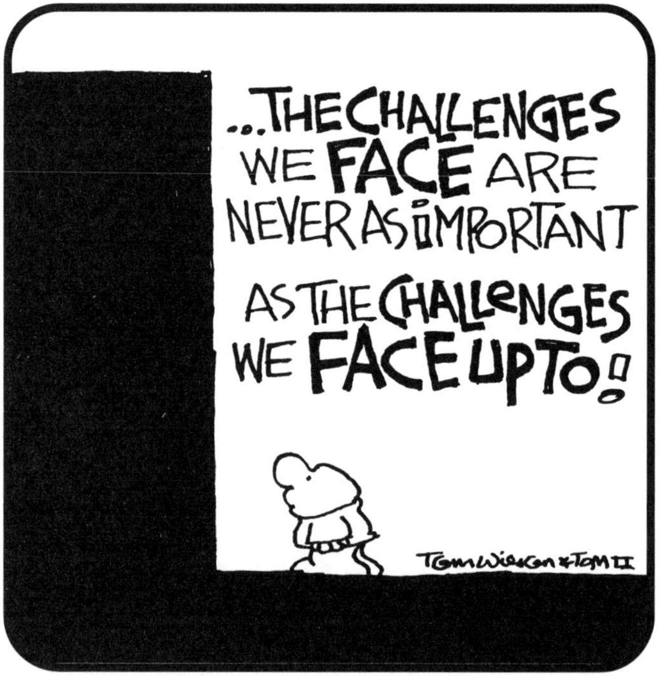
..THE CHALLENGES WE FACE ARE NEVER AS IMPORTANT AS THE CHALLENGES WE FACE UP TO!

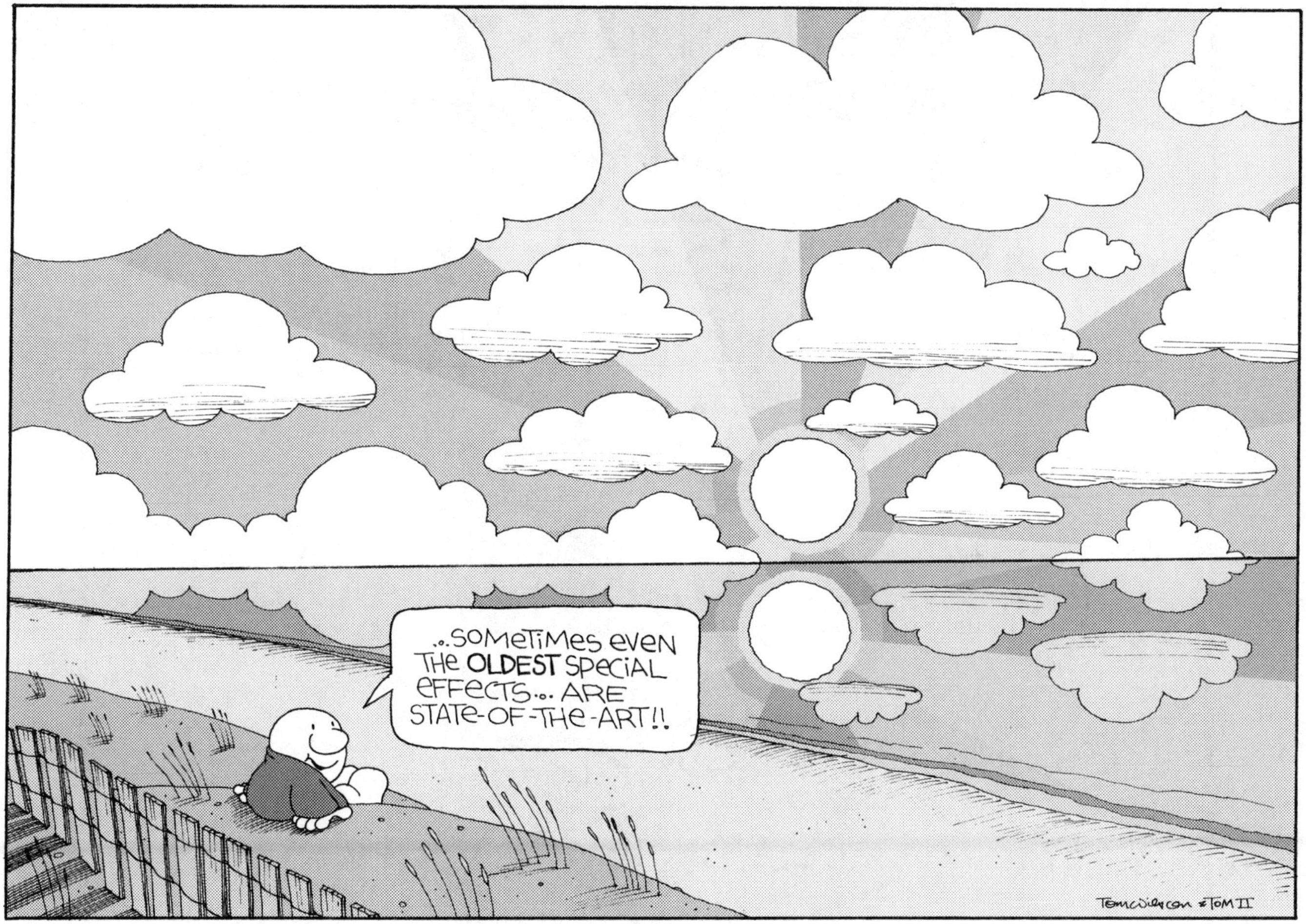

...SOMETIMES EVEN THE **OLDEST** SPECIAL EFFECTS... ARE STATE-OF-THE-ART!!

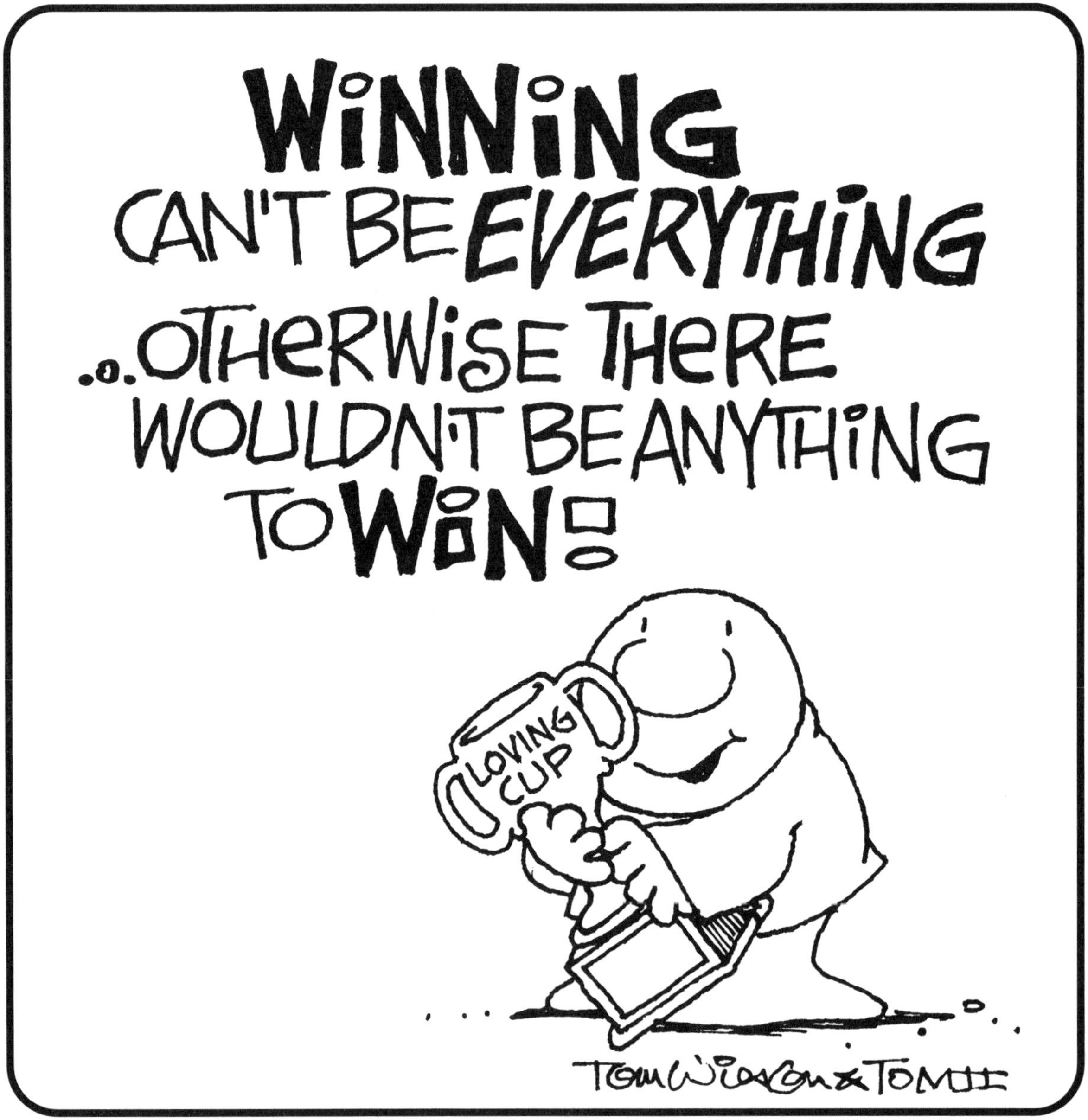
WINNING CAN'T BE EVERYTHING
...OTHERWISE THERE WOULDN'T BE ANYTHING TO WIN!!
LOVING CUP
TOM WILSON & TOM II

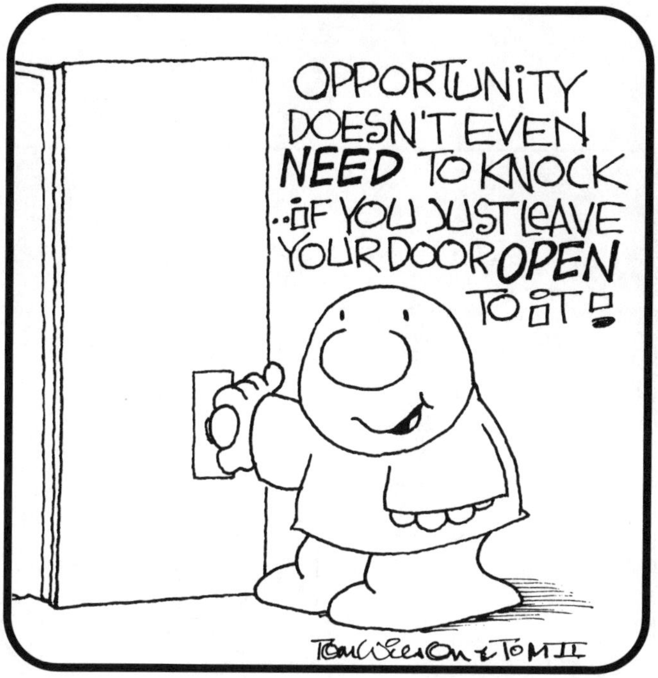
OPPORTUNITY DOESN'T EVEN NEED TO KNOCK ..IF YOU JUST LEAVE YOUR DOOR OPEN TO IT!
TOM WILSON & TOM II

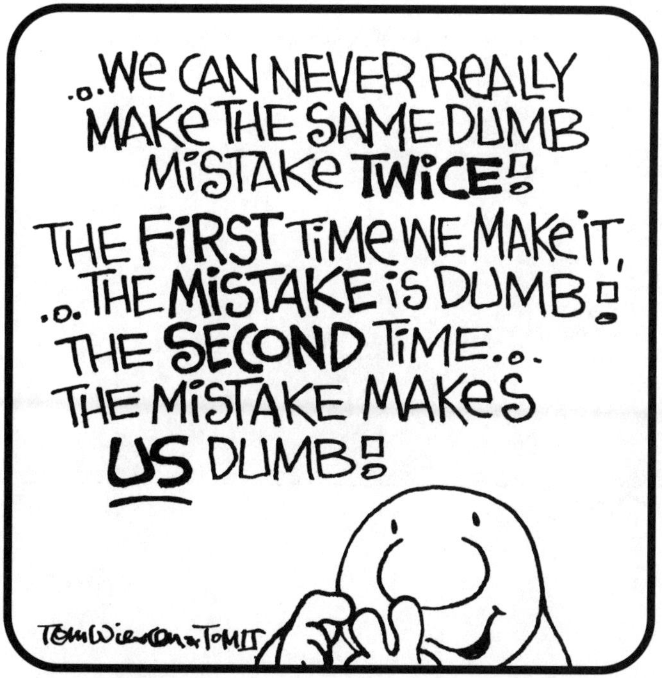
..WE CAN NEVER REALLY MAKE THE SAME DUMB MISTAKE TWICE!
THE FIRST TIME WE MAKE IT, ..THE MISTAKE IS DUMB!
THE SECOND TIME... THE MISTAKE MAKES US DUMB!
TOM WILSON & TOM II

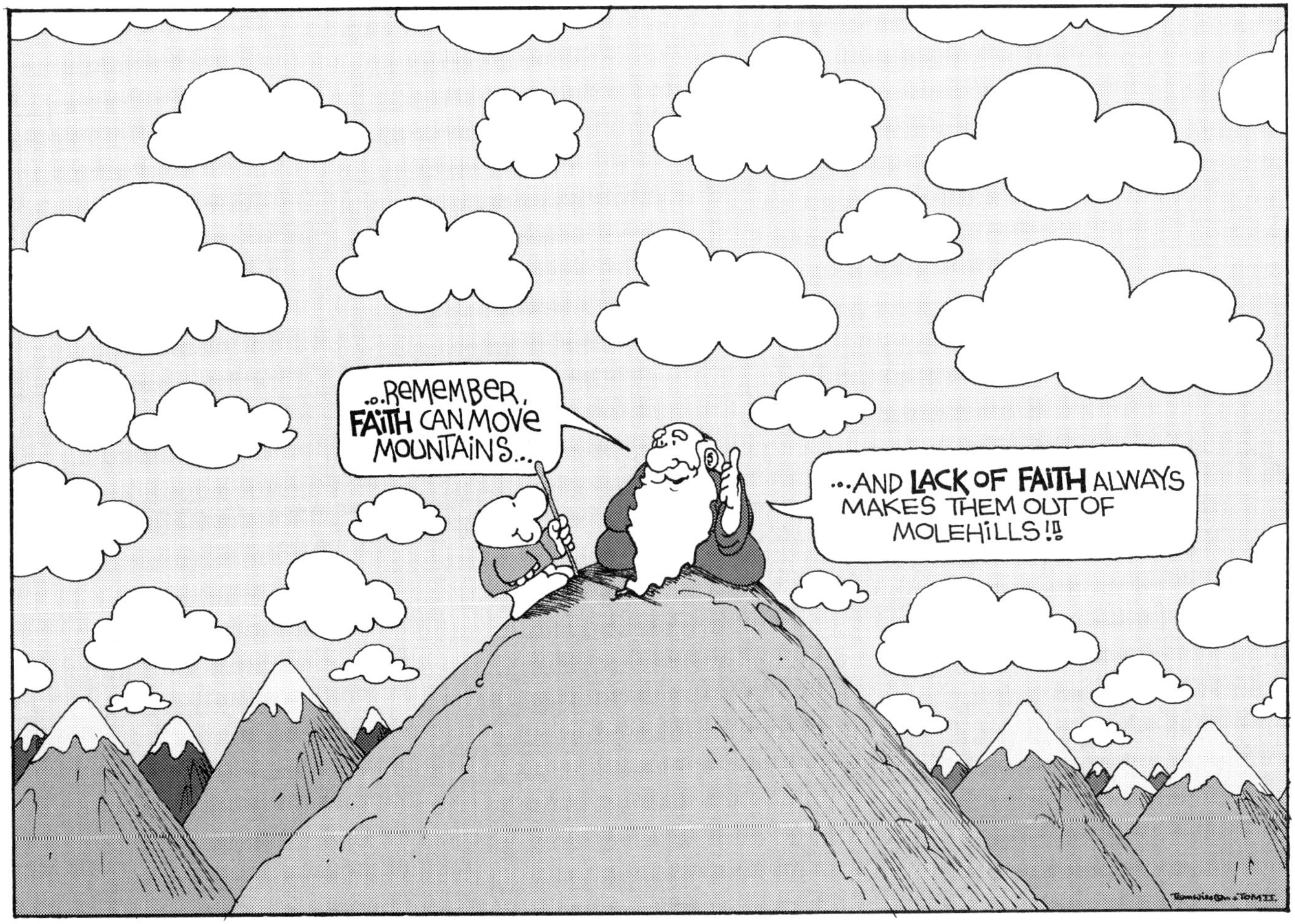
...REMEMBER, FAITH CAN MOVE MOUNTAINS...
...AND LACK OF FAITH ALWAYS MAKES THEM OUT OF MOLEHILLS!!

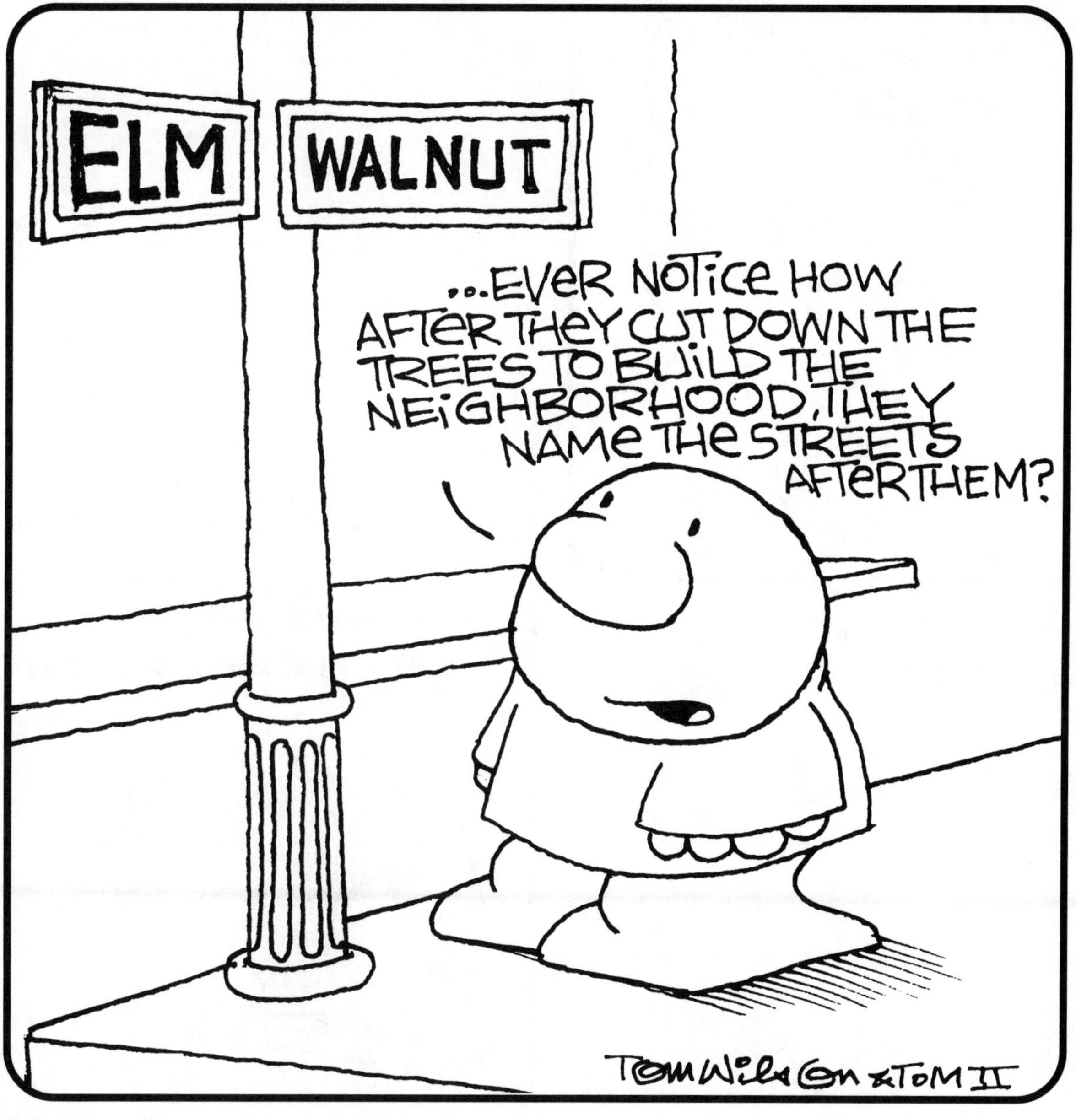
ELM
WALNUT
...EVER NOTICE HOW AFTER THEY CUT DOWN THE TREES TO BUILD THE NEIGHBORHOOD, THEY NAME THE STREETS AFTER THEM?
TOM WILSON & TOM II

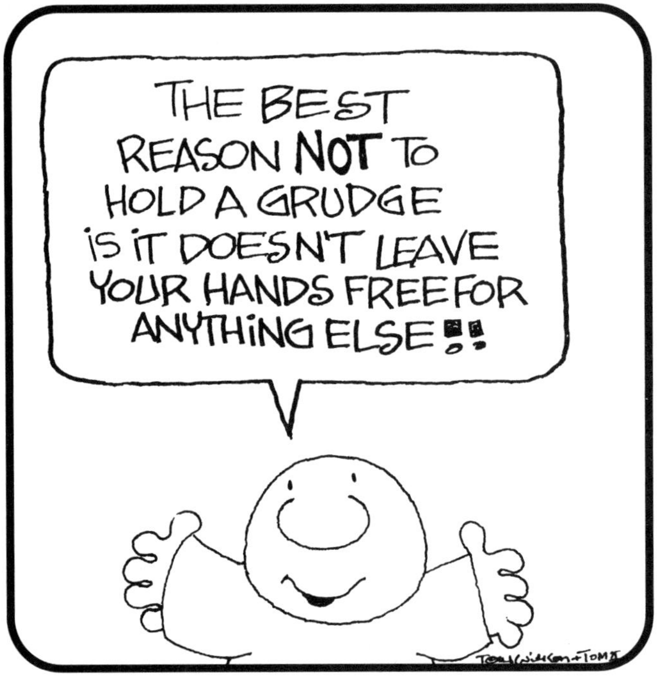
THE BEST REASON **NOT** TO HOLD A GRUDGE IS IT DOESN'T LEAVE YOUR HANDS FREE FOR ANYTHING ELSE!!

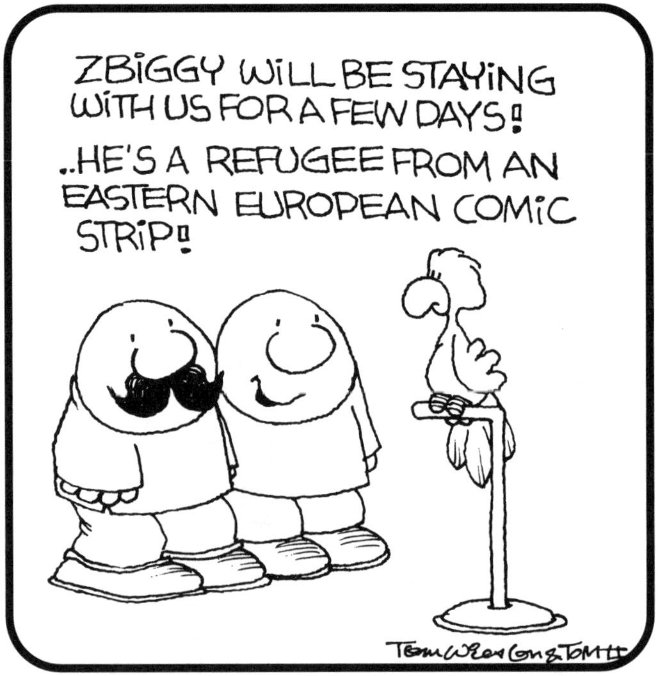
ZBIGGY WILL BE STAYING WITH US FOR A FEW DAYS! ..HE'S A REFUGEE FROM AN EASTERN EUROPEAN COMIC STRIP!

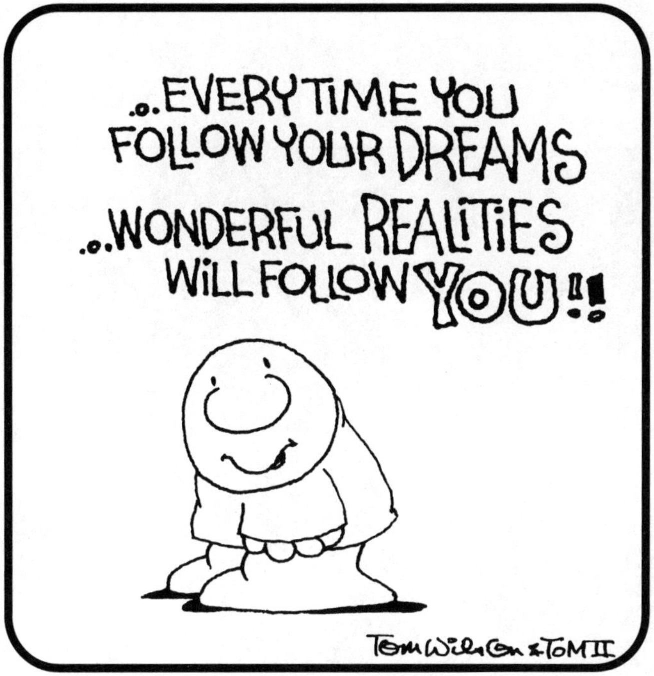
..EVERYTIME YOU FOLLOW YOUR DREAMS ..WONDERFUL REALITIES WILL FOLLOW YOU!!
TOM WILSON & TOM II

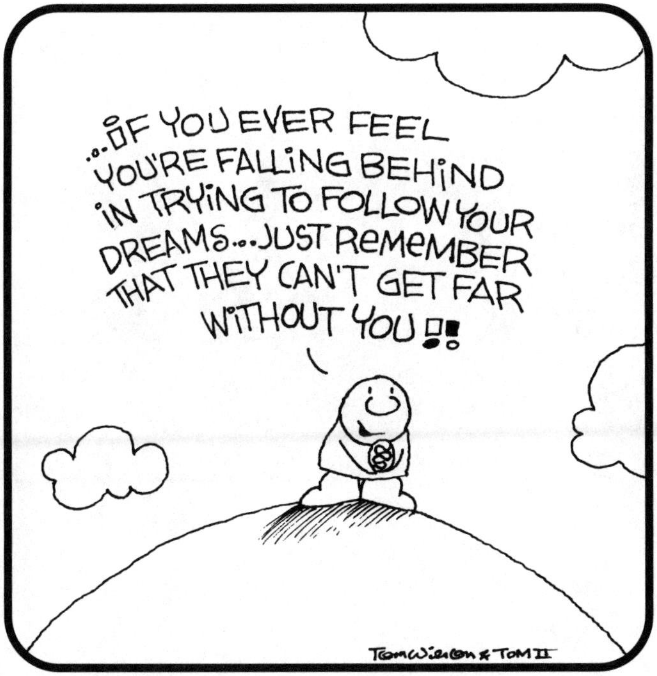
..IF YOU EVER FEEL YOU'RE FALLING BEHIND IN TRYING TO FOLLOW YOUR DREAMS...JUST REMEMBER THAT THEY CAN'T GET FAR WITHOUT YOU!!
TOM WILSON & TOM II

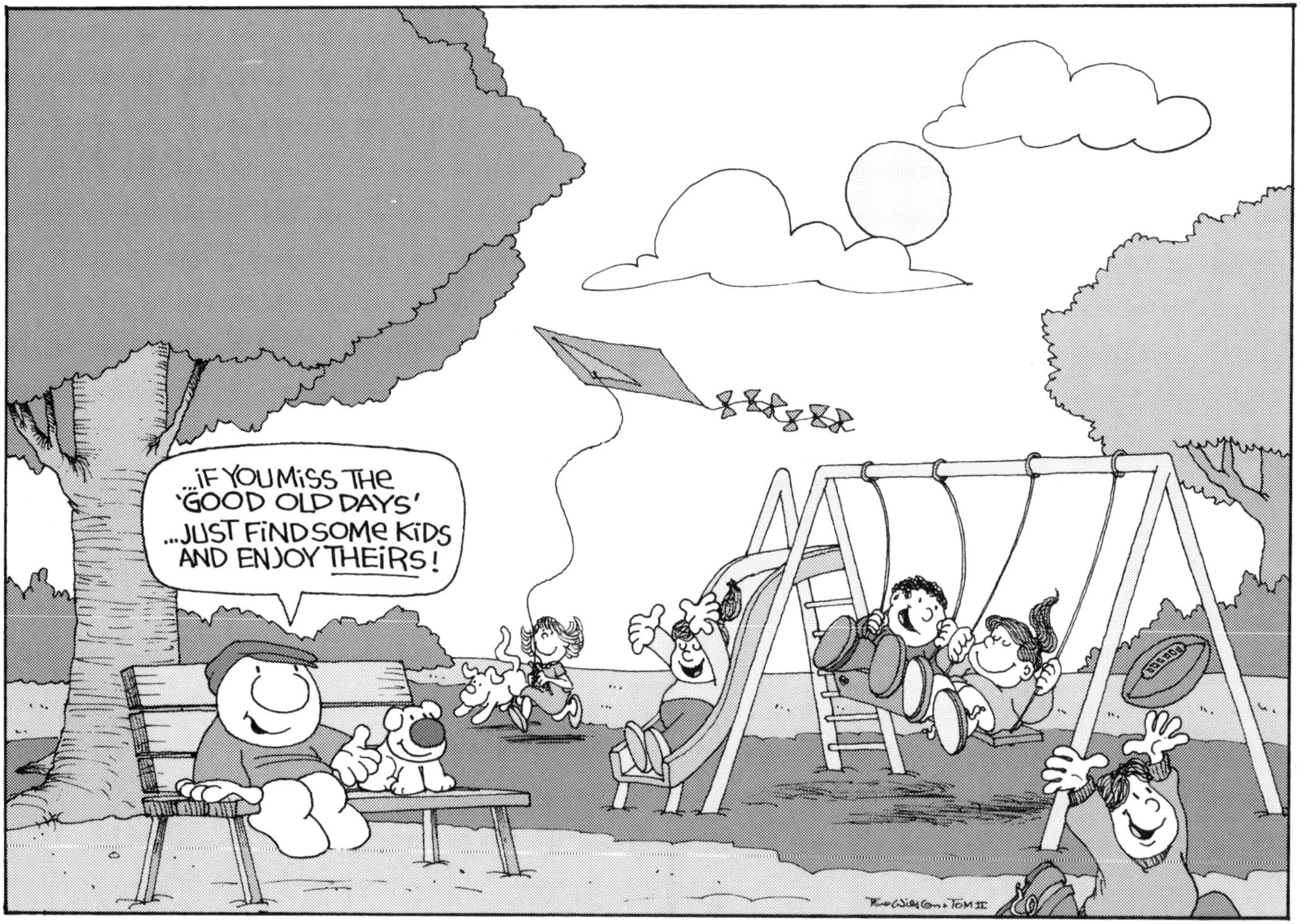
...IF YOU MISS THE 'GOOD OLD DAYS' ...JUST FIND SOME KIDS AND ENJOY THEIRS!

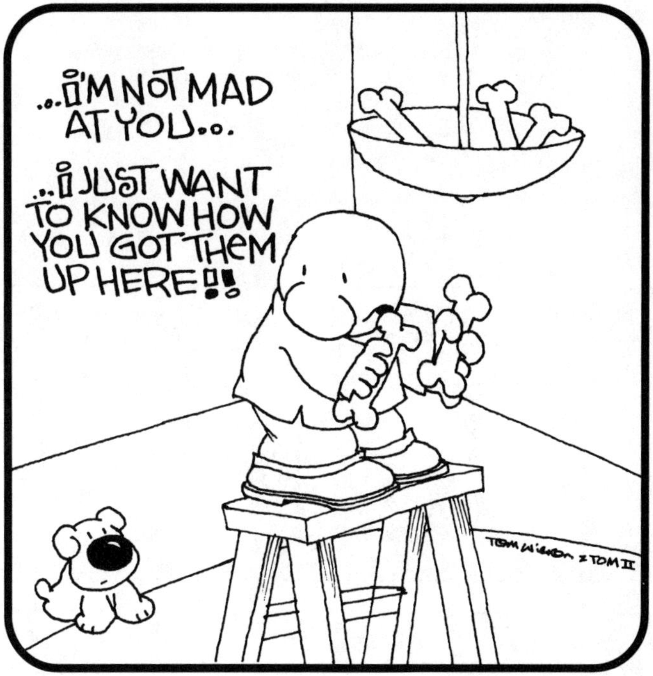
...I'M NOT MAD AT YOU...
...I JUST WANT TO KNOW HOW YOU GOT THEM UP HERE!!
TOM WILSON & TOM II

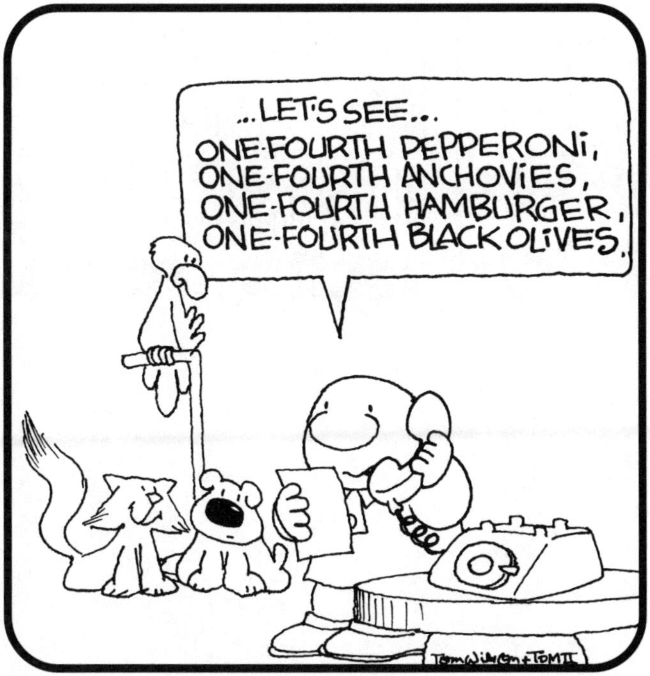
...LET'S SEE... ONE-FOURTH PEPPERONI, ONE-FOURTH ANCHOVIES, ONE-FOURTH HAMBURGER, ONE-FOURTH BLACK OLIVES,
TOM WILSON & TOM II

THANK YOU FOR THIS WONDERFUL FEAST...
THANK YOU FOR ALL OF MY GREAT FRIENDS..
...ON BOTH SIDES OF THE COMIC STRIP...
...AND, MOST OF ALL,...
...THANK YOU FOR MY DAILY BLESSINGS...
CRASH
SIGH
...AND THE PATIENCE TO ENDURE THEM!

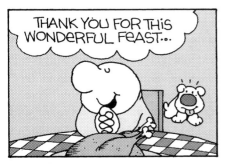

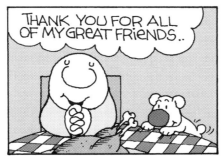

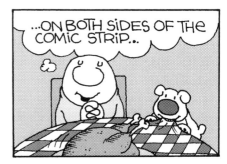

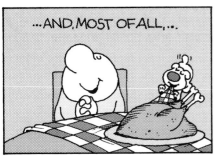

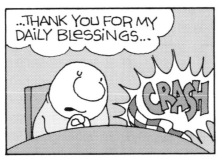

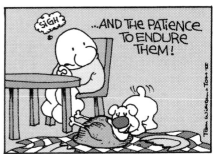

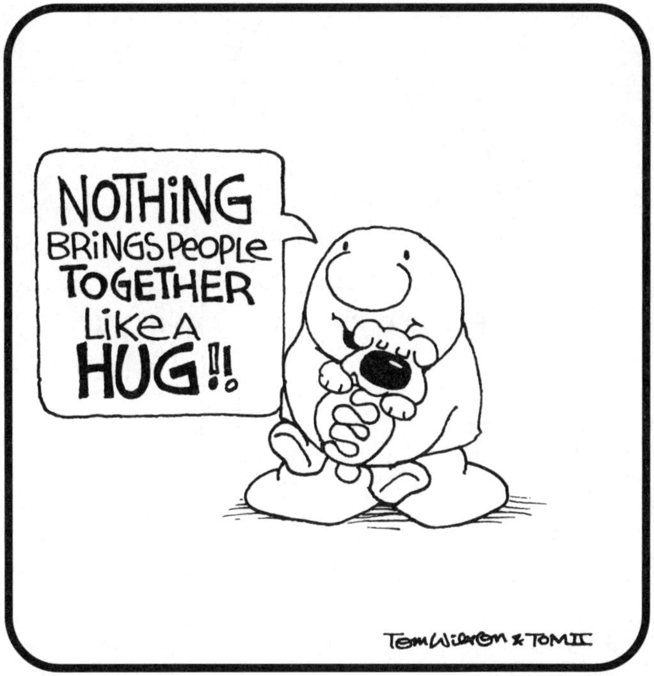
NOTHING BRINGS PEOPLE TOGETHER LIKE A HUG!!
TOM WILSON & TOM II

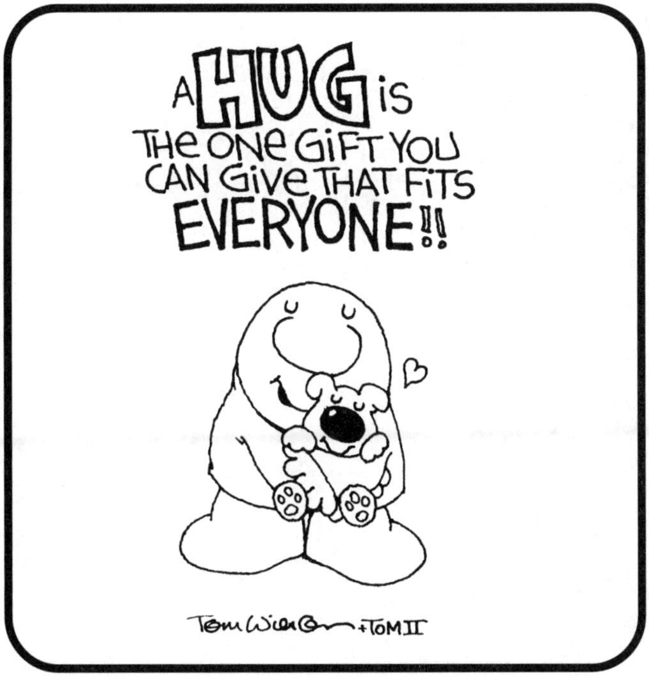
A HUG IS THE ONE GIFT YOU CAN GIVE THAT FITS EVERYONE!!
TOM WILSON + TOM II

LIFE CAN BE A REAL TRIP!!
..IT'S A JOURNEY FULL OF CHOICES, EXPERIENCES AND NEW MEETINGS...
...SOMETIMES IT CAN THROW YOU SO MANY TWISTS AND TURNS...YOU CAN LOSE YOUR WAY...
...AND SOMETIMES ONE PATH ENDS AND WE HAVE TO TURN AROUND AND FIND ANOTHER.
DEAD END
...BUT IN ALL OF MY TRAVELS I'VE DISCOVERED ONE VERY IMPORTANT THING ABOUT LIFE'S JOURNEY...
..WHERE WE BEGIN, WHERE WE ARE NOW AND WHERE WE END UP.. REALLY DOESN'T MATTER...
?
..WHAT MATTERS MOST ARE THE LOVED ONES WE MEET ALONG THE WAY AND WHO MAKE THE JOURNEY WITH US!!
for Susan, In Loving Memory -Tom

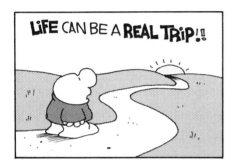

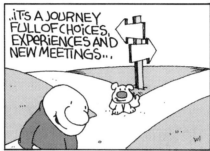

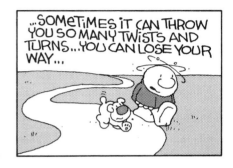

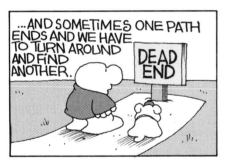

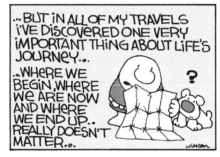

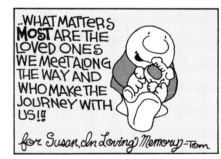

...WHY ARE WE HERE?
WHERE DID WE COME FROM?
WHAT IS THE MEANING OF LIFE?
UH,OH
FWOMP
WHAT IS THE MEANING OF LIFE?
...I THINK I BETTER LAY OFF THINKING THESE 'HEAVY' THOUGHTS FOR A WHILE!!
WHY ARE

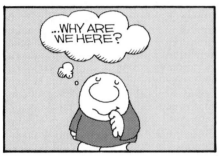

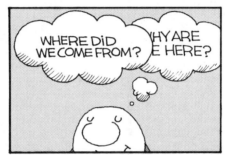

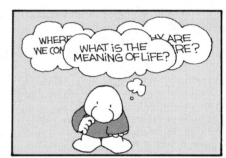

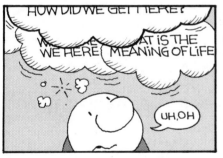

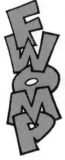

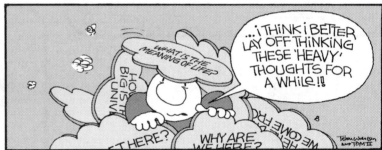

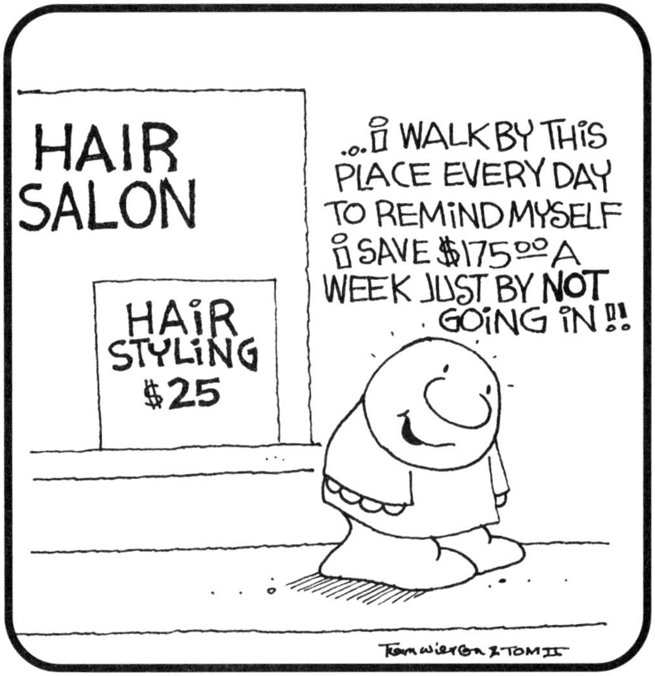
HAIR SALON
HAIR STYLING $25
...I WALK BY THIS PLACE EVERY DAY TO REMIND MYSELF I SAVE $175.00 A WEEK JUST BY **NOT** GOING IN!!
TOM WILSON & TOM II

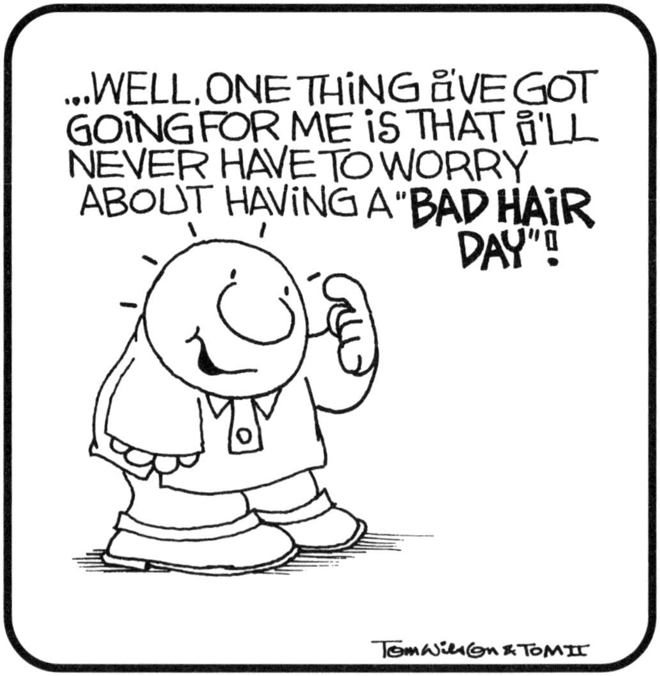
...WELL, ONE THING I'VE GOT GOING FOR ME IS THAT I'LL NEVER HAVE TO WORRY ABOUT HAVING A "**BAD HAIR DAY**"!
TOM WILSON & TOM II

..STAR LiGHT ..STAR BRiGHT.. FiRST STAR i SEE TONiGHT...
...i WiSH i MAY ..i WiSH i MiGHT HAVE THE WiSH i MAKE TONiGHT!
!
PEAS?
eR..EXCUSE Me... THAT WiSH WAS FOR PEACE ON EARTH!

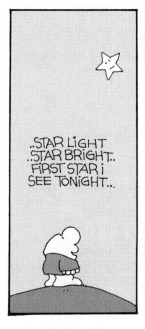

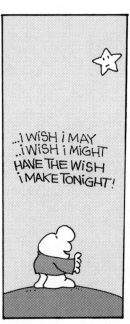

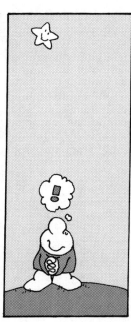

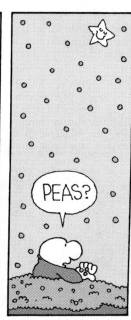

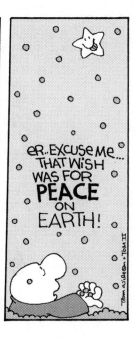

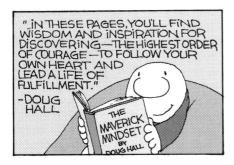

"..IN THESE PAGES, YOU'LL FIND WISDOM AND INSPIRATION FOR DISCOVERING—THE HIGHEST ORDER OF COURAGE—TO FOLLOW YOUR OWN HEART AND LEAD A LIFE OF FULFILLMENT."
-DOUG HALL
THE MAVERICK MINDSET BY DOUG HALL
...MAYBE MR. HALL IS RIGHT! ..MAYBE A LITTLE COURAGE IS ALL I REALLY NEED "TO JOURNEY FROM FEAR TO FREEDOM"!
THE MAVERICK MINDSET BY
..MAYBE I CAN FIGURE OUT WHAT I WANT TO DO WITH MY LIFE!
...MAYBE I CAN FIGURE OUT HOW TO OVERCOME SOME OF THE FEARS I HAVE AND THE LIMITS I'VE PLACED ON MYSELF!
..AND MAYBE, JUST MAYBE, I CAN GET UP OFF MY REAR, GO OUT THERE AND MAKE A DIFFERENCE IN THIS WORLD!
...MAYBE I CAN FIGURE OUT A WAY TO GET OUT OF THIS CHAIR!

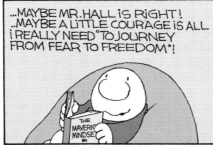

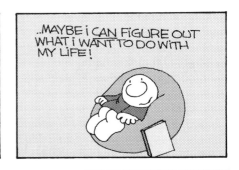

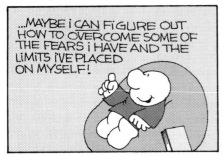

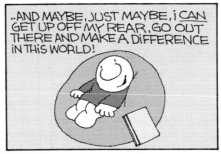

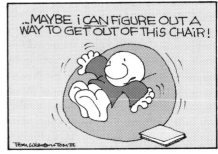

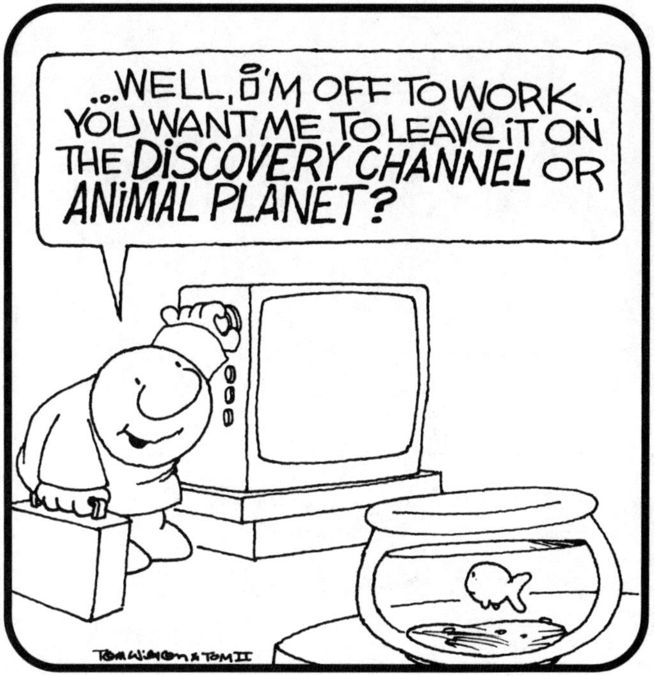
...WELL, I'M OFF TO WORK. YOU WANT ME TO LEAVE IT ON THE DISCOVERY CHANNEL OR ANIMAL PLANET?

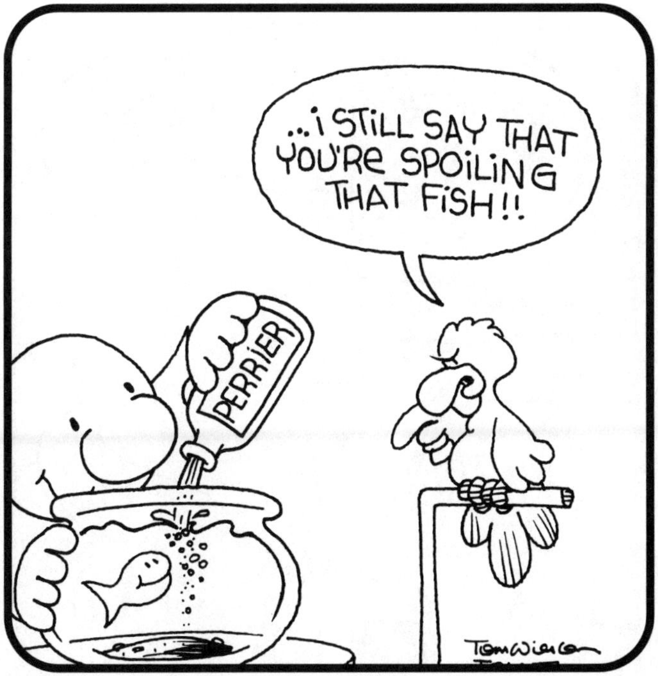
...I STILL SAY THAT YOU'RE SPOILING THAT FISH!!
PERRIER

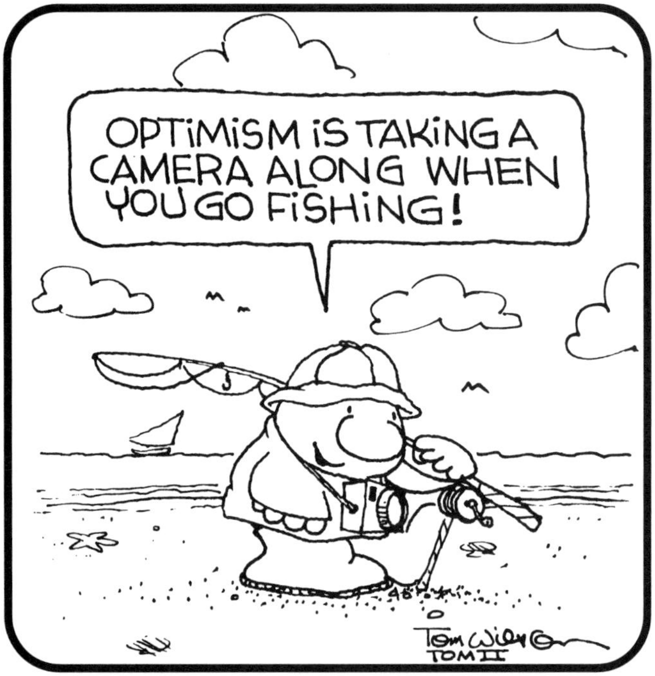
OPTIMISM IS TAKING A CAMERA ALONG WHEN YOU GO FISHING!
TOM WILSON TOM II

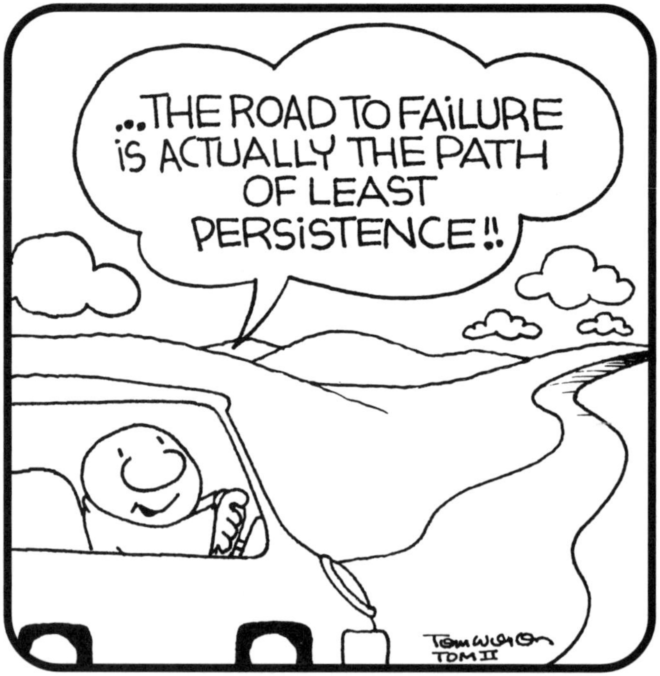
...THE ROAD TO FAILURE IS ACTUALLY THE PATH OF LEAST PERSISTENCE!!
TOM WILSON TOM II

THE TIE ?...IT'S PART OF MY "NEW IMAGE"!! ...I FIGURED IT'S TIME I STARTED TO DRESS FOR SUCCESS!
?
..AFTER ALL, PEOPLE SEE US THE WAY WE SEE OURSELVES.
..A POSITIVE, SUCCESSFUL SELF-IMAGE CAN REALLY MAKE A DIFFERENCE!!
...FROM NOW ON, LET'S TRY TO THINK OF OURSELVES AS SUCCESSES...AND MAYBE OTHERS WILL THINK OF US THAT WAY TOO!
HEY! IT'S YOU!!
..THAT FAMOUS CARTOON CHARACTER!!
..I LOVE YOU!!
IT'S WORKIN'! FUZZ!
OOO...YOU'RE EVEN CUTER IN PERSON!
..I READ YOUR COMIC EVERY DAY!
AND I'VE GOT ALL YOUR BOOKS.
MMPHANKYOU!
...HEAR THAT, FUZZ?
...AND THIS LI'L FELLA MUST BE DOGBERT!!
PAT PAT

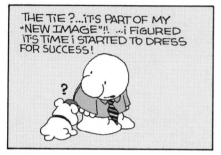

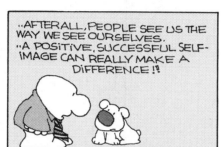

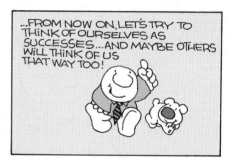

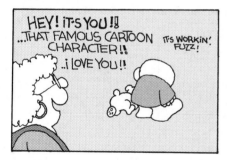

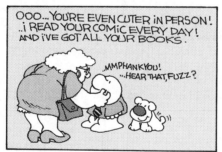

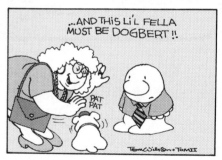

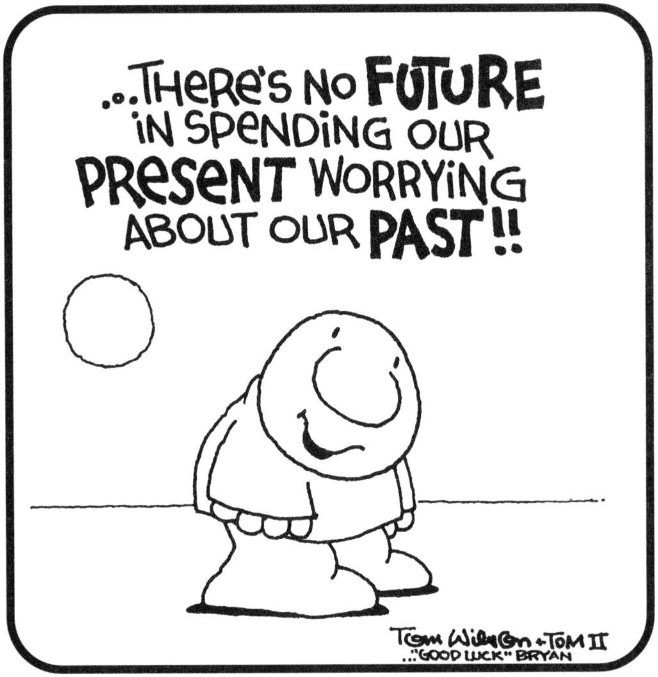
...THERE'S NO FUTURE IN SPENDING OUR PRESENT WORRYING ABOUT OUR PAST!!
Tom Wilson + TOM II
..."GOOD LUCK" BRYAN

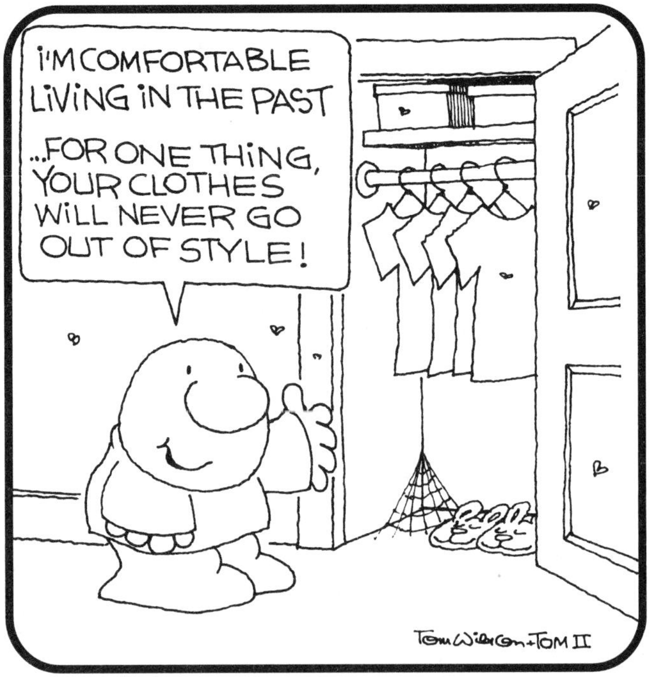
I'M COMFORTABLE LIVING IN THE PAST
...FOR ONE THING, YOUR CLOTHES WILL NEVER GO OUT OF STYLE!
Tom Wilson + TOM II

HIYA MR. PENDLETON!
MMPH!
...HOW'RE YOU FEELING TODAY?
MUMMPH
WHAT'S WRONG, MR. PENDLETON?
...MMPHNN...
...WHY ARE YOU SO DOWN IN THE MOUTH?
MUY MEEPH!
HUH?
MUYM MMNOT MMwerrin MUYM MMEEPH!!
OH, SORRY!...
...I DIDN'T REALIZE YOU DIDN'T HAVE YOUR TEETH IN!!

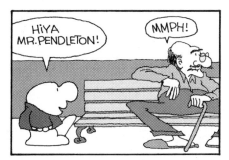

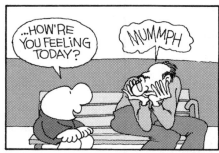

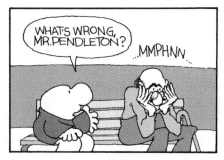

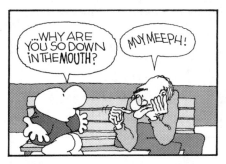

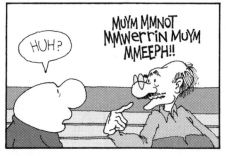

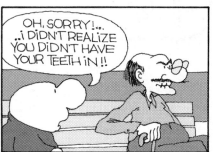

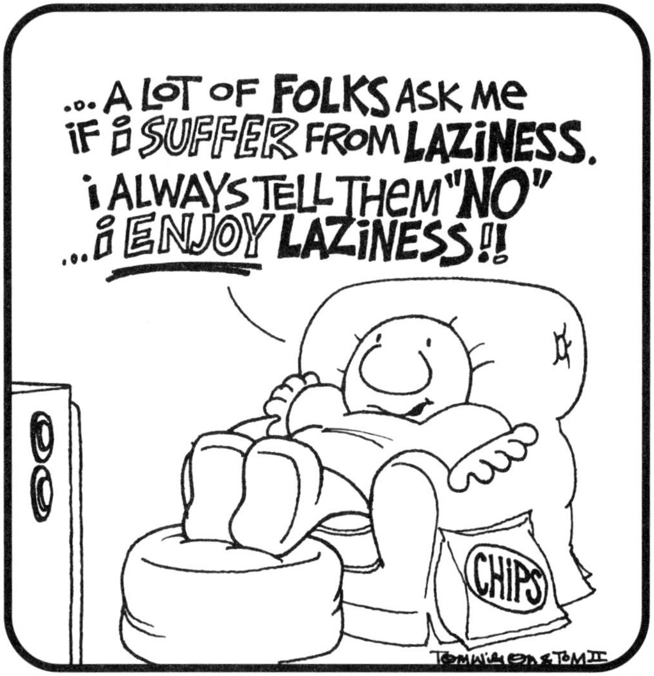
...A LOT OF FOLKS ASK ME IF I SUFFER FROM LAZINESS. I ALWAYS TELL THEM "NO" ...I ENJOY LAZINESS!!
CHIPS
TOM WILSON & TOM II

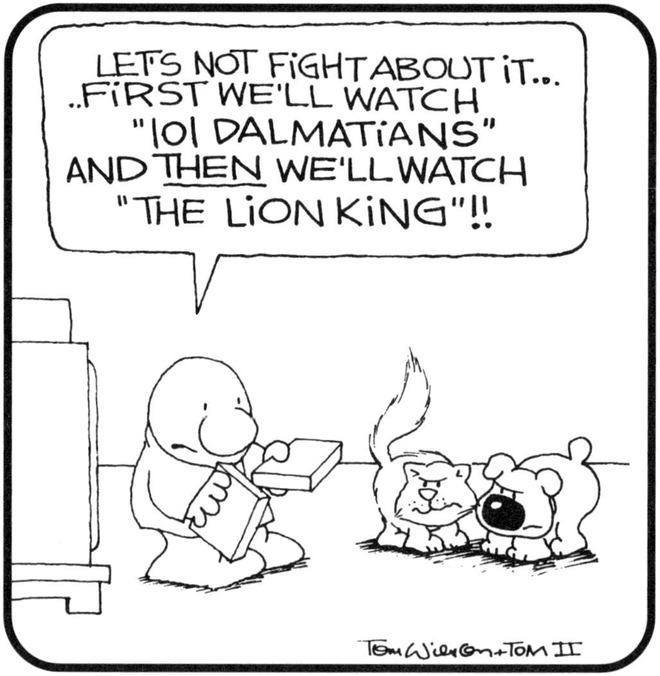
LET'S NOT FIGHT ABOUT IT... ..FIRST WE'LL WATCH "101 DALMATIANS" AND THEN WE'LL WATCH "THE LION KING"!!
TOM WILSON + TOM II

...I'LL NEVER UNDERSTAND WHY "GO FLY A KITE" IS CONSIDERED SUCH AN INSULT!!

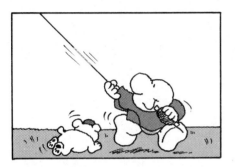

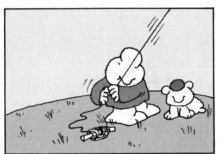

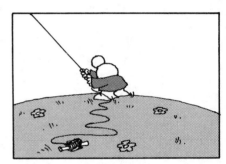

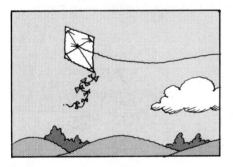

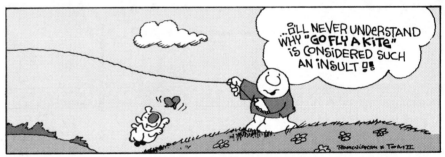

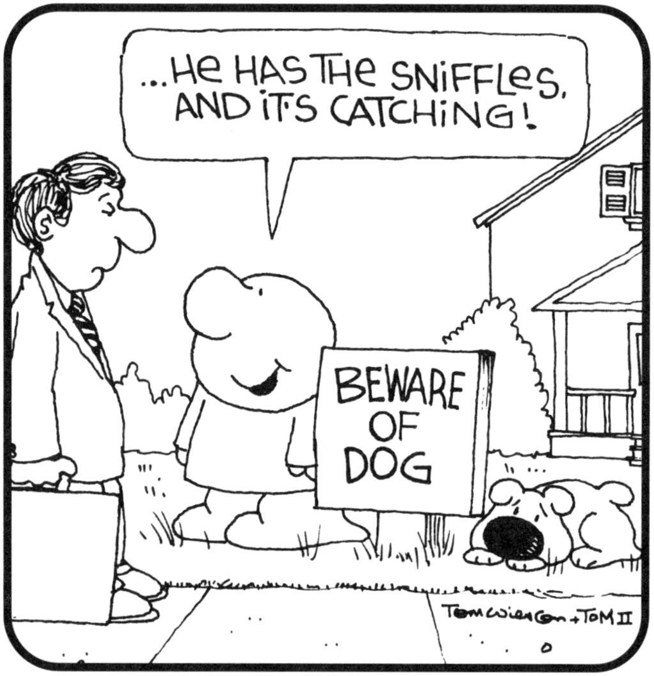
...HE HAS THE SNIFFLES, AND IT'S CATCHING!
BEWARE OF DOG
TOM WILSON + TOM II

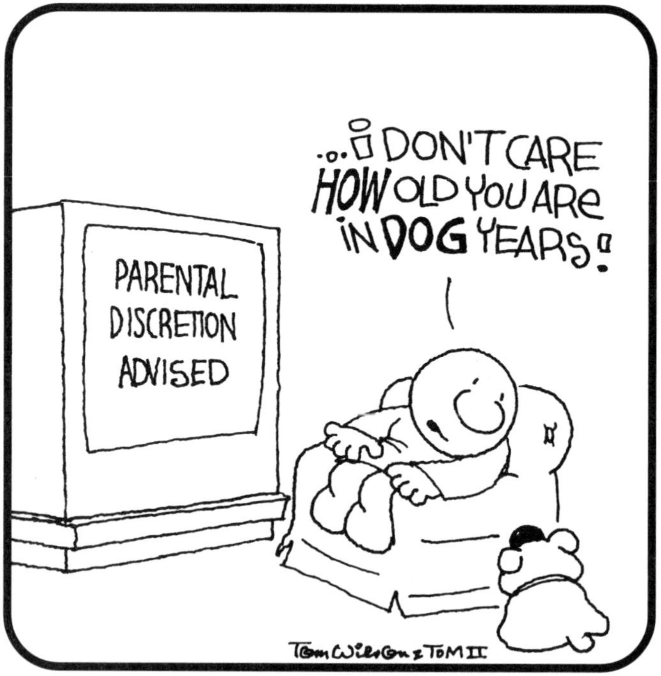
...I DON'T CARE HOW OLD YOU ARE IN DOG YEARS!
PARENTAL DISCRETION ADVISED
TOM WILSON & TOM II

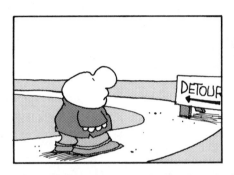

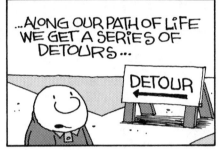

DETOUR
...ALONG OUR PATH OF LIFE WE GET A SERIES OF DETOURS...
DETOUR
..AND WE ALL GET FRUSTRATED AND IMPATIENT WHEN WE FEEL WE HAVE TO LEAVE THE PATH WE'VE CHOSEN!
DETOUR
..BUT WHAT IF THE REAL PATH OF LIFE...
DETOUR
...IS REALLY MADE UP OF ALL THESE DETOURS
..AND INSTEAD OF LEARNING THE REAL LESSONS OF LIFE, WE MISS THEM BECAUSE WE WERE TOO BUSY BEING FRUSTRATED & IMPATIENT!!
TOM WILSON & TOM II

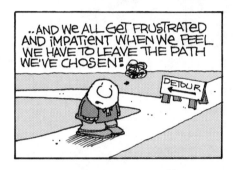

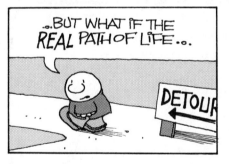

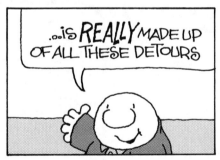

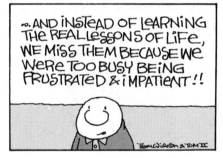

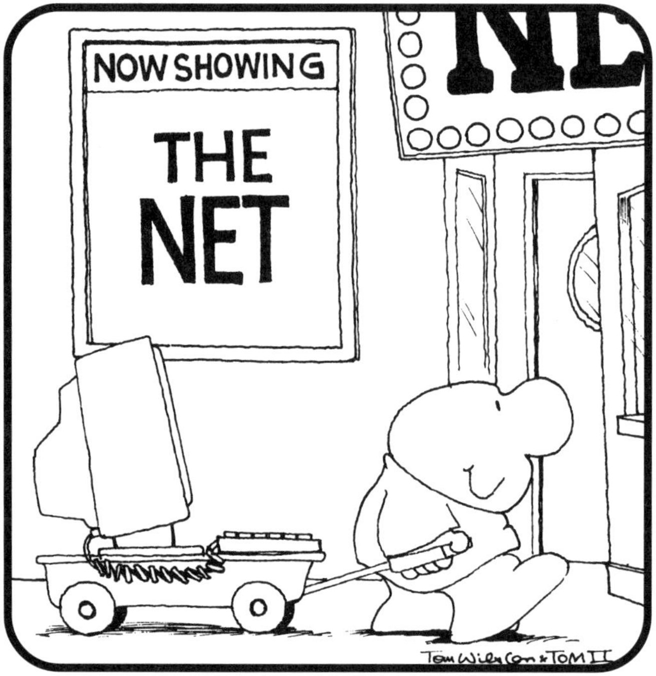
NOW SHOWING
THE NET
Tom Wilson & TOM II

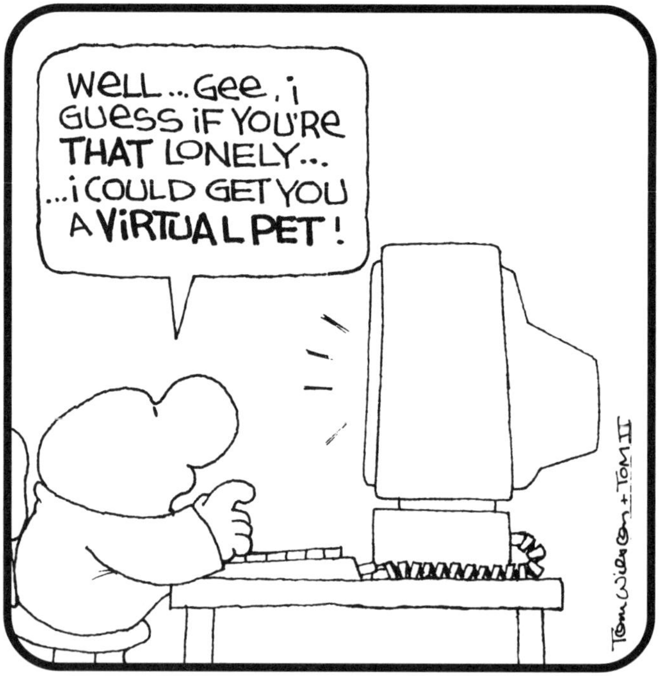
WELL...GEE, i GUESS iF YOU'RE THAT LONELY... ...i COULD GET YOU A VIRTUAL PET!
Tom Wilson + TOM II

STARLIGHT...STARBRIGHT
I WISH I MAY...I WISH I MIGHT...
I WISH I HAD GREAT WISDOM!!
...WHO AM I KIDDING? WISDOM ISN'T SOMETHING YOU GET BY WISHING FOR IT!!
...IT'S SOMETHING YOU HAVE TO EARN WITH YEARS OF EXPERIENCE!!
...AS WELL AS LOTS OF MATURITY AND PATIENCE AND...SAY!!
...MAYBE THAT WISH WORKED AFTER ALL!!

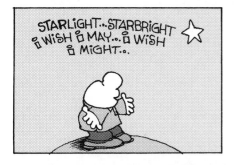

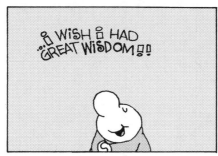

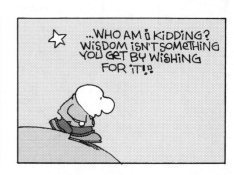

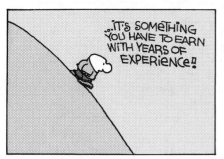

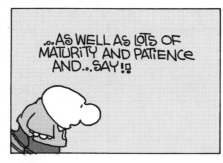

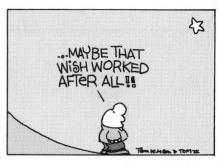

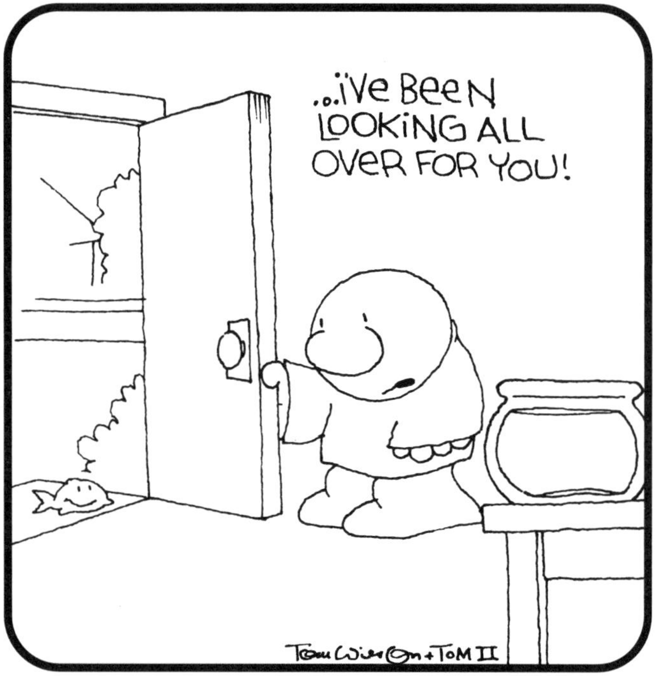
..o..i'Ve Been LOOKiNG ALL OVER FOR YOU!
Tom Wilson + Tom II

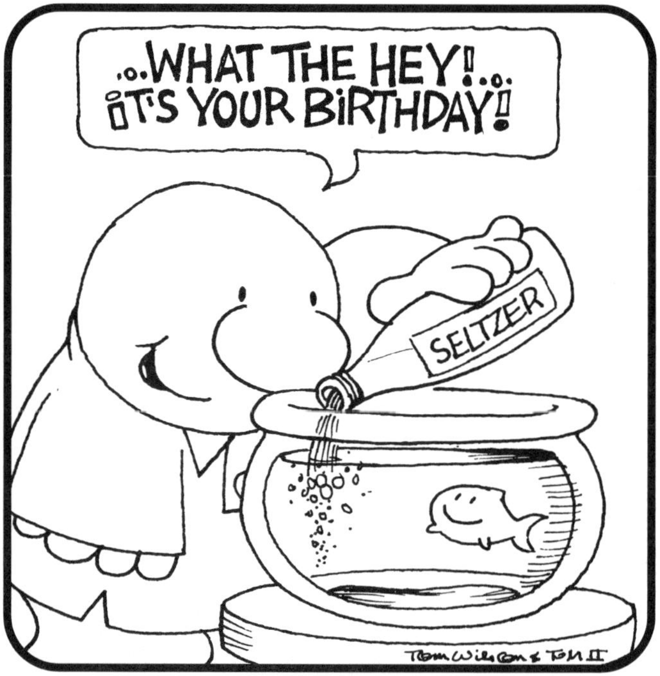
..o..WHAT THE HEY!..o.. iT'S YOUR BiRTHDAY!
SELTZER
Tom Wilson + Tom II

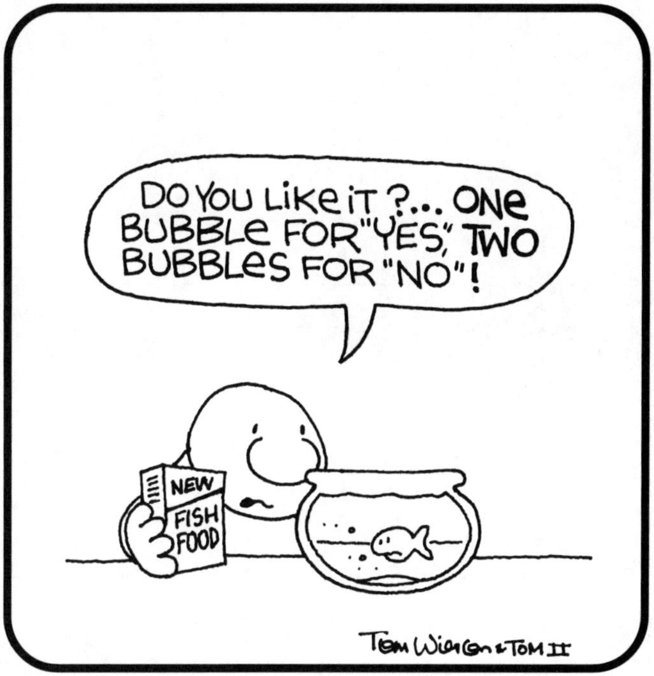
DO YOU LIKE IT?... ONE BUBBLE FOR "YES," TWO BUBBLES FOR "NO"!
NEW FISH FOOD

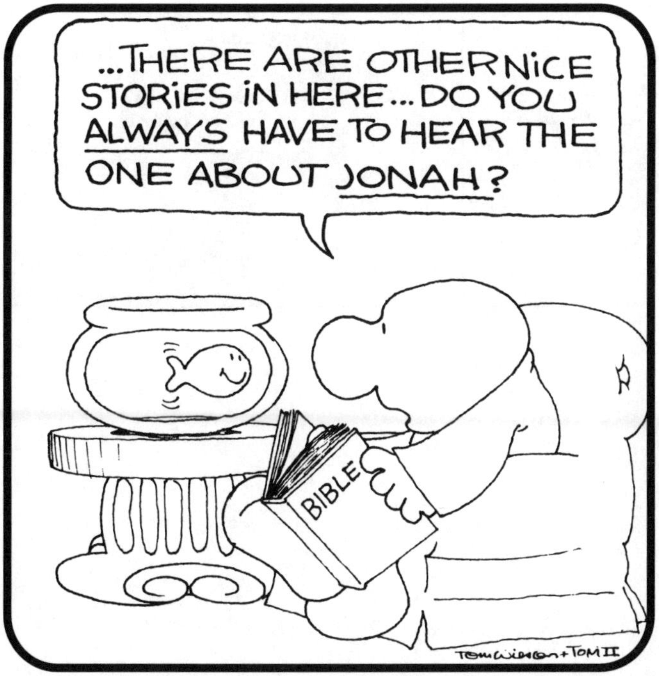
...THERE ARE OTHER NICE STORIES IN HERE... DO YOU ALWAYS HAVE TO HEAR THE ONE ABOUT JONAH?
BIBLE

...SOMETIMES WE IMAGINE THAT THE WORLD IS SO BIG...

...AND SOMETIMES WHEN THAT HAPPENS IT MAKES US FEEL SO SMALL...

...THAT'S WHEN WE GET AFRAID AND FEEL SO HELPLESS...

...AND SOMETIMES WE FORGET...

...THAT THE WORLD IS ONLY AS BIG AS WE IMAGINE IT IS... AND WE ARE ONLY AS SMALL AS WE IMAGINE WE ARE...

...SO REMEMBER THAT WHEN THE WORLD MAKES US FEEL AFRAID AND HELPLESS... IT'S JUST OUR IMAGINATION!!

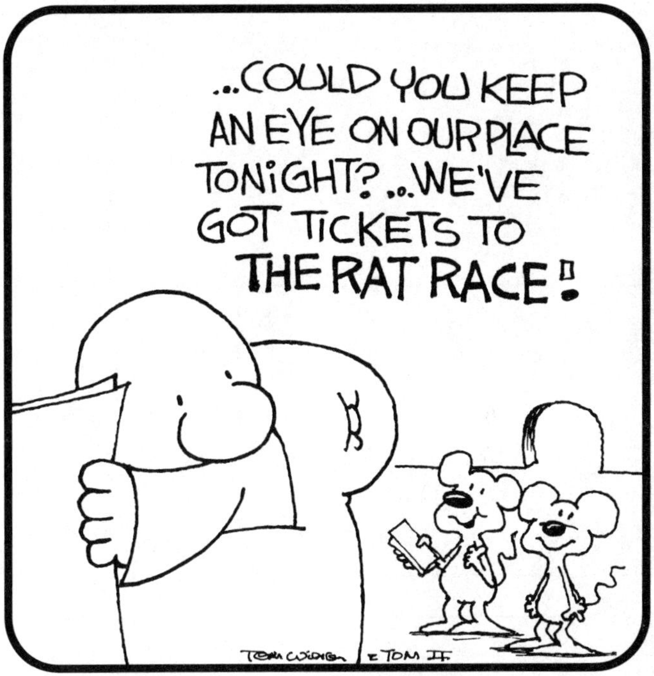
...COULD YOU KEEP AN EYE ON OUR PLACE TONIGHT? ...WE'VE GOT TICKETS TO THE RAT RACE!!
Tom Wilson & TOM II

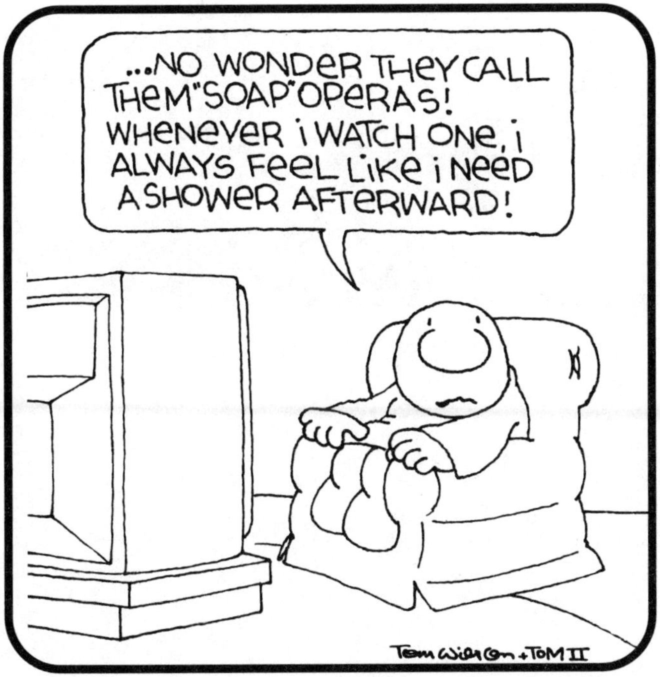
...NO WONDER THEY CALL THEM "SOAP" OPERAS! WHENEVER I WATCH ONE, I ALWAYS FEEL LIKE I NEED A SHOWER AFTERWARD!
Tom Wilson + TOM II

?
?
Nope
NOT HERE!
ZIGGY
NOT HERE!!
..o.. THERE YOU ARE!!
I'VE BEEN LOOKING EVERYWHERE FOR YOU!!
LOVE

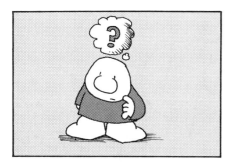

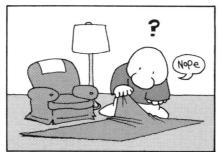

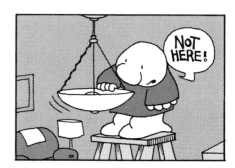

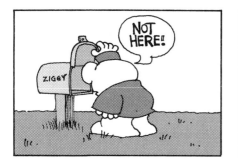

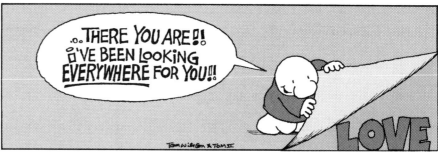

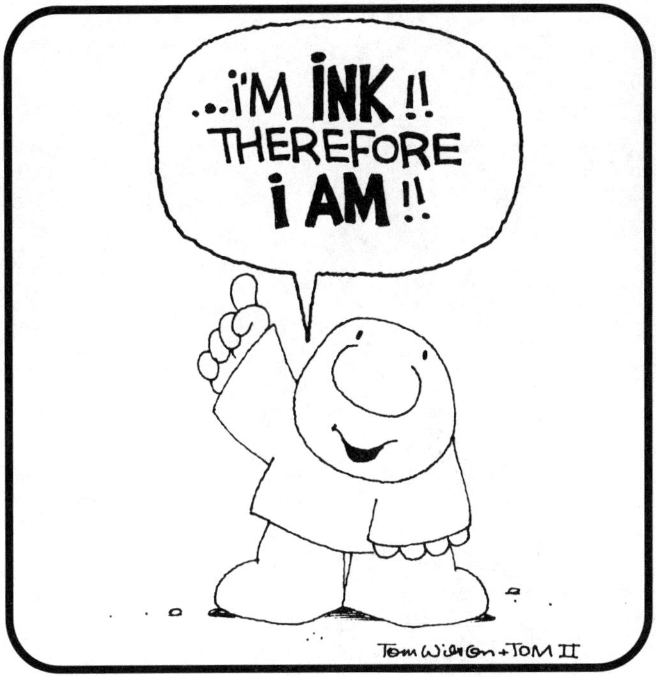
..I'M INK !!
THEREFORE
I AM !!
Tom Wilson + TOM II

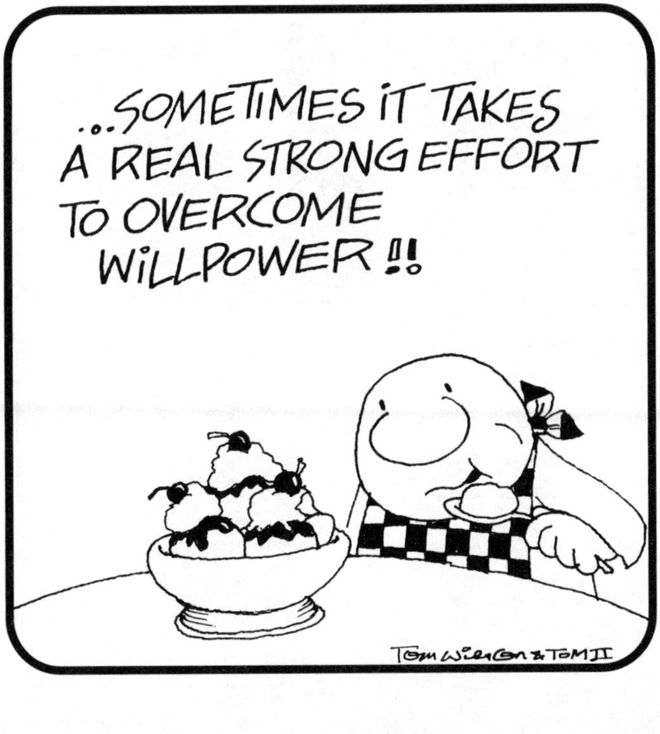
...SOMETIMES IT TAKES
A REAL STRONG EFFORT
TO OVERCOME
WILLPOWER !!
Tom Wilson & TOM II

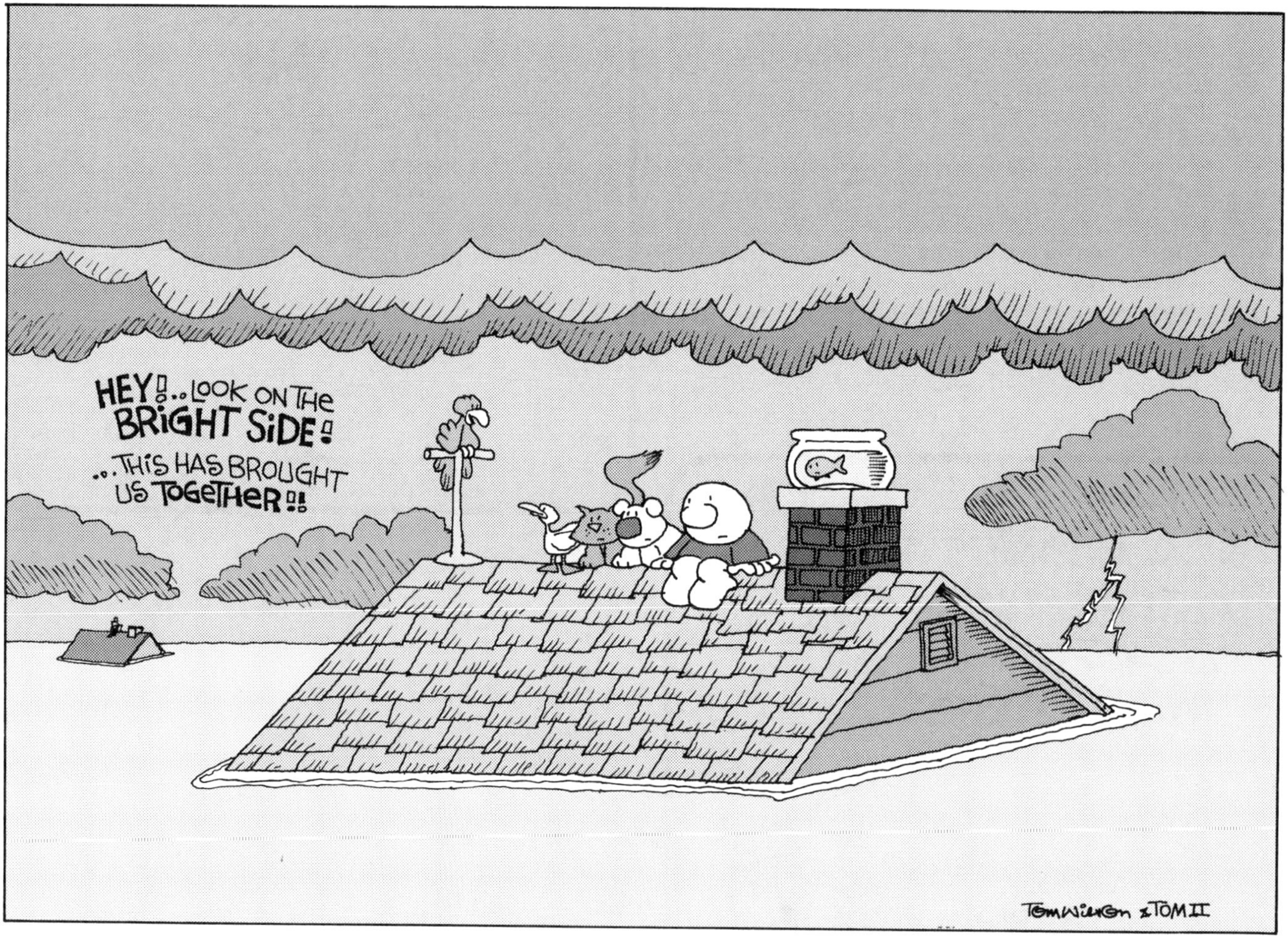
HEY!..LOOK ON THE BRIGHT SIDE!
..THIS HAS BROUGHT US TOGETHER!!
Tom Wilson & TOM II

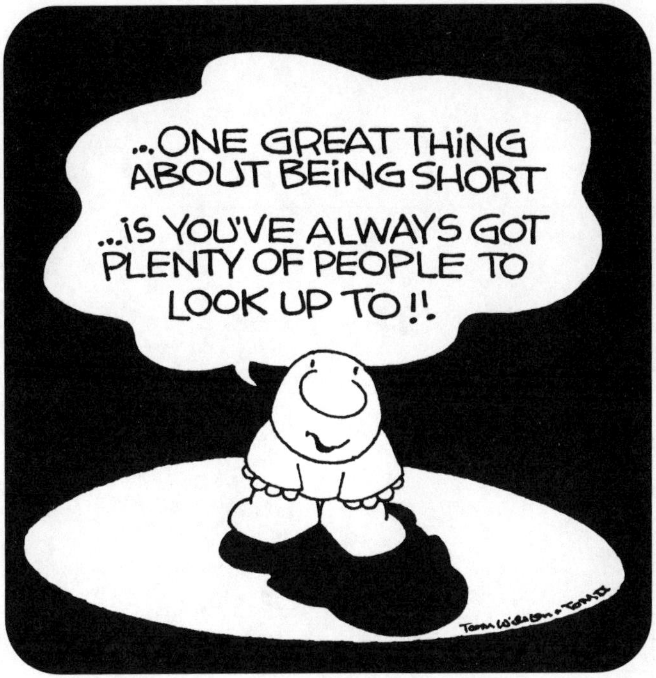
...ONE GREAT THiNG ABOUT BEiNG SHORT
...iS YOU'VE ALWAYS GOT PLENTY OF PEOPLE TO LOOK UP TO!!
TOM WILSON & TOM II

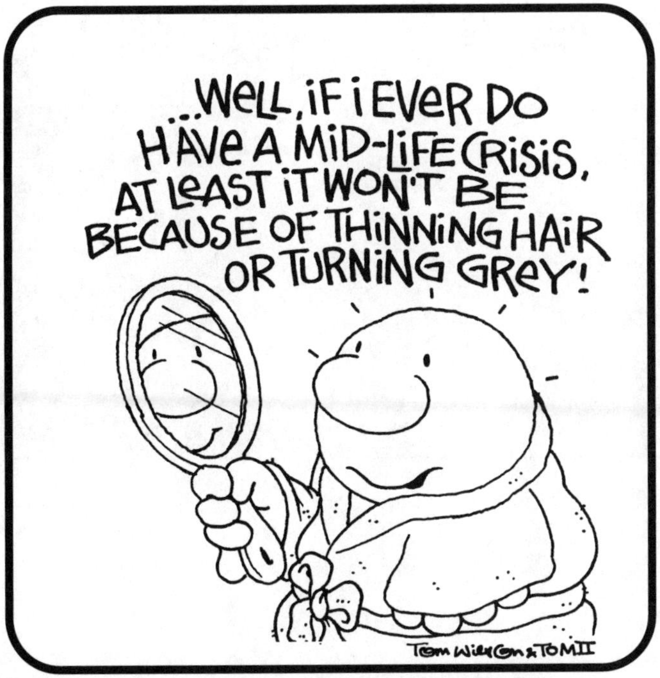
...WeLL, iF i EVeR DO HAVe A MiD-LiFE CRiSiS, AT LeAST iT WON'T BE BECAUSE OF THiNNiNG HAiR OR TURNiNG GReY!
TOM WILSON & TOM II

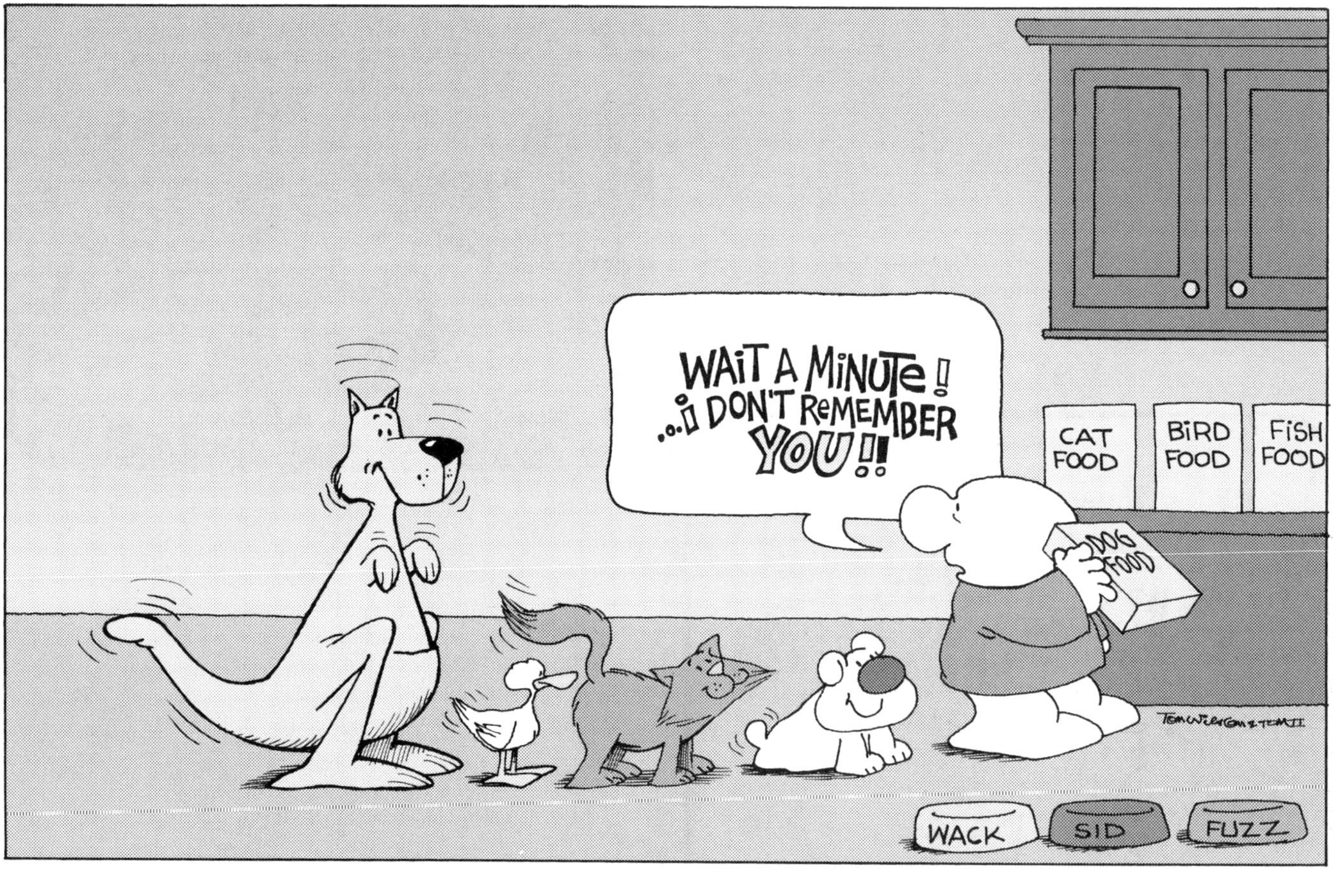
WAIT A MINUTE! ..I DON'T REMEMBER YOU!!
CAT FOOD
BIRD FOOD
FISH FOOD
DOG FOOD
WACK
SID
FUZZ

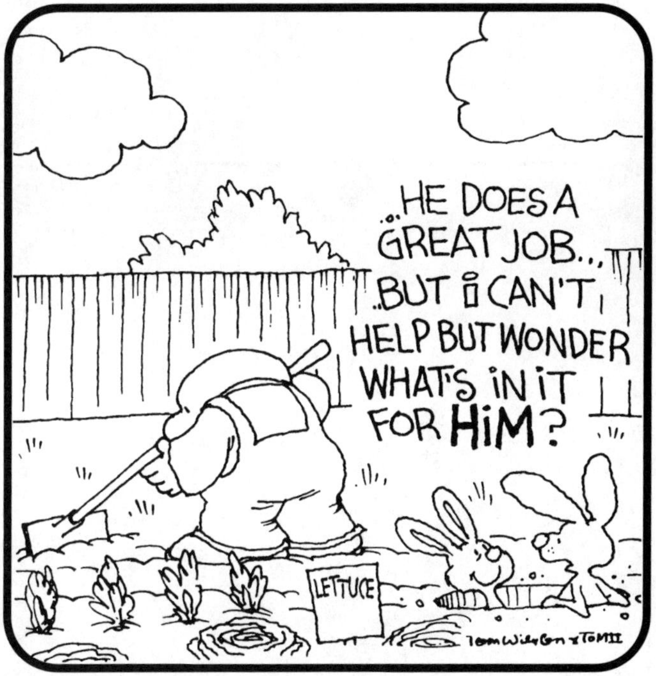
..HE DOES A GREAT JOB..,
..BUT I CAN'T HELP BUT WONDER WHAT'S IN IT FOR HIM?
LETTUCE
TOM WILSON & TOM II

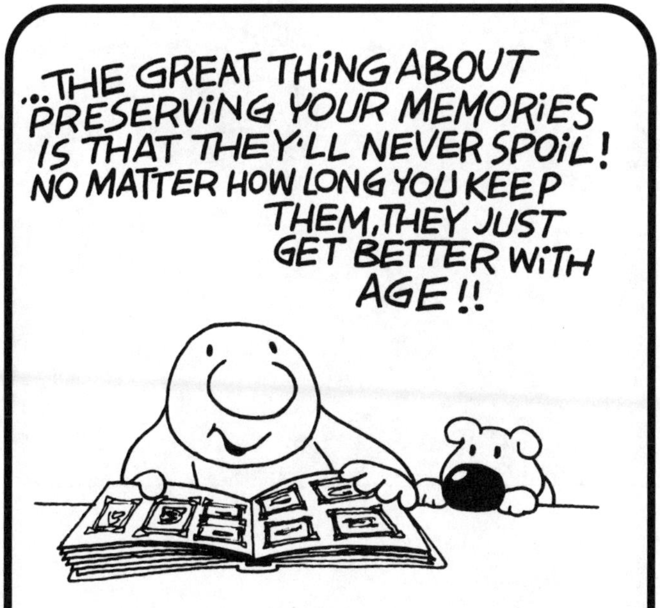
..THE GREAT THING ABOUT PRESERVING YOUR MEMORIES IS THAT THEY'LL NEVER SPOIL! NO MATTER HOW LONG YOU KEEP THEM, THEY JUST GET BETTER WITH AGE!!
TOM WILSON

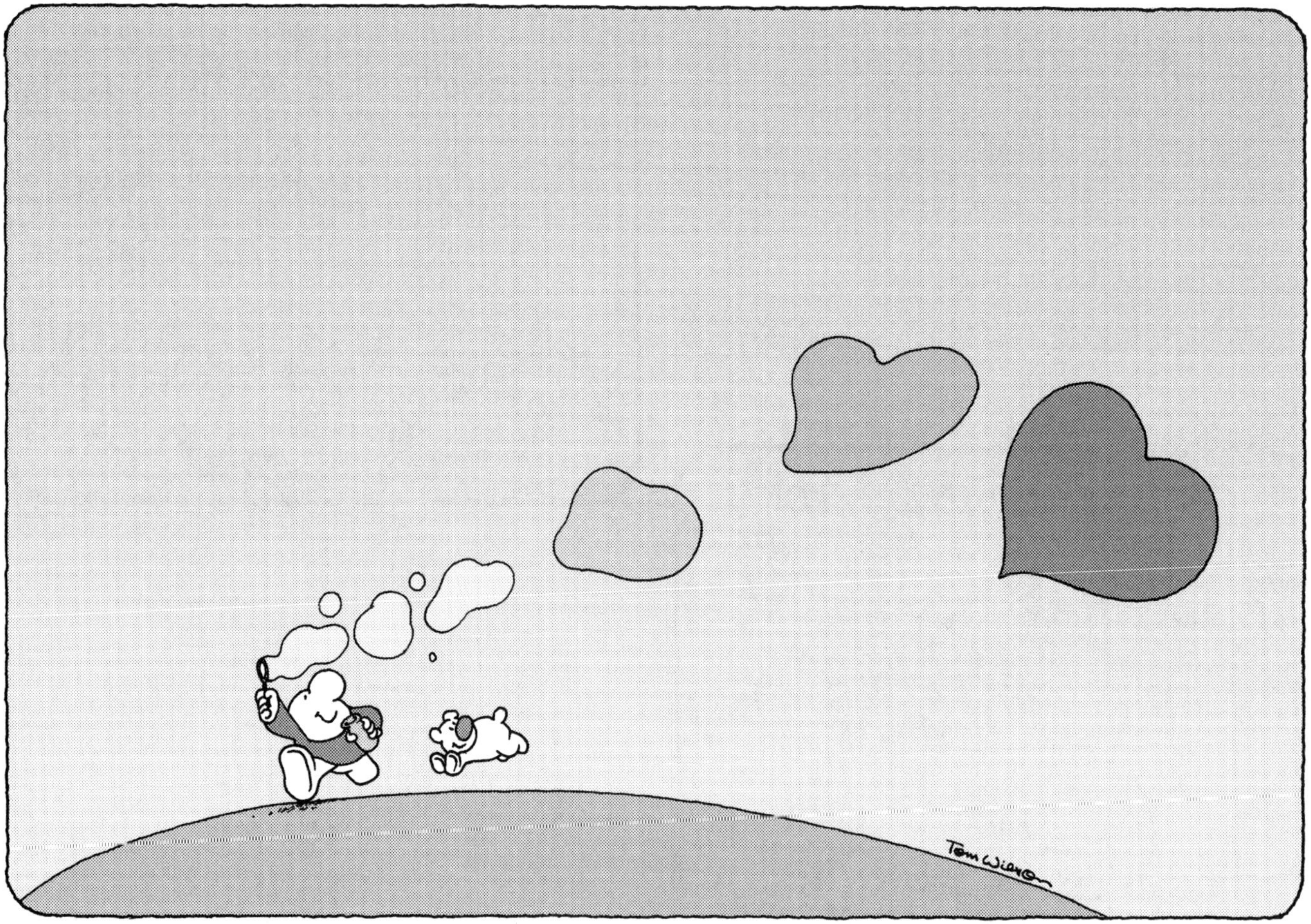
Tom Wilson

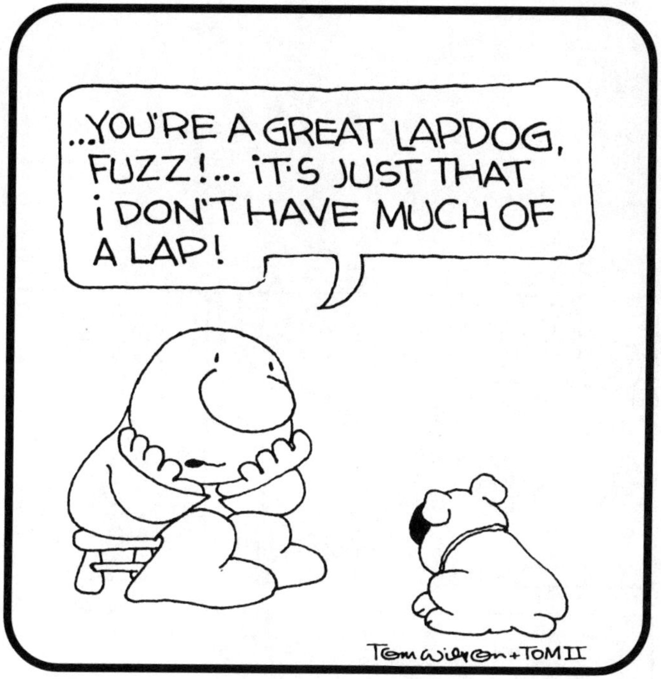
...YOU'RE A GREAT LAPDOG, FUZZ!... iT'S JUST THAT i DON'T HAVE MUCH OF A LAP!
Tom Wilson + TOM II

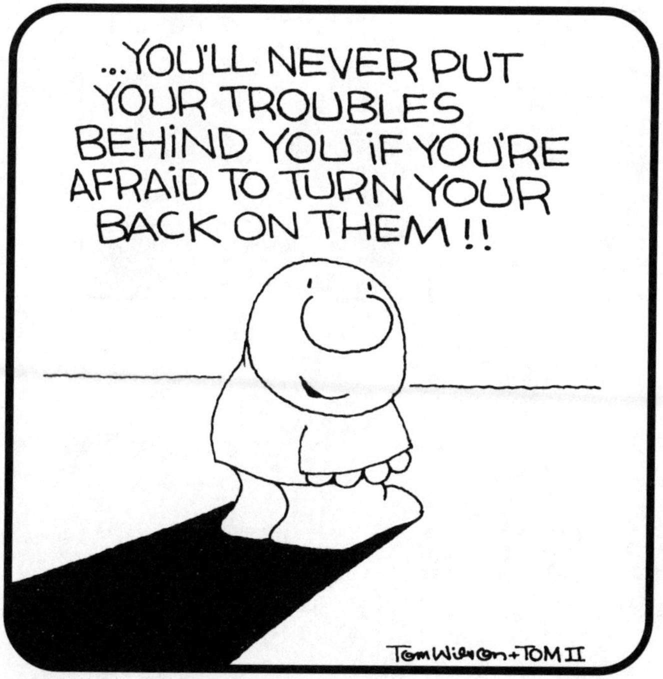
...YOU'LL NEVER PUT YOUR TROUBLES BEHiND YOU iF YOU'RE AFRAiD TO TURN YOUR BACK ON THEM!!
Tom Wilson + TOM II

IT DOESN'T GET ANY BETTER THAN THIS!!
ROSEBUD
THERE'S A LOT MORE TO FISHING THAN ALL THIS STRENUOUS PHYSICAL EXERCISE...
..IT'S A MENTAL GAME, ALSO!
...A SUPREME BATTLE OF WITS AND CUNNING AS THE FISHERMAN ATTEMPTS TO OUTSMART HIS PREY IN AN ULTIMATE BATTLE BETWEEN LIFE AND DEATH!!
ROSEBUD
YEP! THERE'S NOTHING MORE AWE-INSPIRING THAN SOME GUY WHO CAN OUTWIT A LARGE-MOUTH BASS!
ROSEBUD

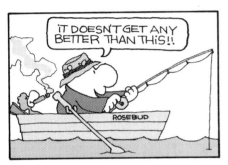

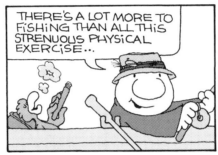

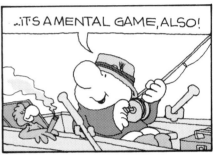

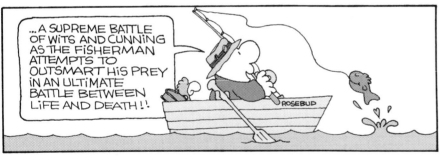

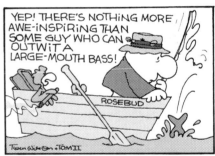

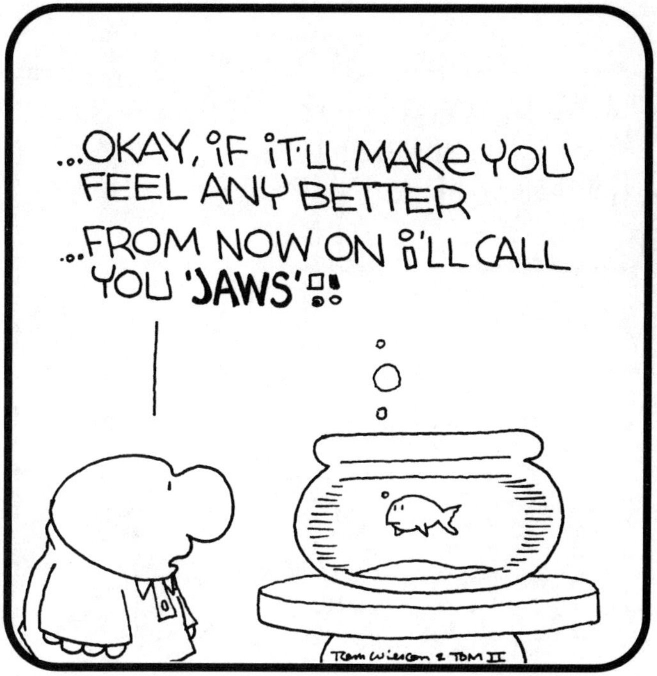
...OKAY, IF IT'LL MAKE YOU FEEL ANY BETTER
...FROM NOW ON I'LL CALL YOU 'JAWS'!!
TOM WILSON & TOM II

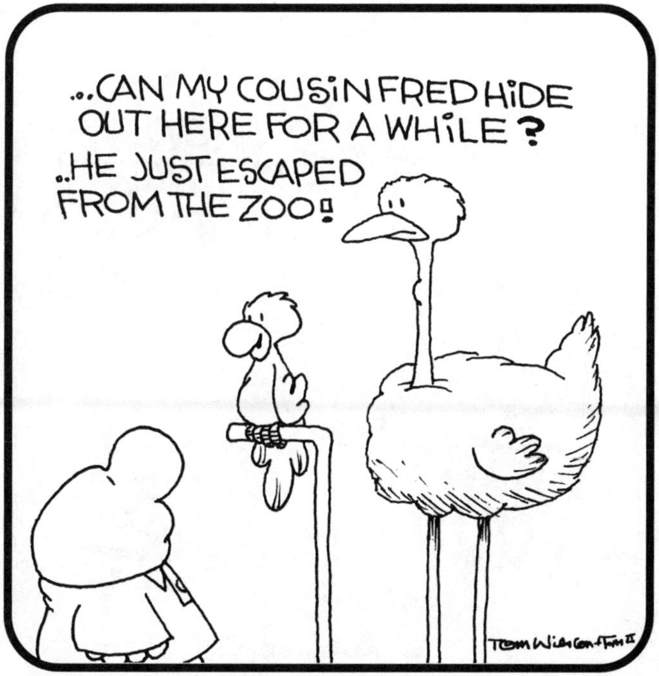
...CAN MY COUSIN FRED HIDE OUT HERE FOR A WHILE?
..HE JUST ESCAPED FROM THE ZOO!
TOM WILSON & TOM II

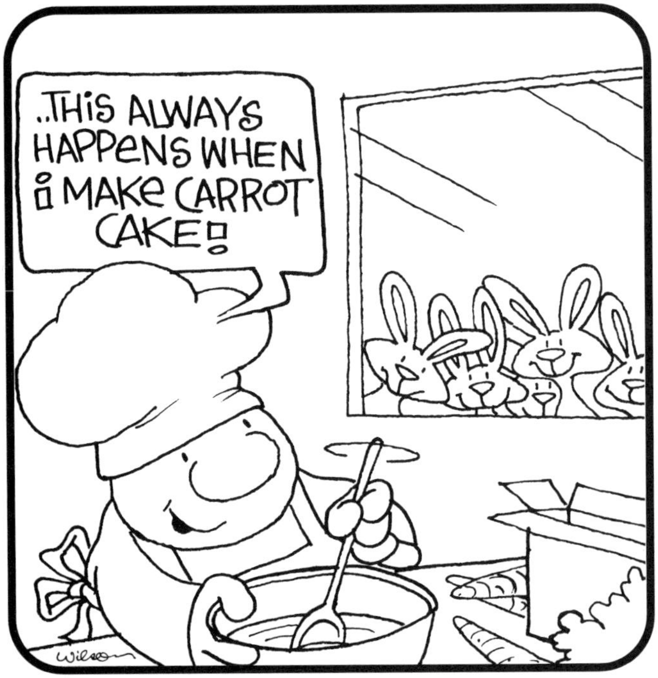
..THIS ALWAYS HAPPENS WHEN I MAKE CARROT CAKE!
Wilson

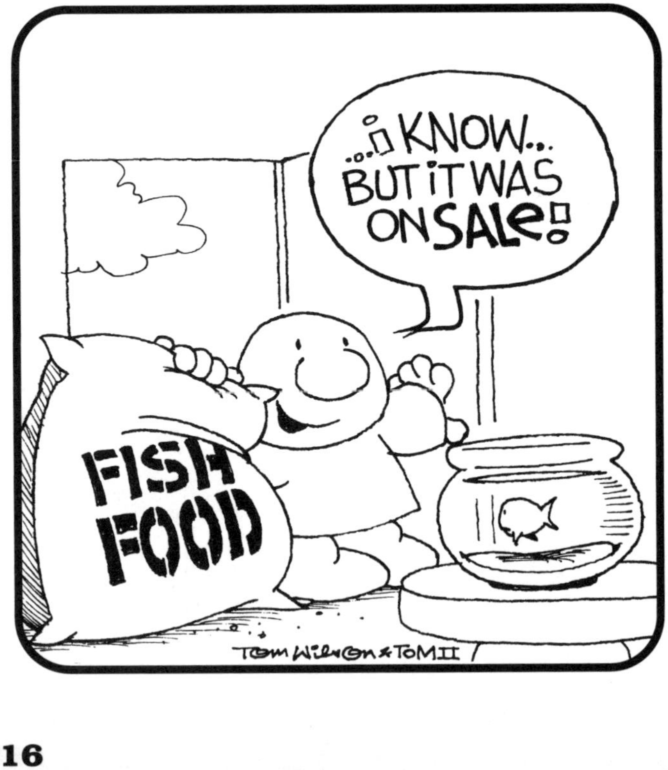
...I KNOW... BUT IT WAS ON SALE!
FISH FOOD
TOM WILSON & TOM II

THIS WAY TO THE FUTURE
THE FUTURE STRAIGHT AHEAD
THE
NEXT STOP THE FUTURE
NEXT STOP THE FUTURE
THE PRESENT
..IF YOU SPEND ALL OF YOUR TIME RACING AHEAD TO THE FUTURE..
..YOU'RE LIABLE TO DISCOVER YOU'VE LEFT A GREAT PRESENT BEHIND!!

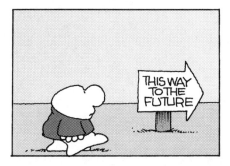

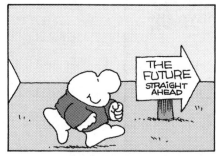

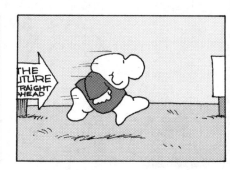

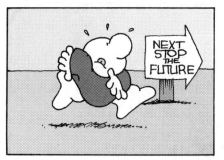

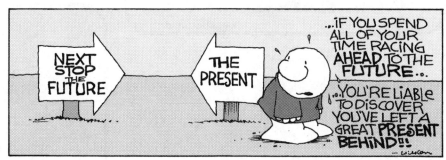

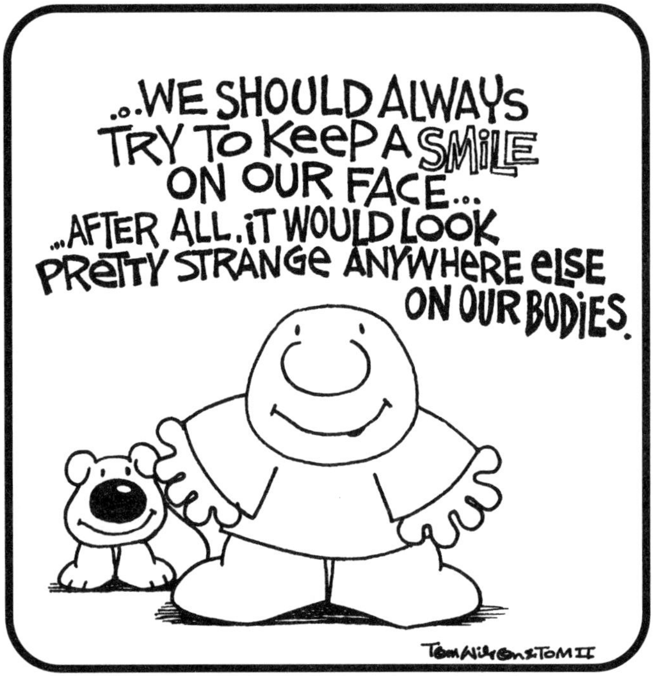
...WE SHOULD ALWAYS TRY TO KEEP A SMILE ON OUR FACE... ...AFTER ALL, IT WOULD LOOK PRETTY STRANGE ANYWHERE ELSE ON OUR BODIES.
TOM WILSON & TOM II

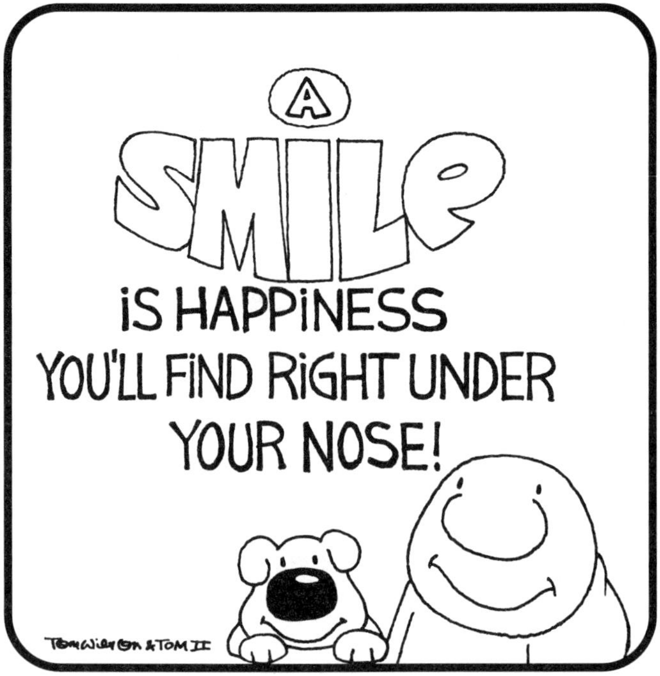
A SMILE IS HAPPINESS YOU'LL FIND RIGHT UNDER YOUR NOSE!
TOM WILSON & TOM II

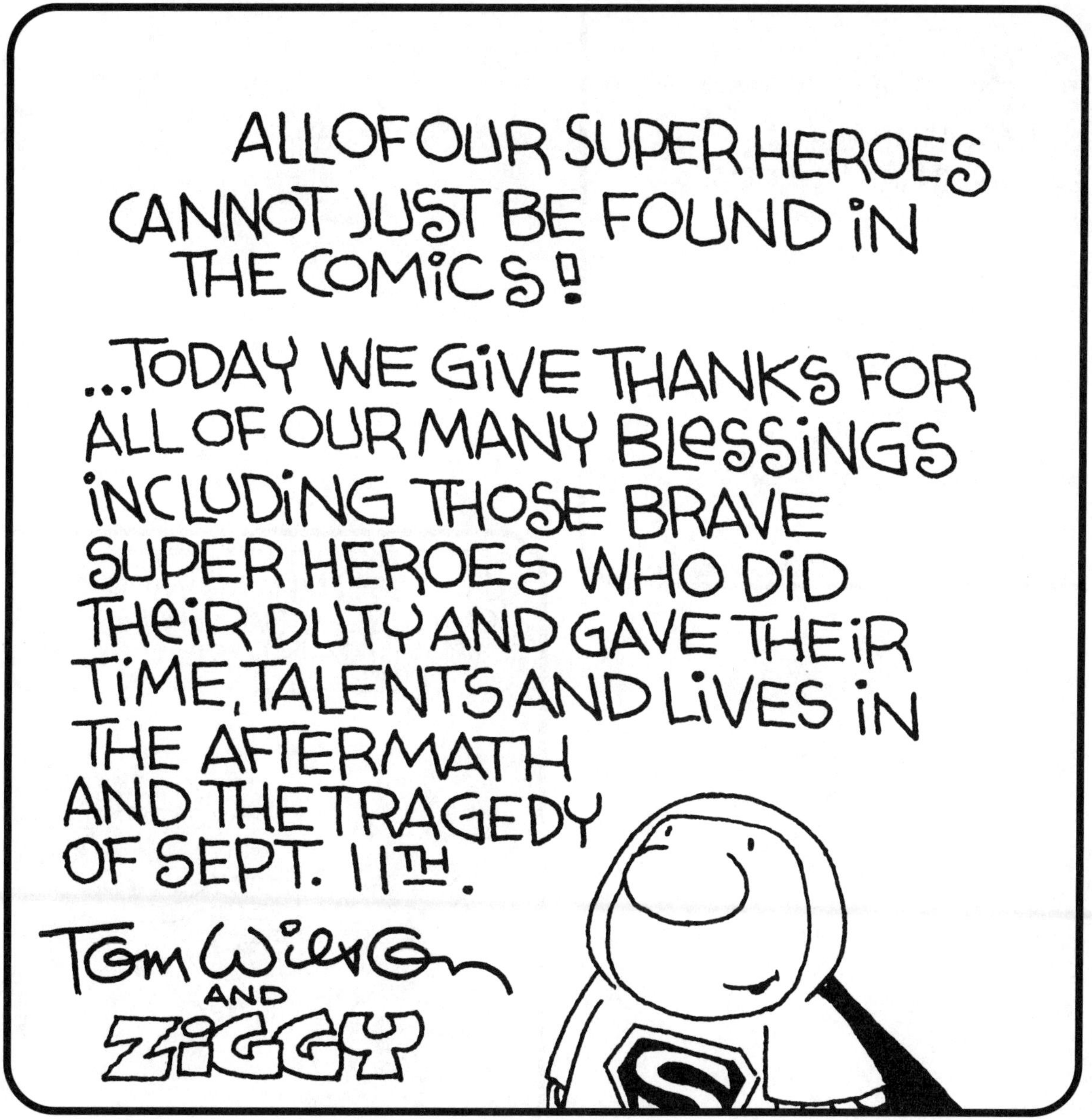
ALL OF OUR SUPER HEROES CANNOT JUST BE FOUND IN THE COMICS!
...TODAY WE GIVE THANKS FOR ALL OF OUR MANY BLESSINGS INCLUDING THOSE BRAVE SUPER HEROES WHO DID THEIR DUTY AND GAVE THEIR TIME, TALENTS AND LIVES IN THE AFTERMATH AND THE TRAGEDY OF SEPT. 11TH.
Tom Wilson
AND
ZIGGY

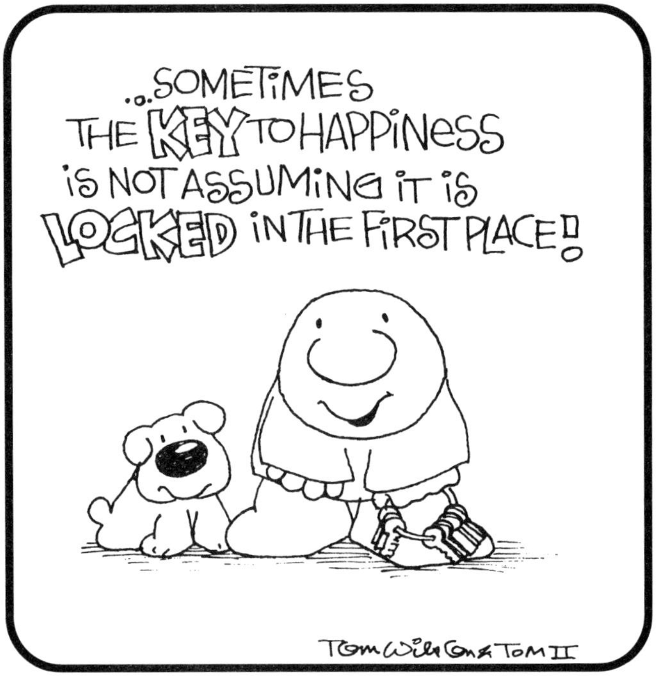
..SOMETIMES THE KEY TO HAPPINESS IS NOT ASSUMING IT IS LOCKED IN THE FIRST PLACE!!
TOM WILSON & TOM II

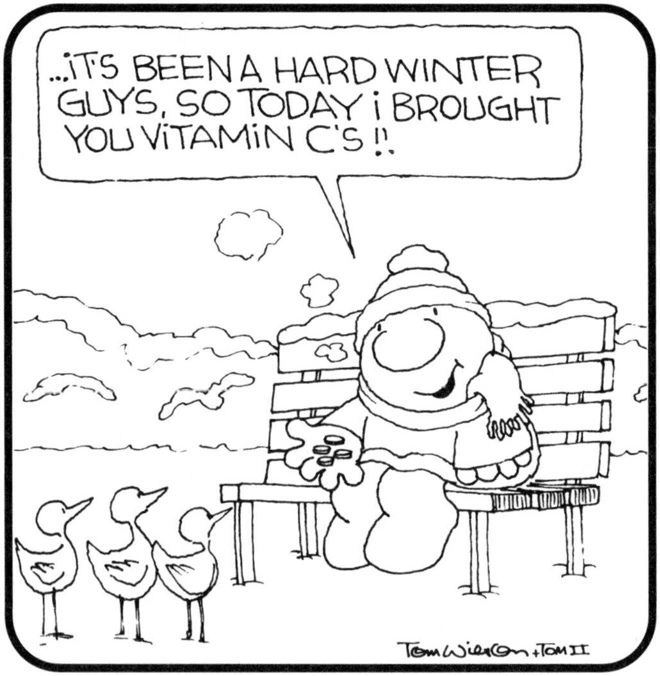
...IT'S BEEN A HARD WINTER GUYS, SO TODAY I BROUGHT YOU VITAMIN C'S !!
TOM WILSON + TOM II

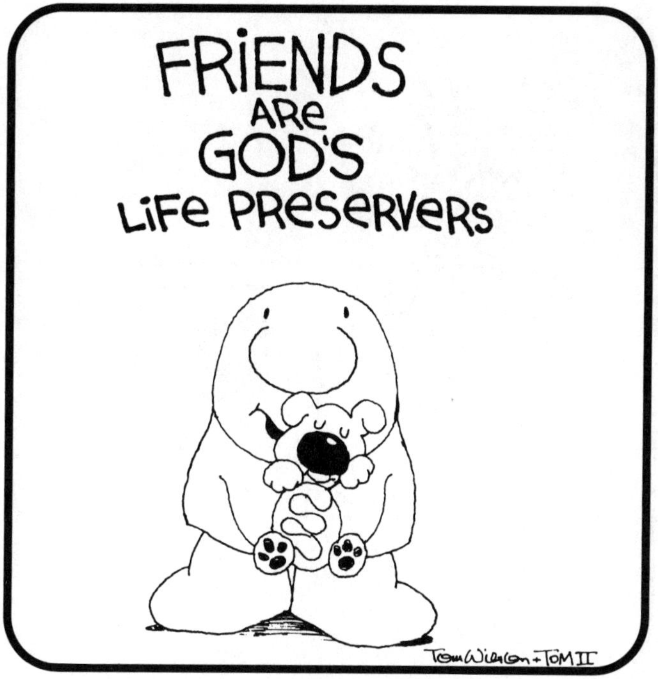
FRIENDS
ARE
GOD'S
LIFE PRESERVERS
Tom Wilson + TOM II

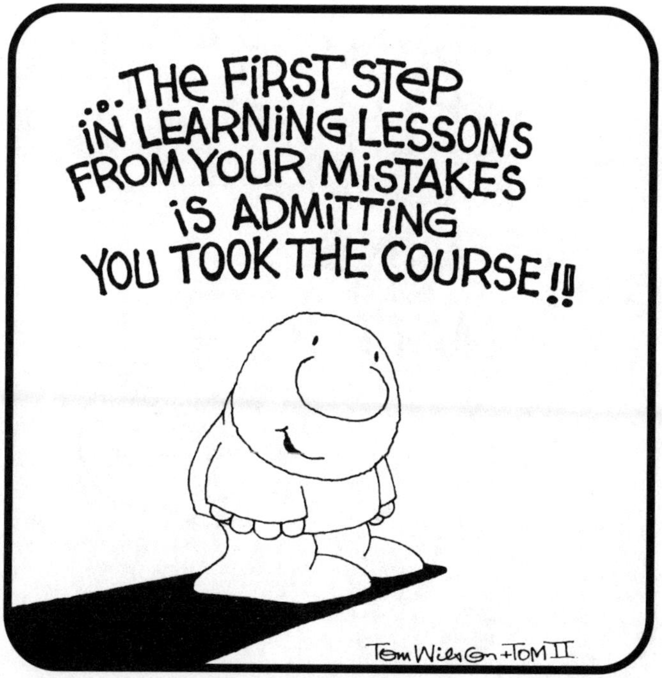
...THE FIRST STEP
IN LEARNING LESSONS
FROM YOUR MISTAKES
IS ADMITTING
YOU TOOK THE COURSE!!
Tom Wilson + TOM II

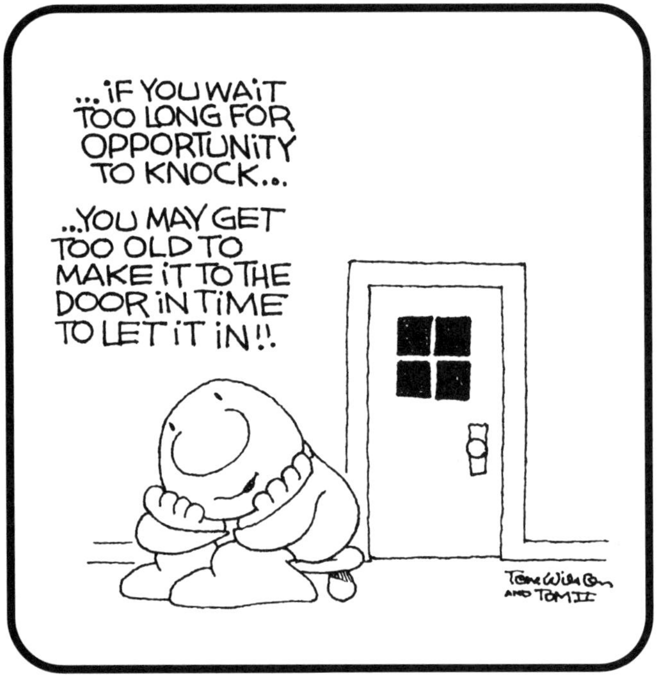
...iF YOU WAiT TOO LONG FOR OPPORTUNiTY TO KNOCK...
...YOU MAY GET TOO OLD TO MAKE iT TO THE DOOR iN TiME TO LET iT iN!!
Tom Wilson and Tom II

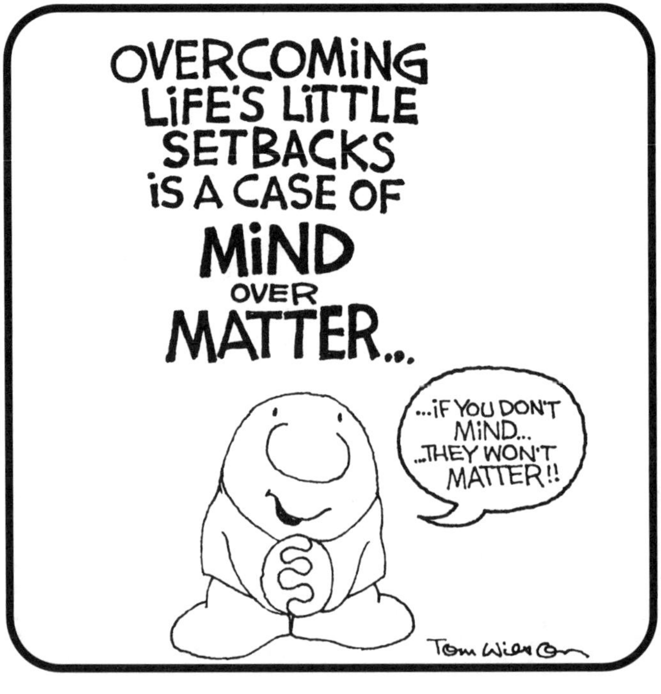
OVERCOMiNG LiFE'S LiTTLE SETBACKS iS A CASE OF MiND OVER MATTER...
...iF YOU DON'T MiND... ...THEY WON'T MATTER!!
Tom Wilson

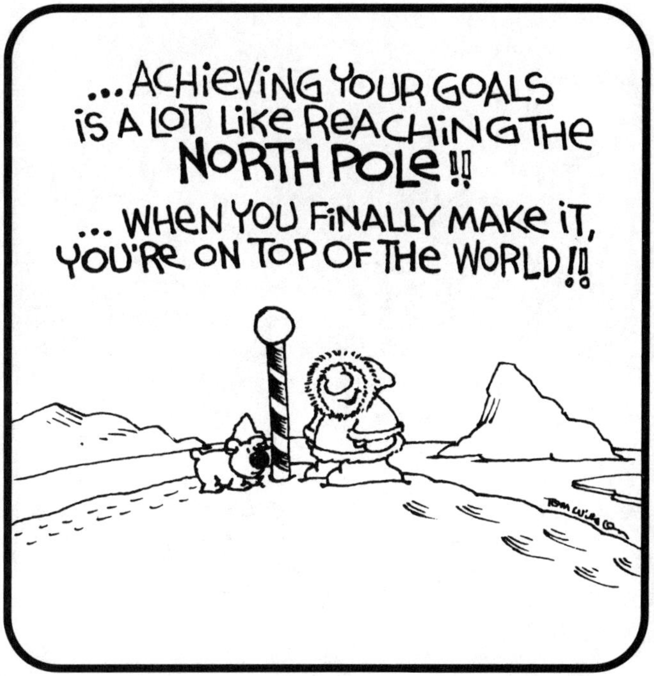
...ACHIEVING YOUR GOALS IS A LOT LIKE REACHING THE NORTH POLE !!
... WHEN YOU FINALLY MAKE IT, YOU'RE ON TOP OF THE WORLD !!
TOM WILSON

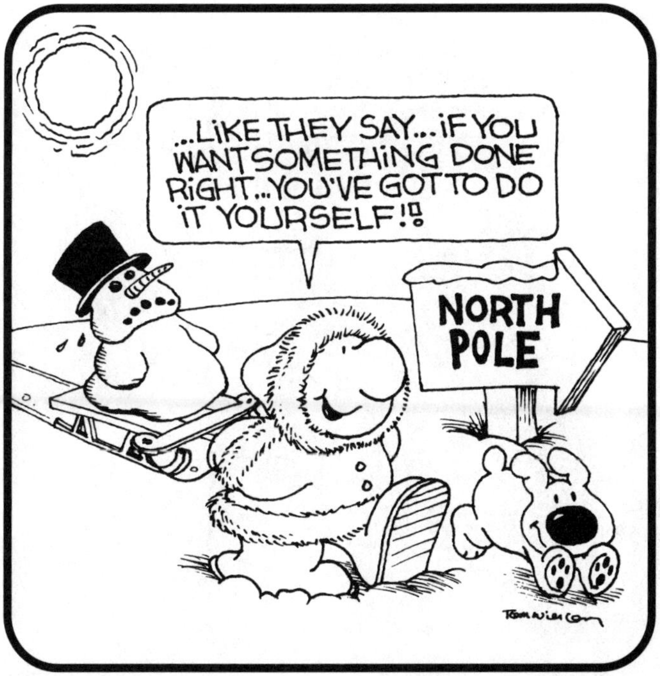
...LIKE THEY SAY... IF YOU WANT SOMETHING DONE RIGHT... YOU'VE GOT TO DO IT YOURSELF !!
NORTH POLE
TOM WILSON

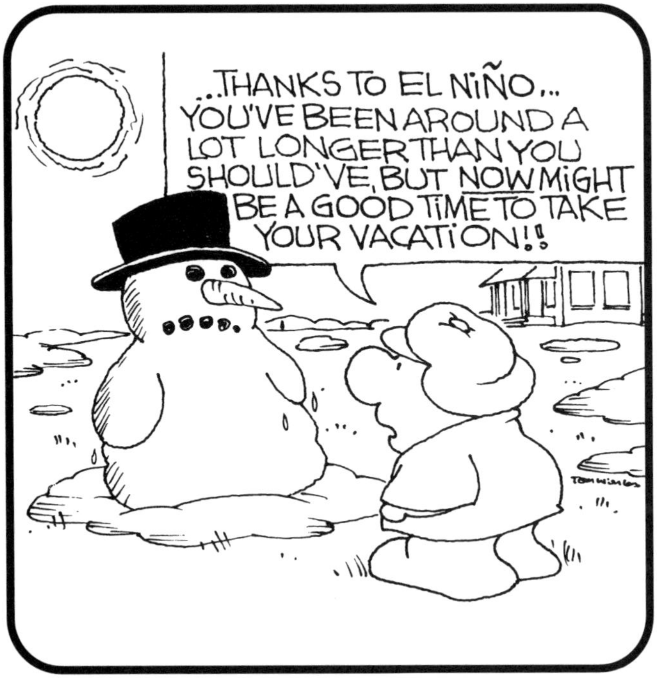
...THANKS TO EL NIÑO... YOU'VE BEEN AROUND A LOT LONGER THAN YOU SHOULD'VE, BUT NOW MIGHT BE A GOOD TIME TO TAKE YOUR VACATION!!

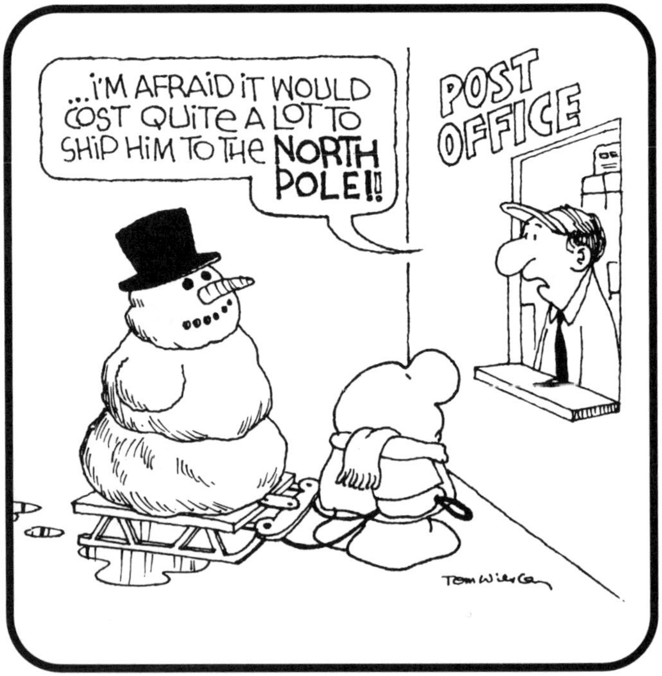
...I'M AFRAID IT WOULD COST QUITE A LOT TO SHIP HIM TO THE NORTH POLE!!
POST OFFICE

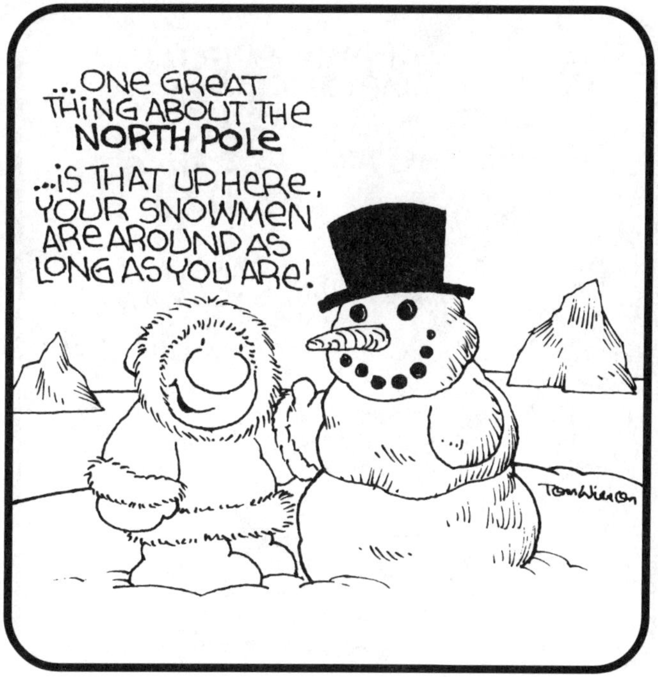
...ONE GREAT THING ABOUT THE NORTH POLE ...IS THAT UP HERE, YOUR SNOWMEN ARE AROUND AS LONG AS YOU ARE!
TOM WILSON

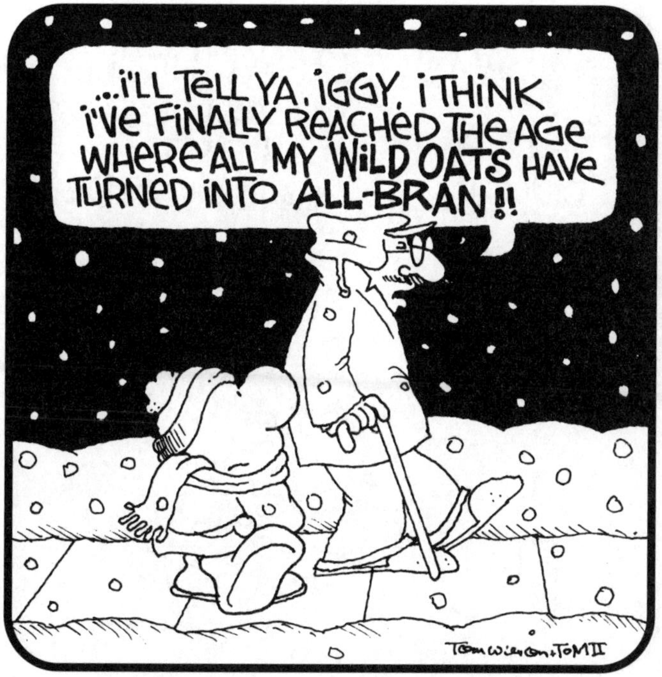
...I'LL TELL YA, IGGY, I THINK I'VE FINALLY REACHED THE AGE WHERE ALL MY WILD OATS HAVE TURNED INTO ALL-BRAN!!
TOM WILSON & TOM II

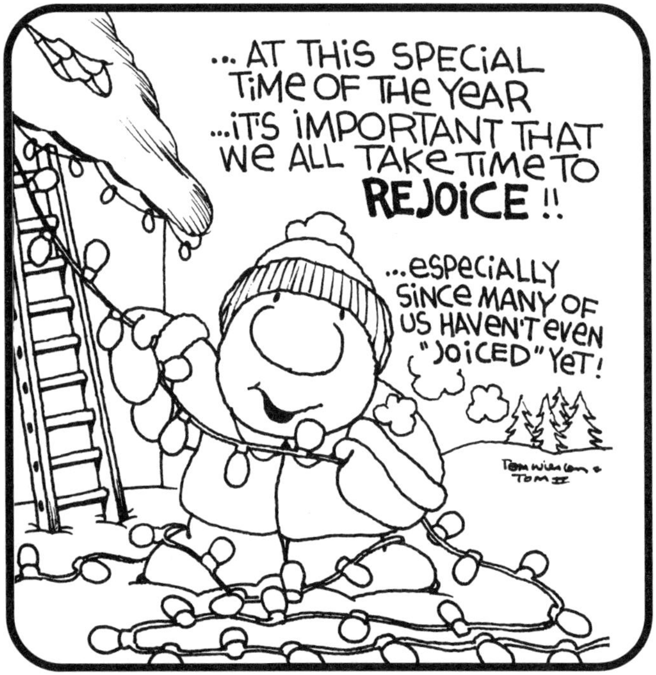

...AT THIS SPECIAL TIME OF THE YEAR ...IT'S IMPORTANT THAT WE ALL TAKE TIME TO REJOICE!!
...ESPECIALLY SINCE MANY OF US HAVEN'T EVEN "JOICED" YET!

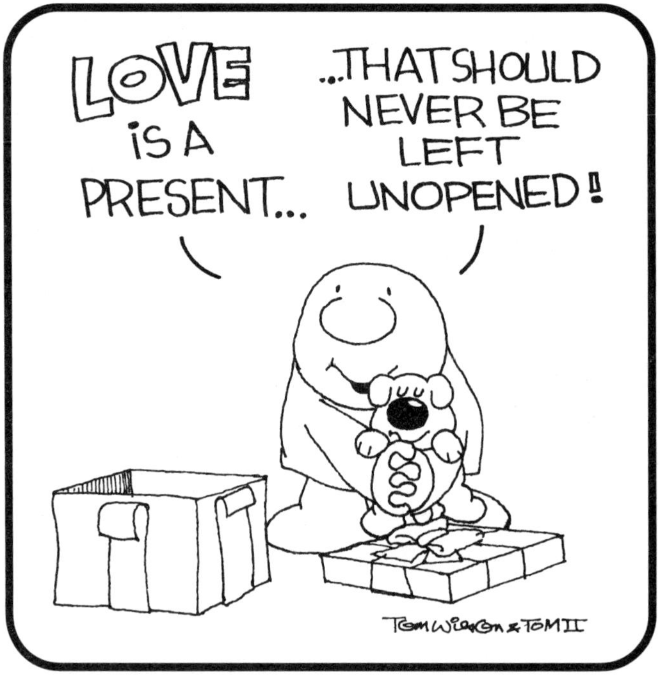

LOVE IS A PRESENT...
...THAT SHOULD NEVER BE LEFT UNOPENED!

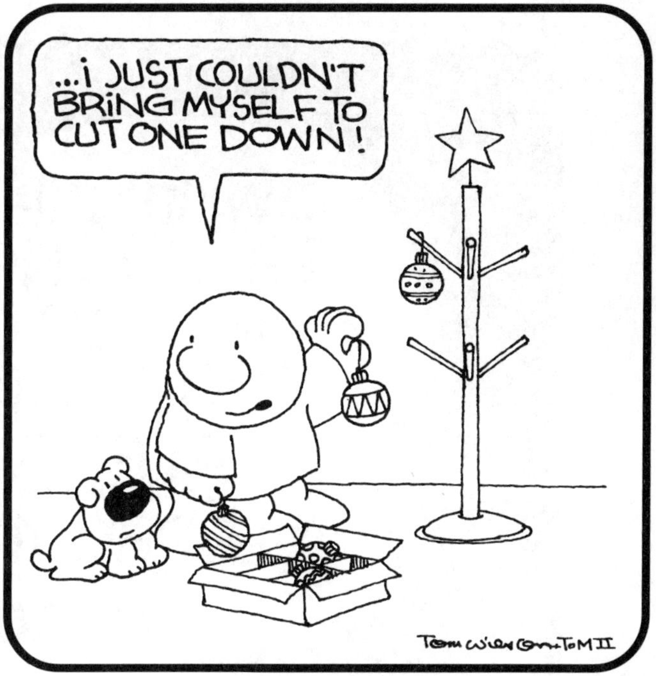
...i JUST COULDN'T BRiNG MYSELF TO CUT ONE DOWN!
Tom Wilson + ToM II

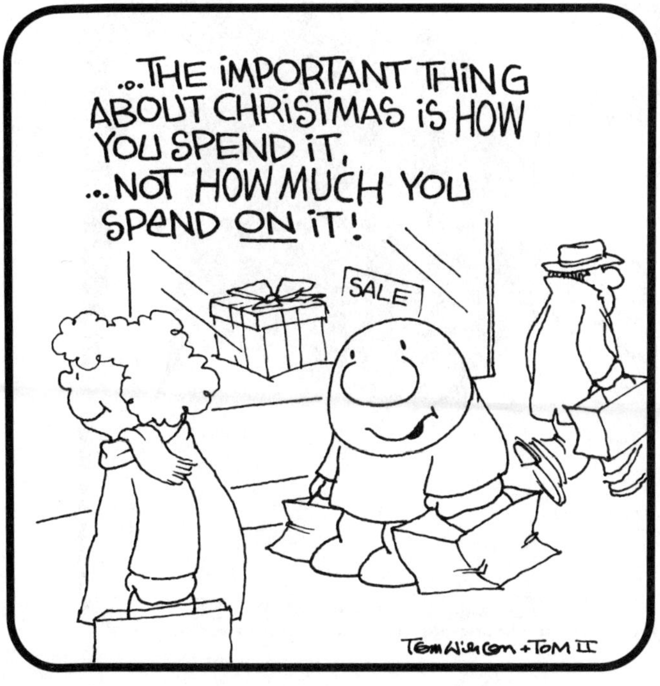
...THE iMPORTANT THiNG ABOUT CHRiSTMAS iS HOW YOU SPEND iT, ...NOT HOW MUCH YOU SPEND ON iT!
SALE
Tom Wilson + ToM II

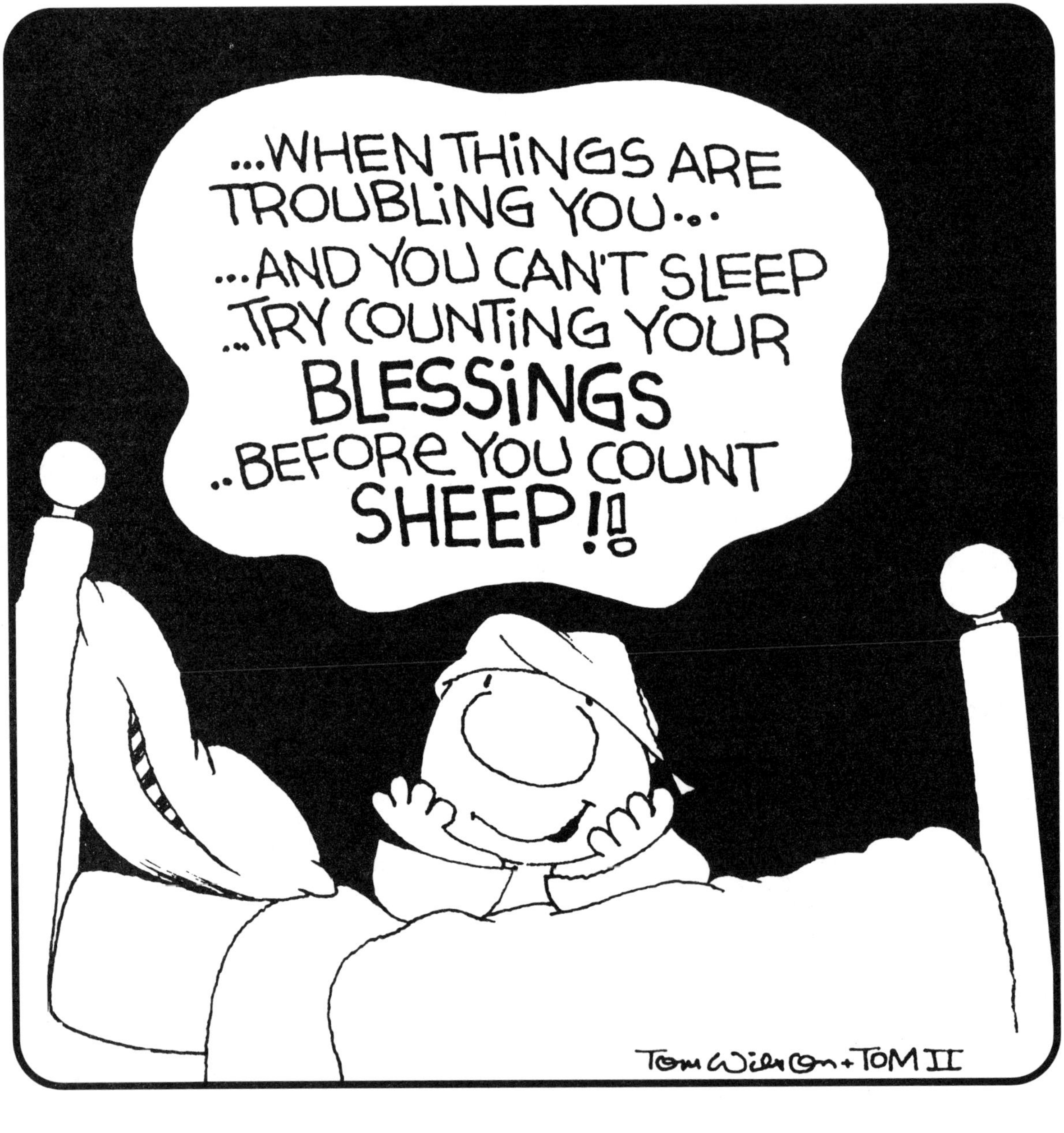
...WHEN THINGS ARE TROUBLING YOU...
...AND YOU CAN'T SLEEP
...TRY COUNTING YOUR BLESSINGS
..BEFORE YOU COUNT SHEEP!!
Tom Wilson + TOM II